Redis Stack for Application Modernization

Build real-time multi-model applications at any scale with Redis

Luigi Fugaro

Mirko Ortensi

BIRMINGHAM—MUMBAI

Redis Stack for Application Modernization

Group Product Manager: Kaustubh Manglurkar

Publishing Product Manager: Heramb Bhavsar

Book Project Manager: Kirti Pisat

Content Development Editor: Manikandan Kurup

Technical Editor: Kavyashree K S

Copy Editor: Safis Editing

Proofreader: Safis Editing

Indexer: Rekha Nair

Production Designer: Alishon Mendonca

Senior DevRel Marketing Coordinator: Nivedita Singh

First published: December 2023

Production reference: 1151223

Published by Packt Publishing Ltd.

Grosvenor House

11 St Paul's Square

Birmingham

B3 1RB, UK.

ISBN 978-1-83763-818-5

`www.packtpub.com`

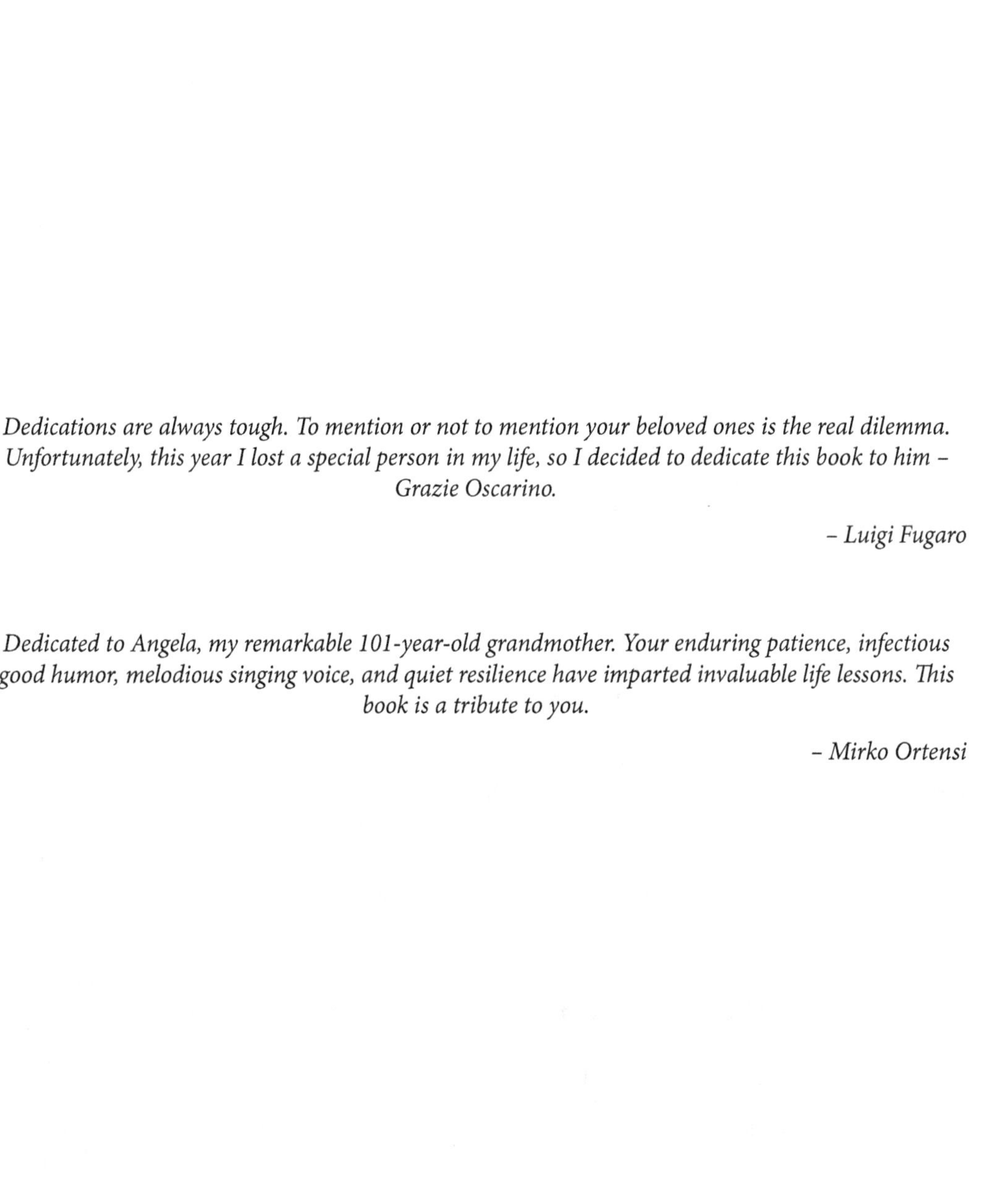

Dedications are always tough. To mention or not to mention your beloved ones is the real dilemma. Unfortunately, this year I lost a special person in my life, so I decided to dedicate this book to him – Grazie Oscarino.

– Luigi Fugaro

Dedicated to Angela, my remarkable 101-year-old grandmother. Your enduring patience, infectious good humor, melodious singing voice, and quiet resilience have imparted invaluable life lessons. This book is a tribute to you.

– Mirko Ortensi

Contributors

About the authors

Luigi Fugaro's computer science career began with a fascination for video games on the Vic 20 and Atari ST1040, where he enjoyed manipulating game code. This interest sparked his journey into programming, leading to a varied career in mastering numerous languages, including Fortran, Java, Go, Delphi, Visual Basic, and Python. While he is ambivalent about JavaScript and doesn't consider HTML a programming language, he appreciates its utility.

Luigi's career expanded into observability, monitoring, and data management, with significant experiences at Red Hat and Redis, where he understood the importance of application performance. Despite many side projects, most unfinished, Luigi's notable contributions to literature reflect his enduring passion and drive for technology and innovation in computer science.

In the journey of crafting a book, a myriad of dynamics come into play, mirroring the numerous individuals who grace our daily lives. This holds particularly true for my family, including my children, Giada, Filippo, and Viola. I've borrowed time from them – moments that I couldn't spend by their side. Yet, they are the spark that kindles my hope and fuels my drive to be better. For this gift, my gratitude and love for them knows no bounds.

Mirko Ortensi wrote his first lines of code on a Commodore 64 in Basic when he was 10. It was love at first sight. Eventually, he earned a degree in electronic engineering and a master's degree in software engineering at Università Politecnica delle Marche in Italy in 2002, with a thesis about pattern recognition at UPC in Barcelona, Spain. Mirko's career has spanned several roles in software and services businesses, encompassing development and testing, system management, and support, mainly centered around databases and distributed systems. As a senior technical enablement architect at Redis, Mirko shares technical knowledge about Redis's products, services, and features.

I extend heartfelt thanks to my incredible family – my loving wife, children, and Gizmo the cat – for their unwavering patience and support during the countless hours I disappeared into the world of writing and coding. Your understanding and encouragement were my pillars throughout this journey.

Luigi and Mirko express their deep gratitude to everyone at Redis who contributed to this book. They extend special thanks to Alexandre Vasseur, David Maier, Tal Shkolnik, Raffaele Landoni, Cody Henshaw, Myra El-Bayoumi, Claudia Di Martino, and all the contributors to Redis open source. Additionally, they thank Packt for believing in this project, particularly Heramb Bhavsar, Kirti Pisat, and Manikandan Kurup for their support throughout Luigi and Mirko's journey.

About the reviewer

Sumit Shatwara, a solution architect, brings a wealth of expertise from his previous role at Redis, the global leader in real-time data platforms. At Redis, Sumit led the charge in designing and building cutting-edge, real-time data solutions, driving technology sales, and serving as a trusted advisor to enterprise clients within the banking, financial services, and digital native sectors. Sumit's extensive career spans experiences with renowned companies such as Red Hat, NetApp, and Capgemini, where he facilitated the adoption of cloud-native technologies for numerous clients. Sumit's future aspirations include becoming an artificial intelligence specialist and ultimately establishing himself as a thought leader in the realms of data and AI.

Table of Contents

3

Getting Started with Redis Stack 63

4

Setting Up Client Libraries 77

Part 2: Data Modeling

5

Redis Stack as a Document Store 129

6

7

8

Part 3: From Development to Production

9

The Programmability of Redis Stack 219

10

RedisInsight – the Data Management GUI 241

11

Using Redis Stack as a Primary Database 255

12

Preface

Redis Stack for Application Modernization is written by industry experts from Redis, making this an insightful reference for database administrators and developers, with best practices to administer and manage the server, scalability, high availability, data integrity, stored functions, and more.

Modern applications require efficient operational and analytical capabilities and must ensure predictable performance regardless of the workload. Redis is a de facto standard caching system, with real-time response and flexible data types that fulfill all the different data modeling requirements. This book introduces you to Redis Stack, an extension of Redis presented in 2022, and it guides you through the multiple data modeling capabilities, together with examples to perform real-time queries and searches. Redis Stack represents a new approach to providing a rich data modeling experience all within the same database server.

You will learn how to model and search your data in the JSON and hash data types and work with features such as vector search, which adds semantic search capabilities to your application (for example, to search for similar texts, images, or audio files). You will understand how to use the probabilistic Bloom filters to resolve efficiently recurrent big data problems. Next, we dive into the strengths of Redis Stack as a data platform, show use cases to manage database events, and introduce stream processing features. Scenarios to use Redis Stack in microservices architectures complete the picture.

Who this book is for

This book is for software developers, software architects, and database administrators who want to discover the powerful real-time, multi-model capabilities of the Redis Stack database.

You will work with JSON and hash documents, vectors, time series models, probabilistic data structures, and stream processing, with an eye on the performance and security of the database and the integrity of the data.

The prerequisite to reading this book is a basic understanding of Redis and databases in general and software development skills in at least one of the Java, Python, C#, Golang, or JavaScript languages.

What this book covers

Chapter 1, Introducing Redis Stack, introduces you to Redis Stack, its differences with Redis, and why Redis can't be considered as a caching system only, but a full-fledged database, augmenting and replacing relational databases in many use cases.

Chapter 2, Developing Modern Use Cases with Redis Stack, explores how Redis Stack extends Redis's well-known capabilities thanks to its modular architecture, thus becoming a document store, a vector database, and a time series database. The probabilistic data types help to efficiently resolve many problems. Redis Stack is a modern real-time solution that can replace traditional relational databases in many use cases.

Chapter 3, Getting Started with Redis Stack, teaches you how Redis Stack can be installed in a variety of methods and on the most popular operative systems. This means that Redis Stack can be installed easily on Linux, macOS, and Windows systems using native installation packages (Linux tarballs are also available). Docker images are also available in Docker Hub. In addition, Redis Stack is available as a service with Redis Cloud.

Chapter 4, Setting Up Client Libraries, describes how the Redis Stack ecosystem provides a set of client libraries to ease developers' lives. Those include libraries for the most used programming languages such as Python, Java, GoLang, C#, and JavaScript. In addition to client libraries, Redis provides a framework used for object mapping: Redis OM.

Chapter 5, Redis Stack as a Document Store, presents Redis Stack's capability to perform real-time queries and searches against the hash and JSON types. From full-text to tagging, from aggregation to auto-completion, and the new vector search, Redis Stack can be used as a document store with advanced features.

Chapter 6, Redis Stack as a Vector Database, highlights why, among the advanced search features of Redis Stack, Vector Search stands as a core feature and deserves a chapter on its own. You will learn data modeling concepts and how to perform similarity searches for recommendation engines.

Chapter 7, Redis Stack as a Time Series Database, explains how Redis Stack, as a multi-model, real-time data structure server, can store data using data points for time series. Each data point can be enriched by adding metadata, known as labels. Each data point can have multiple labels that can be used for filtering, searching, querying, and aggregations using the built-in reducer functions.

Chapter 8, Understanding Probabilistic Data Structures, explores probabilistic data structures, which are a group of data structures that give a very reasonable approximation of an answer in just a fraction of the usual time and use very little memory. Questions such as "Has the user paid from this location already?", "What are the 10 players with the highest score?", or "How many unique users have played this song?" address the typical use cases for these data structures

Chapter 9, The Programmability of Redis Stack, describes how, in addition to the traditional Redis Lua scripts and functions, Redis Stack includes a JavaScript serverless engine for transaction, batch, and event-driven data processing, allowing users to write and run their functions on data stored in Redis. With this capability, the database reacts to events occurring in the data while taking advantage of different Redis data structures and modules and promoting interoperability between them.

Chapter 10, RedisInsight – the Data Management GUI, covers RedisInsight, which is a graphical desktop manager that connects to Redis Stack databases and offers useful visualization tools for the different data models that can be stored.

Chapter 11, Using Redis Stack as a Primary Database, explains how Redis, as the leading real-time database, is used often as an in-memory cache, backed by a primary database. However, Redis Stack extends Redis with multi-model capabilities and is a good fit in many use cases to replace a traditional relational database. In this chapter, you will learn about the configuration to work with Redis Stack as the only primary database serving multi-model applications

Chapter 12, Managing Development and Production Environments, explains how moving from a development environment to deploying and running Redis at scale and monitoring the systems where the databases are running requires effort and the implementation of several maintenance duties. Redis Enterprise and Redis Cloud alleviate system and database administrators from their duties and can be managed using an intuitive UI.

To get the most out of this book

It is important that you have an understanding of database platforms, specifically in the areas of data insertion, updating, and deletion. Additionally, having a basic knowledge of SQL would be beneficial. You should also be comfortable with executing commands using a command-line interface, and familiarity with Unix-like systems is a plus. Prior experience with Redis or similar technologies is not required.

Software/hardware covered in the book	**Operating system requirements**
Redis Stack 7.2 or later	Windows, macOS, or Linux
RedisInsight 2.36 or later	Windows, macOS, or Linux

If you are using the digital version of this book, we advise you to type the code yourself or access the code from the book's GitHub repository (a link is available in the next section). Doing so will help you avoid any potential errors related to the copying and pasting of code.

Download the example code files

You can download the example code files for this book from GitHub at `https://github.com/PacktPublishing/Redis-Stack-for-Application-Modernization`. If there's an update to the code, it will be updated in the GitHub repository.

We also have other code bundles from our rich catalog of books and videos available at `https://github.com/PacktPublishing/`. Check them out!

Conventions used

There are a number of text conventions used throughout this book.

`Code in text`: Indicates code words in text, database table names, folder names, filenames, file extensions, pathnames, dummy URLs, user input, and Twitter handles. Here is an example: "However, since Python version 3.3, a tool named `virtualenv` was integrated into Python's standard library."

A block of code is set as follows:

```
client = redis.Redis(host='127.0.0.1', port=6379,
username='<YOUR_USERNAME>',
password='<YOUR_PASSWORD>')
client.set("Redis", "Stack")
print(client.get("Redis"))
```

When we wish to draw your attention to a particular part of a code block, the relevant lines or items are set in bold:

```
<dependency>
    <groupId>redis.clients</groupId>
    <artifactId>jedis</artifactId>
    <version>5.0.0</version>
</dependency>
```

Any command-line input or output is written as follows:

```
$ apt install python3.9-venv
```

Bold: Indicates a new term, an important word, or words that you see onscreen. For instance, words in menus or dialog boxes appear in **bold**. Here is an example: "The application prompts you first to establish a connection with a Redis database. Start this process by clicking on the **ADD REDIS DATABASE** button."

> **Tips or important notes**
> Appear like this.

Get in touch

Feedback from our readers is always welcome.

General feedback: If you have questions about any aspect of this book, email us at `customercare@packtpub.com` and mention the book title in the subject of your message.

Errata: Although we have taken every care to ensure the accuracy of our content, mistakes do happen. If you have found a mistake in this book, we would be grateful if you would report this to us. Please visit `www.packtpub.com/support/errata` and fill in the form.

Piracy: If you come across any illegal copies of our works in any form on the internet, we would be grateful if you would provide us with the location address or website name. Please contact us at `copyright@packt.com` with a link to the material.

If you are interested in becoming an author: If there is a topic that you have expertise in and you are interested in either writing or contributing to a book, please visit `authors.packtpub.com`.

Share Your Thoughts

Once you've read *Redis Stack for Application Modernization*, we'd love to hear your thoughts! Scan the QR code below to go straight to the Amazon review page for this book and share your feedback.

`https://packt.link/r/1-837-63818-7`

Your review is important to us and the tech community and will help us make sure we're delivering excellent quality content.

Download a free PDF copy of this book

Thanks for purchasing this book!

Do you like to read on the go but are unable to carry your print books everywhere?

Is your eBook purchase not compatible with the device of your choice?

Don't worry, now with every Packt book you get a DRM-free PDF version of that book at no cost.

Read anywhere, any place, on any device. Search, copy, and paste code from your favorite technical books directly into your application.

The perks don't stop there, you can get exclusive access to discounts, newsletters, and great free content in your inbox daily

Follow these simple steps to get the benefits:

1. Scan the QR code or visit the link below

`https://packt.link/free-ebook/9781837638185`

2. Submit your proof of purchase
3. That's it! We'll send your free PDF and other benefits to your email directly

Part 1: Introduction to Redis Stack

Redis Stack combines the core features of Redis with its most successful capabilities, offering a comprehensive understanding of Redis fundamentals and advanced functionalities. It distinguishes itself from Redis by its modular architecture, expanding its capabilities to serve as a document store, vector database, and time-series database. Redis Stack is versatile, functioning as an in-memory real-time cache, session store, leaderboard storage, and message broker. Its probabilistic data types enhance problem-solving efficiency, positioning it as a modern alternative to traditional relational databases for various applications.

The installation of Redis Stack is straightforward across popular operating systems such as Linux, macOS, and Windows, with native packages and Docker images available. To support developers, Redis Stack includes client libraries for major programming languages such as Python, Go, C#, Java, and JavaScript, along with the Redis OM framework for object mapping. This makes Redis Stack a user-friendly and adaptable solution for real-time data processing and management needs.

This part contains the following chapters:

- *Chapter 1, Introducing Redis Stack*
- *Chapter 2, Developing Modern Use Cases with Redis Stack*
- *Chapter 3, Getting Started with Redis Stack*
- *Chapter 4, Setting Up Client Libraries*

1

Introducing Redis Stack

Redis has achieved several important milestones since its inception in 2009, from taking the lead as the most popular key-value data store, according to the ranking published every month by the website DB-Engines (and the sixth among all database systems), up to establishing the record as the most downloaded container image on Docker. Not to mention that Redis has been the most loved database for five years in a row, according to the Developer Survey published by Stack Overflow in the years 2016-2021. And, for sure, you, or a friend of yours, have used it for some reason, work, or hobby.

If you are reading this book, chances are you have programmed an application using a Redis server, or at least you know what it is and what it is used for. In this chapter, we'll recap what made Redis the most famous caching system in the world and we'll share some anecdotes about the development undertaken by its creator, Salvatore Sanfilippo. We won't stay long on the story of Redis, though, because this book is about application modernization. As you read through, you will discover how the original database, designed for speed and simplicity, has evolved to resolve many of the new challenges of this age, without compromising on the ease of adoption, flexibility, and, above all, speed.

Redis Stack is an extension of Redis presented in 2022, which introduces JSON, vector, and time series data modeling capabilities, all supporting real-time queries and searches. Redis Stack represents a new approach to providing a rich data modeling experience all within the same database server. It introduces features such as vector similarity search to query structured and unstructured data (for example, text, images, or audio files) and delivers probabilistic Bloom filters to efficiently resolve recurrent big data problems. Redis Stack is also a data platform that supports event-driven programming and introduces stream processing features. By the end of this chapter, you will understand what Redis Stack is and how it enhances the Redis server with many new capabilities. Above all, you will learn the motivation behind Redis Stack and why multi-model databases can increase the speed of technological innovation for organizations of all sizes. In this chapter, we are going to cover the following topics:

- Exploring the history of Redis
- The open source project
- From key-value to multi-model real-time databases
- Redis Stack deployment types

Technical requirements

To follow along with the examples in the chapter, you will need the following:

- Redis Stack Server version 7.2 or later installed on your development environment. Alternatively, you can create a free Redis Cloud subscription to achieve a free plan and use a managed Redis Stack database. Refer to *Chapter 3, Getting Started with Redis Stack*.
- The dataset used in the examples – a conversion of the rows in the popular MySQL World database to Redis Hash data types. Find and download it from this book's repository if you'd like to test the examples that we propose in this chapter: `https://github.com/PacktPublishing/Redis-Stack-for-Application-Modernization`.

Exploring the history of Redis

Redis was conceived and designed in 2009 by the Italian software engineer Salvatore Sanfilippo as a solution to scaling LLOOGG, an online analytics server co-founded with Fabio Pitrola that empowered web admins to track user activities. Challenged by the scalability limitations of MySQL, Salvatore decided to rethink the concept of key-value storage and design something that would (admittedly) be different from Memcached, while preserving its simplicity and speed. The first beta release was shared on Google Code on February 25, 2009. A few months later, in September 2009, the first stable release, Redis 1.0, was published as a tar package of less than 200 KB.

Redis has been designed to offer an alternative for problems where **relational databases** (**RDBMSs**) are not a good fit because *there is something wrong if we use an RDBMS for all kinds of work*. However, in comparison to other data storage options that became popular when the NoSQL wave shook the world of databases (Memcached, the key-value data store released in 2003, or MongoDB, the document store released in 2009, and many more), Redis has its roots in computer science and makes a rich variety of data structures available. This is one of the distinguishing features of Redis and the likely reason that fostered its adoption by software engineers and developers – presenting data structures such as hashes, lists, sets, bitmaps, and so on that are familiar to software engineers so they could transfer the programming logic to data modeling without any lengthy and computationally expensive data transformation. Viewed in this light, we could say that Redis is about persisting the data structures of a programming language. An example of the simplicity of storing a Python dictionary in a Redis hash data structure follows:

```
user = {"name":"John",
        "surname":"Smith",
        "company":"Redis",
        "department":"Sales"}
r.hset("user:{}".format(str(2345)), mapping=user)
```

In the same way, adding elements to a Redis Set can be done using Python lists:

```
languages = ['Python', 'C++', 'JavaScript']
r.sadd("coding", *languages)
```

In these examples, the `user` dictionary and the `languages` list are stored without transformations, and this is one of the advantages that Redis data structures offer to developers: simplifying data modeling and reducing the transformational overhead required to convert the data in a format that can be mapped to the data store (thus reducing the so-called impedance mismatch).

There was a short gap between the first release and its adoption by Instagram and GitHub. If we try to dig into the reasons that made Redis so popular, we can mention a few, among which we count the speed and simplicity of deployment. Beyond the user experience, Redis is an act of dedication and passion, and as we read in Redis's own manifesto, code is like poetry; it's not just something we write to reach some practical result. People love beautiful stories and simplicity and everybody should fight against complexity.

What is surely true is that Redis is an idea to solve problems where relational databases, still tied to rigid paradigms, wouldn't fit the purpose. It is the product of creativity, inspiration, and love for things done manually, where good design and craftsmanship intertwine to accomplish something that simply works. An intimate artwork. And we like to recall Salvatore's words about the creative approach when writing Redis:

My wife claims I wrote it mostly while sitting on the WC for the first years, on a MacBook Air 11. Would be nice to tell her she is wrong, but she happens to be perfectly right about the matter.

From the most-used thinking room in Sicily to becoming the most-loved and used key-value database in the world, this is the story we have decided to tell in this book, and we are sure you will find the journey through the pages an exciting adventure.

One of the guiding principles behind Redis is being open source and driven by a community of enthusiast contributors. We'll explore that in the next section.

The open source project

The success of a technical project is always measurable in terms of the innovation of the proposal, simplicity of use, exhaustive documentation, high performance, low footprint, and stability, among other aspects. However, and this is true for many things, at the end of the day what matters is the capacity to resolve a problem and the impact of the solution. Organizations that decide to add new technology to their stack face several challenges to understand, prototype, validate, and set up a plan to deploy test environments together with a release strategy, a maintenance plan, and, finally, a plan to develop competence. Success stories require careful planning. From these many perspectives,

Redis is considered first-in-class, and in this book, we will expose many of the reasons that made Redis the de-facto standard among the in-memory data stores in the world. But even before digging into the features of Redis Stack, Redis, as an open source project, has undoubtedly added value to many businesses:

- A variety of options exist to get it running close to the application. It is available as a managed service in every public cloud provider, it can be installed from the source code or as a binary file, and Docker images are available for all the versions and flavors.
- It has good documentation and a command reference, together with examples (from the `https://redis.io/` website).
- It is straightforward to set up and test. The source code is self-contained and does not depend on external libraries.
- Client libraries for the most popular programming languages are available and supported (Java, JavaScript, Python, Go, and C#/.NET).
- The well-known and permissive BSD license grants the freedom to use, modify, and distribute Redis, among other advantages. Users can test and run Redis in production without any concerns.

These reasons, together with the fact that it's very easy to learn Redis, make it an attractive option to set up and use. On a computer configured to build C projects, pulling the source code from the GitHub repository, compiling it, and running the server can be done in less than a minute:

```
git clone https://github.com/redis/redis.git
cd redis/
make
./src/redis-server &
./src/redis-cli PING
PONG
```

The open source project delivers the core Redis server plus additional utilities, such as these:

- `redis-cli`, the command-line interface to administer the server and manage the data. This utility assists also in configuring scalable deployments with Redis Cluster and high availability with replication and Sentinel. Among other features, it includes auto-completion, online help for single commands (for example, `HELP HSET`), or by group of commands (for example, `HELP @hash`, to learn about the commands that can be used with the Hash data structure). Just type `HELP` to understand how to make use of the online help.
- `redis-benchmark`, a simple benchmarking utility to perform batches of tests for different data structures. Useful to evaluate how well the server performs on determined hardware.
- `redis-sentinel`, the agent that automates the management of replicated topologies and provides clients with a discovery service.

- `create-cluster`, a utility useful to set up a Redis Cluster environment for testing.
- `redis-check-rdb` and `redis-check-aof`, utilities to health check AOF and RDB persistence files.

Now that we have reviewed the basic principles behind Redis and its utilities, we are ready to dive into the world of data modeling. This journey will take us from relational databases to Redis core data structures, and we will see how the multi-model capabilities of Redis Stack simplify many data modeling problems.

From key-value to multi-model real-time databases

The core data structures that are available out of the box in the Redis server solve a variety of problems when it comes to mapping entities and relationships. To start with concrete examples of modeling using Redis, the usual option to store an object is the Hash data structure, while collections can be stored using Sets, Sorted Sets, or Lists (among other options because a collection can be modeled in several other ways). In this section, we will introduce the multi-model features of Redis Stack using a comprehensive approach, which may be useful for those who are used to storing data using the relational paradigm, which implies organizing the data in rows and columns of a table.

Consider the requirement to model a list of cities. Using the relational data model, we can define a table using the SQL **data definition language** (**DDL**) instruction `CREATE TABLE` as follows:

```
CREATE TABLE `city` (
  `ID` int NOT NULL AUTO_INCREMENT,
  `Name` char(35) NOT NULL DEFAULT '',
  `CountryCode` char(3) NOT NULL DEFAULT '',
  `District` char(20) NOT NULL DEFAULT '',
  `Population` int NOT NULL DEFAULT '0',
  PRIMARY KEY (`ID`),
  KEY `CountryCode` (`CountryCode`)
)
```

This table definition defines attributes for the `city` entity and specifies a primary key on an integer identifier (a surrogate key, in this case, provided the uniqueness of the attributes is not guaranteed for the `city` entity). The DDL command also defines an index on the `CountryCode` attribute. Data encoding, collation, and the specific technology adopted as the storage engine are not relevant in this context. We are focused on understanding the model and the ability that we have to query it.

Primary key lookup

Primary key lookup is the most efficient way to access data in a relational table. Filtering the table on the primary key attribute is as easy as executing the SQL SELECT statement:

```
SELECT * FROM city WHERE ID=653;
+-----+--------+-------------+----------+------------+
| ID  | Name   | CountryCode | District | Population |
+-----+--------+-------------+----------+------------+
| 653 | Madrid | ESP         | Madrid   |    2879052 |
+-----+--------+-------------+----------+------------+
1 row in set (0.00 sec)
```

Modeling a city using one of the Redis core data structures leads to mapping the data in the SQL table to Hashes, so we can store the attributes as field-value pairs, with the key name including the primary key:

```
127.0.0.1:6379> HSET city:653 Name "Madrid" CountryCode "ESP" District
"Madrid" Population 2879052
```

The HGETALL command can be used to retrieve the entire hash with minimal overhead (HGETALL has direct access to the value in the Redis keyspace):

```
HGETALL city:653
1) "Name"
2) "Madrid"
3) "CountryCode"
4) "ESP"
5) "District"
6) "Madrid"
7) "Population"
8) "2879052"
```

In addition, we can limit the bandwidth usage caused by the entire row transfer to the client and select only specific attributes. The SQL syntax is as follows:

```
SELECT Name, Population FROM city WHERE ID=653;
+--------+------------+
| Name   | Population |
+--------+------------+
| Madrid |    2879052 |
+--------+------------+
1 row in set (0.00 sec)
```

In this analogy between the relational model and Redis, the command is HGET (or HMGET for multiple values):

```
127.0.0.1:6379> HMGET city:653 Name Population
1) "Madrid"
2) "2879052"
```

While we need to extract data based on the primary key identifier, the solution is at hand in both the relational database and in Redis. Things get more complicated if we want to perform lookup and search queries on the dataset. In the next examples, we'll see how the complexity and performance of such operations may vary substantially.

Secondary key lookup

Primary key lookups are efficient: after all, the primary key is an index, and it guarantees direct access to the table row. But what if we want to search for cities by filtering on an attribute? Let's try an indexed search against our relational database over the CountryCode column, which has a secondary index:

```
mysql> SELECT Name FROM city WHERE CountryCode = "ESP";
+-----------------------------------+
| Name                              |
+-----------------------------------+
| Madrid                            |
| Barcelona                         |
| [...]                             |
+-----------------------------------+
59 rows in set (0.02 sec)
```

This is an efficient search because the table defines an index on the CountryCode column. To continue the comparison of the relational database versus Redis, we will need to execute the same query against the stored Hashes. For this demonstration, we will assume that we have migrated the city table to Hashes in the Redis server. By design, Redis has no secondary indexing feature for any of the core data structures, which means that we should scan all the Hashes prefixed by the "city:" namespace, then read the city name from every Hash and check whether it matches our search term. The following example performs a non-blocking scan of the keyspace, filtering on the key name ("city:*") in batches of configurable size (three, in the example):

```
127.0.0.1:6379> SCAN 0 MATCH city:* COUNT 3
1) "512"
2) 1) "city:4019"
   2) "city:9"
   3) "city:103"
```

The client should now extract the `CountryCode` value from every city, compare it to the search term, and repeat until the scan is concluded. This is obviously a time-consuming and expensive approach. There are ways to improve the efficiency of such batched operations. We will explore three standard options and then show how to resolve the problem using the Redis Stack capabilities:

- Pipelining
- Using functions
- Using indexes
- Redis Stack capabilities

We will look at these in detail next.

Pipelining

The first approach to reducing the overhead of the search operation is to use pipelining, which is supported by all major client libraries. Pipelining collects a batch of commands, delivers them to the server, and collects the outputs from the server immediately before returning the result to the client. This option dramatically reduces the latency of the overall operation, as it saves on the roundtrip time to the server (an analogy that works is going to the supermarket once to purchase 30 items rather than going 30 times and purchasing one item on every visit). The pros and cons of pipelining are as follows:

- **Pros**: Saves on roundtrip time and does not block the server, as the server executes a batch of commands and returns the results to the client. Therefore, it increases overall system throughput. Pipelining is especially useful when batching operations.
- **Cons**: The complexity of the operation is proportional to the number and complexity of the operations in the pipeline that are executed by the server. This may increase the memory usage on the server, as it keeps the intermediate results in memory until all commands in the pipeline are processed. The client manages multiple responses, which adds complexity to its business logic, especially when it has to deal with errors of some operations in the pipeline.

Using functions

Lua scripting and functions (functions were introduced in Redis 7.0 and represent an evolution of Lua scripting for remote server execution) help to offload the client and remove network latency. The search is local to the server and close to the data (equivalent to the concept of stored procedures). The following function is an example of local search:

```
#!lua name=mylib

local function city_by_cc(keys, args)
    local match, cursor = {}, "0";
    repeat
```

```
        local ret = redis.call("SCAN", cursor, "MATCH", "city:*",
"COUNT", 100);
        local cities = ret[2];
          for i = 1, #cities do
            local keyname = cities[i];
            local ccode = redis.
call('HMGET',keyname,'Name','CountryCode')
            if ccode[2] == args[1] then
               match[#match + 1] = ccode[1];
            end;
          end;
          cursor = ret[1];
        until cursor == "0";
    return match;
end
redis.register_function('city_by_cc', city_by_cc)
```

In this function, we do the following:

1. We perform a scan of the entire keyspace, filtering by the "`city:*`" prefix, which means that we will iterate through all the keys in the Redis server database.
2. For every key returned by the `SCAN` command, we retrieve the name and `CountryCode` of the city using the `HMGET` command.
3. If `CountryCode` matches our search filter, we add the city to an output array.
4. When the scan is completed, we return the array to the client.

Type the code into the `mylib.lua` file and import the library as follows:

```
cat mylib.lua | redis-cli -x FUNCTION LOAD
```

The function can be invoked using the following command:

```
127.0.0.1:6379> FCALL city_by_cc 0 "ESP"
 1) "A Coru\xf1a (La Coru\xf1a)"
 2) "Almer\xeda"
[...]
59) "Barakaldo"
```

The pros and cons of using functions are as follows:

- **Pros**: The operation is executed on the server, and the client does not experiment with any overhead.
- **Cons**: The complexity of the operation is linear, and the function (like any other Lua script or function) blocks the server. Any other concurrent operation must wait until the execution of the function is completed. Long scans make the server appear stuck to other clients.

Using indexes

Data scans, wherever they are executed (client or server side), are slow and ineffective in satisfying real-time requirements. This is especially true when the keyspace stores millions of keys or more. An alternative approach for search operations using the Redis core data structures is to create a secondary index. There are many options to do this using Redis collections. As an example, we can create an index of Spanish cities using a Set as follows:

```
SADD city:esp "Sevilla" "Madrid" "Barcelona" "Valencia" "Bilbao" "Las
Palmas de Gran Canaria"
```

This data structure has interesting properties for our needs. We can retrieve all the Spanish cities in a single command:

```
127.0.0.1:6379> SMEMBERS city:esp
1) "Madrid"
2) "Sevilla"
3) "Valencia"
4) "Barcelona"
5) "Bilbao"
6) "Las Palmas de Gran Canaria"
```

Or we can check whether a specific city is in Spain using `SISMEMBER`, a constant time-complexity command:

```
127.0.0.1:6379> SISMEMBER city:esp "Madrid"
(integer) 1
```

And we can even search the index for cities having a name that matches a pattern:

```
127.0.0.1:6379> SSCAN city:esp 0 MATCH B*
1) "0"
2) 1) "Barcelona"
   2) "Bilbao"
```

We can refine our search requirements and design an index that considers the population. In such a case we could use a Sorted Set and Set the population as the score:

```
127.0.0.1:6379> ZADD city:esp 2879052 "Madrid" 701927 "Sevilla"
1503451 "Barcelona" 739412 "Valencia" 357589 "Bilbao" 354757 "Las
Palmas de Gran Canaria"
(integer) 6
```

The main feature of the Sorted Set data structure is that its members are stored in an ordered tree-like structure (Redis uses a skiplist data structure), and with that, it is possible to execute low-complexity range searches. As an example, let's retrieve Spanish cities with more than 2 million inhabitants:

```
127.0.0.1:6379> ZRANGE city:esp 2000000 +inf BYSCORE
1) "Madrid"
```

We can also check whether a city belongs to the index of Spanish cities:

```
127.0.0.1:6379> ZRANK city:esp Madrid
(integer) 5
```

In the former example, the `ZRANK` command informs us that the city Madrid belongs to the index and is fifth highest in the ranking. This solution resolves the overhead caused by having to scan the entire keyspace looking for matches.

The drawback of such a manual approach to indexing the data is that indexes need to reflect the data at any time. Considering scenarios where we want to add or remove a city from our database, we need to perform the two operations of removing the city Hash and updating the index, atomically. We can use a Redis transaction to perform atomic changes on both the data and the index:

```
127.0.0.1:6379> MULTI
OK
127.0.0.1:6379(TX)> DEL city:653
QUEUED
127.0.0.1:6379(TX)> ZREM city:esp "Madrid"
QUEUED
127.0.0.1:6379(TX)> EXEC
1) (integer) 1
2) (integer) 1
```

Custom secondary indexes come at a price, though, because complex searches become hard to manage using multiple data structures. Indexes must be maintained, and the complexity of such solutions may get out of hand, putting the consistency of search operations at risk. The pros and cons of using indexing are as follows:

- **Pros**: Simple and fast search operations are possible using Redis core data structures to create a secondary index
- **Cons**: The secondary index needs to be maintained, and search operations on multiple fields (what is called a composite index in relational databases) are not immediate and need thoughtful planning, implementation, and maintenance

Next, we will examine the capabilities of Redis Stack.

Redis Stack capabilities

Caching is one of the frequent use cases for which Redis shines as the best-in-class storage solution. This is because it stores data in memory, and offers real-time performance. It is also lightweight, as data structures are optimized to consume little memory. Redis does not need any complex configuration or maintenance and it is open source, so there is no reason not to give it a try. As a real-time data storage, it seems plausible that complex search operations may not be the primary use case users are interested in when using Redis. After all, fast retrieval of data by key is what made Redis so versatile as a cache or as a session store.

However, if in addition to the ability to use core data structures to store the data, we ensure that fast searches can be performed (besides primary key lookup), it is possible to think beyond the basic caching use case and start looking at Redis as a full-fledged database, capable of high-speed searches.

So far, we have presented simple and common search problems and *both* solutions using the traditional SQL approach *and* possible data modeling strategies using Redis core data structures. In the following sections, we will show how Redis Stack resolves query and search use cases and extends the core features of Redis with an integrated modeling and developing experience. We will introduce the following capabilities:

- Querying, indexing, and searching documents
- Time series data modeling
- Probabilistic data structures
- Programmability

Let's discuss each of these capabilities in detail.

Querying, indexing, and searching documents

Redis Stack complements Redis with the ability to create secondary indexes on Hashes or JSON documents, the two document types supported by Redis Stack. The search examples seen so far can be resolved with the indexing features. To perform an indexed search, we create an index against the hashes modeling the cities using the following syntax:

```
FT.CREATE city_idx
ON HASH
PREFIX 1 city:
SCHEMA Name AS name TEXT
CountryCode AS countrycode TAG SORTABLE
Population AS population NUMERIC SORTABLE
```

The `FT.CREATE` command instructs the server to perform the following operations:

1. Create an index for the desired values of the Hash document.
2. Scan the keyspace and retrieve the documents prefixed by the "`hash:`" string.
3. Create the index corresponding to the desired data structure and, as specified by the `FT.CREATE` command, the Hash in this case. The indexes defined in this example are of the following types:
   - `TEXT`, which enables full-text search on the `Name` field
   - `TAG SORTABLE`, which enables an exact-match search against the `CountryCode` field and enables high-performance sorting by the value of the attribute
   - `NUMERIC SORTABLE`, which enables range queries against the `Population` field and enables high-performance sorting by the value of the attribute

As soon as the indexing operation against the relevant data – all the keys prefixed by "`hash:`"– is completed, we can execute the queries and searches seen so far, and more. The syntax in the following example executes a search of all the cities with the value "`ESP`" in the `TAG` field type and returns only the name of the cities, sorted in lexicographical order. Finally, the first three results are returned using the `LIMIT` option. Note that this query is executed against the new `city_idx` index, and not directly against the data:

```
127.0.0.1:6379> FT.SEARCH city_idx '@countrycode:{ESP}' RETURN 1 name
SORTBY name LIMIT 0 3
1) (integer) 59
2) "city:670"
3) 1) "name"
   2) "A Coru\xc3\xb1a (La Coru\xc3\xb1a)"
4) "city:690"
5) 1) "name"
   2) "Albacete"
6) "city:687"
7) 1) "name"
   2) "Alcal\xc3\xa1 de Henares"
```

It is possible to combine several textual queries/filters in the same index. Using exact-match and full-text search, we can verify whether Madrid is a Spanish city:

```
127.0.0.1:6379> FT.SEARCH city_idx '@name:Madrid @countrycode:{ESP}'
RETURN 1 name
1) (integer) 1
2) "city:653"
3) 1) "name"
   2) "Madrid"
```

In a previous example, the range search was executed using the `ZRANGE` data structure. Using the indexing capability of Redis Stack, we can execute range searches using the `NUMERIC` field type. So, if we want to retrieve the Spanish cities with more than 2 million inhabitants, we will write the following search query:

```
127.0.0.1:6379> FT.SEARCH city_idx '@countrycode:{ESP}' FILTER
population 2000000 +inf RETURN 1 name
1) (integer) 1
2) "city:653"
3) 1) "name"
   2) "Madrid"
```

Redis Stack offers flexibility and concise syntax to combine several field types, of which we have seen only a limited but representative number of examples. Once the index is created, the user can go ahead and use it, and add new documents or update existing ones. The database maintains the indexes updated synchronously as soon as documents are created or changed.

Besides full-text, exact-match, and range searches, we can also perform data aggregation (as we would in a relational database using the `GROUP BY` statement). If we would like to retrieve the three most populated countries, sorted in descending order, we would solve the problem in SQL as follows:

```
SELECT CountryCode,
SUM(Population) AS sum
FROM city
GROUP BY CountryCode
ORDER BY sum DESC
LIMIT 3;
+-------------+-----------+
| CountryCode | sum       |
+-------------+-----------+
| CHN         | 175953614 |
| IND         | 123298526 |
| BRA         |  85876862 |
+-------------+-----------+
3 rows in set (0.01 sec)
```

We can perform complex aggregations with the `FT.AGGREGATE` command. Using the following command, we can perform a real-time search and aggregation to compute the total population of the top three countries by summing up the inhabitants of the cities per country:

```
127.0.0.1:6379> FT.AGGREGATE city_idx * GROUPBY 1 @countrycode REDUCE
SUM 1 @population AS sum SORTBY 2 @sum DESC LIMIT 0 3
1) (integer) 232
2) 1) "countrycode"
   2) "chn"
```

```
    3) "sum"
    4) "175953614"
 3) 1) "countrycode"
    2) "ind"
    3) "sum"
    4) "123298526"
 4) 1) "countrycode"
    2) "bra"
    3) "sum"
    4) "85876862"
```

To summarize this brief introduction where we addressed the search and aggregation capabilities, it is worth mentioning that there are multiple types of searches, such as phonetic matching, auto-completion suggestions, geo searches, or a spellchecker to help design great applications. We will cover them in depth in *Chapter 5, Redis Stack as a Document Store,* where we showcase Redis Stack as a document store.

Besides modeling objects as Hash, it is possible to store, update, and retrieve JSON documents. The JSON format needs no introduction, as it permeates data pipelines including heterogeneous subsystems, protocols, databases, and so on. Redis Stack delivers this capability out of the box and manages JSON documents in a similar way to Hashes, which means that it is possible to store, index, and search JSON objects and work with them using JSONPath syntax:

1. To illustrate the syntax to store, search, and retrieve JSON data along the lines of the previous examples, let's store city objects formatted as JSON:

   ```
   JSON.SET city:653 $ '{"Name":"Madrid", "CountryCode":"ESP",
   "District":"Madrid", "Population":2879052}'
   JSON.SET city:5 $ '{"Name":"Amsterdam", "CountryCode":"NLD",
   "District":"Noord-Holland", "Population":731200}'
   JSON.SET city:1451 $ '{"Name":"Tel Aviv-Jaffa",
   "CountryCode":"ISR", "District":"Tel Aviv",
   "Population":348100}'
   ```

2. We don't need anything else to start working with the JSON documents stored in Redis Stack. We can then perform basic retrieval operations on entire documents:

   ```
   127.0.0.1:6379> JSON.GET city:653
   "{\"Name\":\"Madrid\",\"CountryCode\":\"ESP\",\"District\":\"Ma-
   drid\",\"Population\":2879052}"
   ```

3. We can also retrieve the desired property (or multiple properties at once) stored on a certain path, with fast access guaranteed, because the document is stored in a tree structure:

   ```
   127.0.0.1:6379> JSON.GET city:653 $.Name
   "[\"Madrid\"]"
   127.0.0.1:6379> JSON.GET city:653 $.Name $.CountryCode
   "{\"$.Name\":[\"Madrid\"],\"$.CountryCode\":[\"ESP\"]}"
   ```

4. As we have seen for Hash documents, we can index JSON documents using a similar syntax and perform search operations. The following command creates an index for all the JSON documents with the `city:` prefix in the database:

```
FT.CREATE city_idx ON JSON PREFIX 1 city: SCHEMA $.Name AS name
TEXT $.CountryCode AS countrycode TAG SORTABLE $.Population AS
population NUMERIC SORTABLE
```

5. And using the `FT.SEARCH` command with an identical syntax as seen for the Hash documents, we can perform search operations:

```
127.0.0.1:6379> FT.SEARCH city_idx '@countrycode:{ESP}' FILTER
population 2000000 +inf RETURN 1 name
1) (integer) 1
2) "city:653"
3) 1) "name"
   2) "Madrid"
```

Unlike Hash documents, the JSON supports nested levels (up to 128) and can store properties, objects, arrays, and geographical locations at any level in a tree-like structure, so the JSON format opens up a variety of use cases using a compact and flexible data structure.

Time series data modeling

Time series databases do not need any long introduction: they are data structures that can store data points happening at a certain time, indicated by a Unix timestamp expressed in milliseconds, with an associated numeric data value, typically with double precision. This data structure applies to many use cases, such as monitoring entities over time or tracking user activities for a determined service. Redis Stack has an integrated time series database that offers many useful features to manage the data points, for querying and searching, and provides convenient formatting commands for data processing and visualization. Beginning with time series modeling is straightforward:

1. We can create a time series from the command-line interface (or from any of the client libraries that support time series):

```
TS.CREATE "app:monitor:temp"
```

2. Storing samples into the time series can be done with the `TS.ADD` command. If we would like to store the temperature measured by the sensor of a meteorological station captured every few seconds, the commands would be as follows:

```
127.0.0.1:6379> "TS.ADD" "app:monitor:temp" "*" "20"
(integer) 1675632813307
127.0.0.1:6379> "TS.ADD" "app:monitor:temp" "*" "20"
(integer) 1675632818179
```

```
127.0.0.1:6379> "TS.ADD" "app:monitor:temp" "*" "20"
(integer) 1675632824174
127.0.0.1:6379> "TS.ADD" "app:monitor:temp" "*" "20.1"
(integer) 1675632829519
127.0.0.1:6379> "TS.ADD" "app:monitor:temp" "*" "20"
(integer) 1675632835052
```

3. We are instructing the database to insert the sample at the current time, so we specify the * argument. We can finally retrieve the samples stored in the time series for the desired interval:

```
127.0.0.1:6379> "TS.RANGE" "app:monitor:temp" "1675632818179"
"1675632829519"
1) 1) (integer) 1675632818179
   2) 20
2) 1) (integer) 1675632824174
   2) 20
3) 1) (integer) 1675632829519
   2) 20.1
```

We have just scratched the surface of using time series with Redis Stack, because data may be aggregated, down-sampled, and indexed to address many different uses.

Probabilistic data structures

Deterministic data structures – all those structures that store and return the same data that was stored (such as Strings, Sets, Hashes, and the rest of Redis structures) – are a good solution for standard amounts of data, but they may become inadequate due to the constantly growing volumes of data that systems must handle. Redis offers several options to store and present data to extract different types of insights. Strings are an example because they can be encoded as integers and used as counters:

```
127.0.0.1:6379> INCR cnt
(integer) 1
127.0.0.1:6379> INCRBY cnt 3
(integer) 4
```

Strings can also be managed down to the bit level to store multiple integer counters of variable length and stored at different offsets of a single string to reduce storage overheads using the bitfield data structure:

```
127.0.0.1:6379> BITFIELD cnt INCRBY i5 0 5
1) (integer) 5
127.0.0.1:6379> BITFIELD cnt INCRBY i5 0 5
1) (integer) 10
127.0.0.1:6379> BITFIELD cnt GET i5 0
1) (integer) 10
```

Regular counters, sets, and hash tables perform well for any amount of data but handling large amounts of data represents a challenge to scale the resources of the machine where Redis Stack is running, because of its memory requirements.

Deterministic data structures have given way to probabilistic data structures because of the need to scale up to large quantities of data and give a reasonably approximated answer to questions such as the following:

- How many different pages has the user visited so far?
- What are the top players with the highest score?
- Has the user already seen this ad?
- How many unique values have appeared so far in the data stream?
- How many values in the data stream are smaller than a given value?

In the attempt to give an answer to the first question in the list, we could calculate the hash of the URL of the visited page and store it in a Redis collection, such as a Set, and then retrieve the cardinality of the structure using the `SCARD` command. While this solution works very well (and is deterministically exact), scaling it to many users and many visited pages represents a cost.

Let's consider an example with a probabilistic data structure. `HyperLogLog` estimates the cardinality of a set with minimal memory usage and computational overhead without compromising the accuracy of the results, while consuming only a fraction of memory and CPU, so you would count the visited pages and get an estimation as follows:

```
127.0.0.1:6379> PFADD pages "https://redis.com/" "https://redis.io/
docs/stack/bloom/" "https://redis.io/docs/data-types/hyperloglogs/"
(integer) 1
127.0.0.1:6379> PFCOUNT pages
(integer) 3
```

Redis reports the following memory usage for `HyperLogLog`:

```
127.0.0.1:6379> MEMORY USAGE pages
(integer) 96
```

Attempting to resolve the same problem using a Set and storing the hashes for these URLs would be done as follows:

```
127.0.0.1:6379> SADD hashpages "522195171ed14f78e1f33f84a98f0de6"
"f5518a82f8be40e2994fdca7f71e090d" "c4e78b8c136f6e1baf454b7192e89cd1"
(integer) 3
127.0.0.1:6379> MEMORY USAGE hashpages
(integer) 336
```

Probabilistic data structures trade accuracy for time and space efficiency and give an answer to this and other questions by addressing several data analysis problems against big amounts of data and, most relevantly, efficiently.

Programmability

Redis Stack embeds a serverless engine for event-driven data processing allowing users to write and run their own functions on data stored in Redis. The functions are implemented in JavaScript and executed by the engine upon user invocation or in response to events such as changes to data, execution of commands, or when events are added to a Redis Stream data structure. It is also possible to configure timed executions, so periodical maintenance operations can be scheduled.

Redis Stack minimizes the execution time by running the functions as close as possible to the data, improving data locality, minimizing network congestion, and increasing the overall throughput of the system.

With this capability, it is possible to implement event-driven data flows, thus opening the doors to many use cases, such as the following:

1. A basic library including a function can be implemented in text files, as in the following snippet:

```
#!js api_version=1.0 name=lib
redis.registerFunction('hello', function(){
    return 'Hello Gears!';
});
```

2. The `lib.js` file containing this function can then be imported into Redis Stack:

```
redis-cli -x TFUNCTION LOAD < ./lib.js
```

3. It can then be executed on demand from the command-line interface:

```
127.0.0.1:6379>  TFCALL lib.hello 0
"Hello Gears!"
```

4. Things become more interesting if we subscribe to data changes as follows:

```
redis.registerKeySpaceTrigger("key_logger", "user:",
function(client, data){
    if (data.event == 'del'){
        client.call("INCR", "removed");
        redis.log(JSON.stringify(data));
        redis.log("A user has been removed");
    }
});
```

In this function, we do the following:

- We are subscribing to events against the keys prefixed by the "`user:`" namespace
- We check the command that triggered the event, and if it is a deletion, we act and specify what's going to happen next
- The triggered action will be the increment of a counter, and it will also write a message into the server's log

5. To test this function, we proceed to create and delete a user profile:

```
127.0.0.1:6379> HSET user:123 name "John" last "Smith"
(integer) 2
127.0.0.1:6379> DEL user:123
(integer) 1
```

6. A quick check of the server's log verifies that the condition has been met, and the information logged:

```
299:M 05 Feb 2023 19:13:09.004 * <redisgears_2>
{"event":"del","key":"user:123","key_raw":{}}
299:M 05 Feb 2023 19:13:09.005 * <redisgears_2> A user has been
removed
```

And the counter has increased:

```
127.0.0.1:6379> GET removed
"1"
```

Through this book, we will come to understand the differences between Lua scripts, Redis functions, and JavaScript functions, and we will explore the many possible programmability features along with proposals to resolve challenging problems with simple solutions.

So, what is Redis Stack?

Redis Stack combines the speed and stability of the Redis server with a set of well-established capabilities and integrates them into a compact solution that is easy to install and manage – **Redis Stack Server**. The **RedisInsight** desktop application is a visualization tool and data manager that complements Redis Stack Server with a set of functionalities useful for visualizing data stored by different models as well as providing interactive tutorials with popular examples, and more.

To complete the picture, the **Redis Stack Client SDK** includes the most popular client libraries to develop against Redis Stack in the Java, Python, and JavaScript programming languages.

Figure 1.1 – The Redis Stack logo

Redis Stack empowers users with the liberty to use it for free in development and production environments and merges the open source BSD-licensed Redis with search and query capabilities, JSON support, time series handling, and probabilistic data structures. It is available under a dual license, specifically the **Redis Source Available License** (**RSALv2**) and the **Server Side Public License** (**SSPL**).

So, in a few examples, we have introduced new possibilities to modernize applications, and now we owe you an answer to the original question, "*What is Redis Stack?*"

Key-value storage

To define what Redis Stack is, we need to go back for a moment to its origins, because Redis is the spinal cord of Redis Stack. Redis was born as in-memory storage to accelerate massive amounts of queries and achieve sub-millisecond latency while optimizing memory usage and maximizing the ease of adoption and administration. It appeared at the same time as other solutions taking part in the NoSQL wave and deviating from relational modeling. While the key-value Memcached store was an already established solution, Redis became popular too as a type of key-value storage. So, we can surely say that Redis Stack can be used as a key-value store.

Data structure server

However, considering Redis Stack as a simple key-value data store is reductive. Redis is best known for its flexibility in storing collections such as Hashes, Sets, Sorted Sets or Lists, Bitmaps and Bitfields, Streams, `HyperLogLog` probabilistic data structures, and geo indexes. And, together with data structures, its efficient low-complexity algorithms make storing and searching data a joy for developers. We can certainly say that Redis Stack is also a data structure store.

Multi-model database

The features introduced so far are integrated into Redis Stack Server and extend the Redis server, turning the data structure server into a multi-model database. This provides a rich data modeling experience where multiple heterogeneous data structures such as documents, vectors, and time series coexist in the same database. Software architects will appreciate the variety of possibilities for designing new solutions without multiple specialized databases and software developers will be empowered with a rich set of client libraries that improve the ease of software design. Database administrators will discover how shallow the learning curve is to learn to administer a single database rather than installing, configuring, and maintaining several data stores.

Data platform

The characteristics discussed so far, together with stream processing and the possibility to execute JavaScript functions for event-driven development, push Redis Stack beyond the boundaries of the multi-model database definition. Combining Redis, the key-value data store that is popular as a cache, with advanced data structures and multi-model design, and with the capability of a message broker with event-driven programming features, turns Redis Stack into a powerful data platform.

We have completed the Redis Stack walk-through, and to conclude this chapter, we will briefly discuss how to install it using different methods.

Redis Stack deployment types

We have completed an overview of Redis Stack and its key differentiators from the Redis server. In the next chapters, we will dive into the many use cases that can be solved and will discuss lots of examples and code snippets. For the time being, you can start planning your next Redis Stack-based modern application and think about the platform that will host the data store.

Redis Stack is available on all main operating systems (Linux, Mac, Windows) in binary format. It is also available as a Docker image, so you can start it right now by launching a container on your machine as follows:

```
docker run -d --name redis-stack-server -p 6379:6379 redis/redis-
stack-server:latest
```

Redis Stack is free, and you can install, manage, and deploy it in production without any license fee. It's Redis, after all. You can also install RedisInsight and connect it to Redis Stack Server to see how easy is to bring your data under control.

If you don't want to install Redis Stack, you can also create a free Redis Cloud account at `https://redis.com/try-free/`. You can get a 30 MB forever-free database and a public endpoint to use it from your laptop. No VPN is needed, and no certificate setup is required. You can choose where to create your free instance, for example on Amazon AWS, Google Cloud, or Microsoft Azure.

Be prepared, because if you haven't already thought, "*I didn't know that Redis could do this,*" we will surprise you with the many things you will be able to do, for free, with Redis Stack!

Summary

In this chapter, we have introduced Redis Stack starting from its foundation, the open source Redis server. We have introduced the multi-model approach of Redis Stack with examples, and we have performed simple searches beyond primary key lookup. You have learned about the syntax of the commands to use Redis Stack as a document store capable of storing Hash and JSON documents, and as a time series store, to store data points and search through them. Finally, we explored probabilistic data structures and have shown examples of database programmability.

In *Chapter 2, Developing Modern Use Cases with Redis Stack*, we will see that Redis Stack can be used in many different scenarios. From an in-memory, real-time cache and session store, to storing leaderboards, or being used as a message broker in a microservice architecture, you will learn that Redis Stack can be a better fit than deploying multiple specialized databases and messaging solutions.

2

Developing Modern Use Cases with Redis Stack

Redis Stack can be used in many different scenarios. While Redis is traditionally used as an in-memory real-time cache and as a session store, or it can be used to store leaderboards or act as a message broker using different core data structures, Redis Stack extends Redis's well-known features, thus becoming a flexible solution to many emerging problems. In this chapter, we will present an overview of the traditional use cases so that you will find solutions to classical problems. We will focus on the new use cases that are possible using Redis Stack's multi-model capabilities.

In this chapter, you will learn how Redis Stack can prevent **denial-of-service** (**DoS**) attacks or spot attempts of fraud, thus helping secure the stability of an application and the confidentiality of data. You will also discover how to track the nearest available bikes of the urban bike-sharing service and how to efficiently count all the user authentications over a certain period, from tracking the temperature of thousands of meteorological stations or analyzing massive volumes of trades of a stock market to computing statistical analysis over time series. You will also learn how to build a recommendation engine using object recognition and audio matching. You will understand how Redis Stack can replace monolithic data layers by adapting to the different requirements of a microservice architecture. These and many more problems can be solved using Redis Stack.

In this chapter, we are going to cover the following topics:

- Caching, rate-limiting, geo-positioning, and other Redis traditional use cases
- Going beyond the real-time cache with Redis Stack
- Redis Stack for microservice architectures

Technical requirements

To follow along with the examples in the chapter, you will need to install Redis Stack Server 7.2 or a later version on your development environment. Alternatively, you can create a free Redis Cloud subscription to get a free plan and use a managed Redis Stack database.

Caching, rate-limiting, geo-positioning, and other Redis traditional use cases

Implementing the many use cases that companies demand from their technical staff requires a technological stack and a competence development plan to sustain the efforts of designing, implementing, testing, and maintaining a solution. Evaluating and benchmarking the different options is time-consuming, and introducing a new technology demands processes and often increases the time to market for new features and products, thus slowing down the innovation and competitiveness of a company. Redis Stack is often regarded as a Swiss Army knife when it comes to solving different problems. As a data structures server, it allows you to transfer many responsibilities from application servers or specialized databases to a single, compact database server. In this section, we will recap the classical use cases that made Redis popular. Those uses include the following:

- Caching
- Session store
- Rate limiter
- Leaderboards
- Data deduplication
- Geo-positioning
- Message processing and delivery

Let's go through each of these in turn.

Caching

Speed and flexibility are among the features that made Redis the most popular **cache** in the world. As an in-memory data store, with additional features such as data persistence, high availability, and scalability, Redis can survive massive failures and reload data from disk, failover to a replica, and scale beyond a single machine if configured as a cluster. Redis is also easy to set up and maintain, and it's self-contained: everything you need to set up a full-fledged caching layer is there in the open source package.

Data can be cached using different data structures, each with different trade-offs. It is possible to cache data in strings, as follows:

```
127.0.0.1:6379> GET "wp:posts:3288"
"O:8:\"stdClass\":23:{s:2:\"ID\";s:4:\"3288\";s:11:\"post_
author\";s:1:\"2\";s:9:\"post_date\";s:19:\"2016-03-29
22:15:41\";s:13:\"post_date_gmt\";s:19:\"2016-03-29
21:15:41\";s:12:\"post_content\";s:6519:\"La f\xc3\xadsica cu\xc3\
```

```
xa1ntica indica que\xc2\xa0la realidad es un conjunto de posibilidades
potencialmente infinitas. Con los \xc3\xbaltimos desconcertantes
descubrimientos, nos damos cuenta siempre..."
```

In this example, a single article in a **WordPress** blog is cached using the string data structure, and it will accelerate retrieving the post's content rather than accessing it from the MySQL relational database WordPress uses. Cached data is read from memory and then deserialized, after which it can be returned to the web client and rendered into a web page.

Alternatively, it is possible to cache data in a Hash data structure, with information organized in a dictionary format, which is useful if you only wish to retrieve the metadata of the posts when, for example, you would like to present a list of articles to choose from, without the overhead caused by retrieving and transferring the entire post, thus saving time and bandwidth:

```
127.0.0.1:6379> HMGET "wp:posts:3288" post_status post_modified post_
date_gmt ID
1) "publish"
2) "2016-03-29 22:15:41"
3) "2016-03-29 21:15:41"
4) "3288"
```

Redis is a good fit for the different caching strategies (cache-aside, write-behind, write-through, and read-replica) and is flexible concerning the typical requirements a cache should fulfill, such as flexible expiration (TTL) and eviction policies (LRU or LFU), configurable time-to-live and the already mentioned persistence, high availability, and scalability.

Session store

The HTTP protocol is stateless: every request is independent and unrelated to other requests. Servers ignore the user identity and don't distinguish between new visitors and returning visitors. But what if we need to keep track of a client's activity across multiple requests? **Session management** strategies are used by websites to store session information for a particular user and track their activity. Let's look at a high-level description of user interaction with a website through a browser:

1. The user browses a certain website, and the server receives the request.
2. The server generates a random ID (for example, a UUID).
3. The ID is associated with session data on the server.
4. The ID is delivered to the client and stored in a cookie.
5. The browser attaches the cookie to every subsequent request.
6. The server identifies the returning user from the ID stored in the cookie.

The server, by managing session data associated with the user, can retrieve the user preferences, such as items added to a shopping cart (regardless of whether the user has authenticated to the website). Session information is stored in memory in the application server:

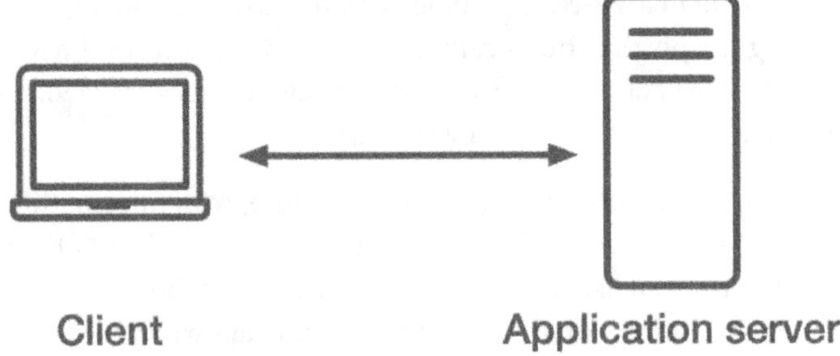

Figure 2.1 – Application servers as session managers

This approach is simplified and may work until we start adding requirements to our service. Guaranteeing the best user experience possible, a typical requirement, becomes challenging during peaks of traffic. Distributing the load to multiple application servers helps us manage increasing workloads:

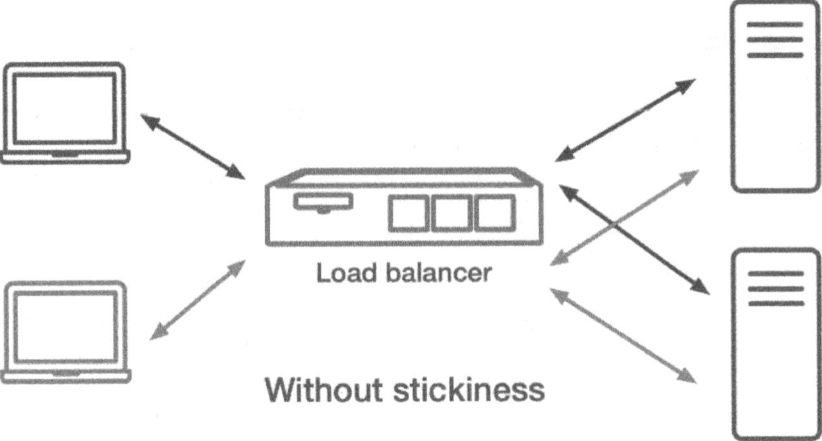

Figure 2.2 – Load balancers in client/server architectures

Scaling application servers is easy: clients are routed by a load balancer to different application servers and the service scales the workload accordingly by relying on multiple machines that receive and process a subset of the user requests. However, this approach has an inconvenience: session data is saved locally to the application server, and a subsequent request from a user will be served by a different application server and will create a new session. One solution to this problem is to use a **sticky session**: load balancers issue a cookie or track information such as the IP address and route requests to the server where the session was first created:

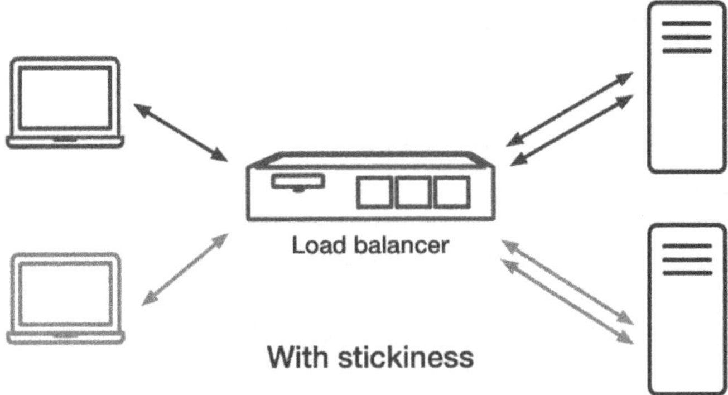

Figure 2.3 – Load balancers map clients to application servers

Sticky sessions resolve the problem of identifying returning users in the presence of multiple application servers, but there are still open points that need to be addressed. What if the service owner wants to collect information about the active sessions? And how can we deal with service outages, which may cause the loss of session data? Application servers are not specialized to persist data and don't have a suitable interface to serve session information to other services for data collection and offline analysis. Wrapping up, session management needs to address the following challenges:

- Applications, application servers, or load balancers can be unavailable, causing the loss of session information
- There may also be the requirement to centralize session data to make it available to other services
- Container-specific sessions generate local session information that's not shared across different application servers in a load-balancing scenario

These challenges pave the way to introducing Redis Stack as a central, scalable, and highly available session store. A session store needs to be fast and requires an in-memory solution. The user is waiting for their details to be retrieved before their unique data can be returned. Writes also need to be fast as sessions need to be updated frequently, at least to extend the time-to-live when the user is active on the website:

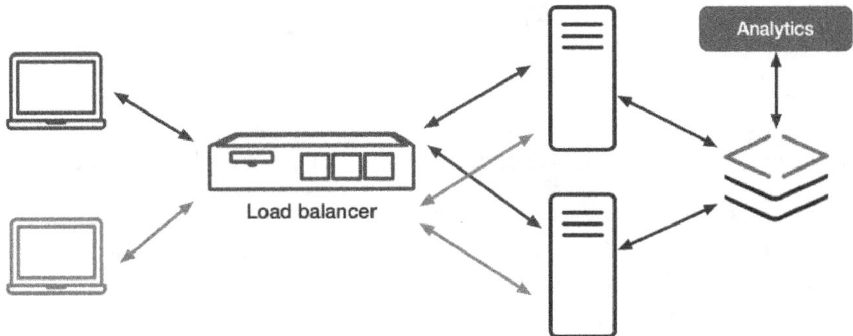

Figure 2.4 – Redis Stack as a distributed session store

Several frameworks can manage Redis as a session store behind the scenes. Let's mention a few:

- Spring with the **Spring Session Data Redis** module
- Express with the **connect-redis** npm package
- Flask, using the **Flask-Session** extension

Having a centralized session store with search, query, and aggregation capabilities enables many new use cases. Relevant data can be extracted from the open sessions (such as the number of users about to buy certain products, the total cost of items in the open shopping cart, and more).

Rate limiter

Redis presents several options to model a counter using the core data structures. Everything can be counted – visits to a website, the number of daily or monthly authentications, transactions per day and user, the number of clicks on a web page, and so on. Redis is a flexible and efficient solution when it's used to implement counters, and in particular rate-limiting policies, which use counters under the hood. A **rate-limiting** mechanism protects against burst traffic inside a time window, attempts to break a password, or a **distributed denial-of-service** (**DDoS**) attack. Rate-limiting mechanisms are usually applied before the request is processed by the application servers and applied at the load balancer or gateway layer, but they can be also applied specifically per service, behind the gateway. A rate limiter that's implemented externally is useful when we want a distributed rate-limiting policy across multiple nodes, as in the case where the API gateway is deployed as a multi-node cluster:

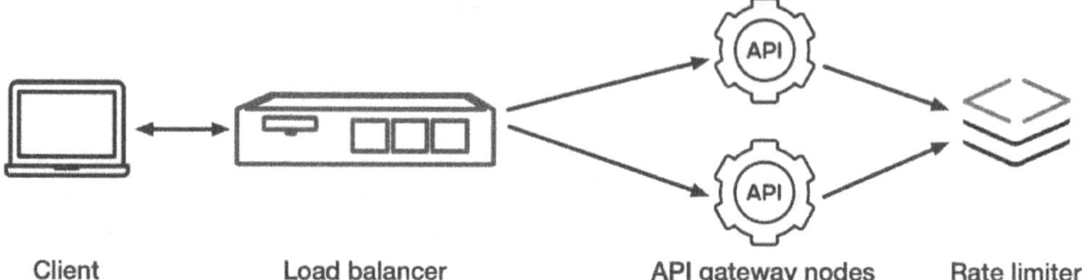

Figure 2.5 – Redis Stack as a rate limiter

We can create a Redis key counter for every minute per user. Every time a request comes in, we'll update the appropriate counter for a determined user (or for the number of overall requests), based on the current minute. To make sure we don't fill up our entire database with junk, we'll expire that key after 1 minute.

The key name can be a combination of the user identity and the minute portion of the current time. The user identity can be expressed as a session identifier, or as an `API-KEY` identifier. So, if we decide to keep the requests of a determined `API-KEY` identifier under control, we would name the key `{API-KEY}:{MINUTE}`. Since we're always expiring the keys, we only need to keep track of the minute; when the hour rolls around from 59 to 00, we can be certain that another limiter for 59 doesn't exist (it would have expired 58 minutes prior).

Let's illustrate this with an example where we allow a maximum of 10 requests per minute. Every time there is a request for a certain `API-KEY` identifier, we check the current usage per minute:

```
GET [user-api-key]:[current minute number]
```

If the number of requests is under a certain threshold (10 requests), we can increase the counter; otherwise, we can reject the request and exit:

```
MULTI
INCR [user-api-key]:[current minute number]
EXPIRE [user-api-key]:[current minute number] 59
QUEUED
EXEC
```

In this example, for every request that is received during a certain minute, the rate limiter will check the value of the related counter and, if allowed, increase its value. When the minute changes, the requests will get checked against a new counter and the old one will expire in a maximum of 60 seconds. This example is a basic fixed time window rate limiter. Using the Redis Sorted Set data structure, it is possible to create a sliding window rate limiter. A sliding window rate limiter can be implemented using the following commands:

```
MULTI
ZREMRANGEBYSCORE [user-api-key] 0 [current-timestamp-ms - 86400000]
ZADD [user-api-key] [current-timestamp-ms] [current-timestamp-
ms:weight]
ZRANGE [user-api-key] "0" "-1"
EXPIRE [user-api-key] [time-to-live]
EXEC
```

This daily rate limiter for a single `API-KEY` with an identifier of `user-api-key` is invoked on every request and performs the following actions:

1. It uses a transaction: all the commands within `MULTI` and `EXEC` are executed atomically.
2. The `ZREMRANGEBYSCORE` command removes all the entries from the Sorted Sets with a score older than the current timestamp expressed in milliseconds minus `86400000`, where `86400000` is the number of milliseconds in a day. After this operation, the Sorted Set will store only those entries that were added within the last 24 hours.
3. The `ZADD` command adds a member-score pair to the Sorted Set, where the score is the current timestamp in milliseconds, and the member is the string composed of the current timestamp plus a weight – for example, `1676895115768:1`. The weight can be any natural number and is used to implement a weighted rate limiter, where certain heavy operations have higher weights than others. If weights are not desired, the weight can be equal to `1` or omitted from the implementation.

4. The `ZRANGE` command fetches all the elements in the Sorted Set, and the application will count the weights and compare them to the threshold. If weights are not required, entries can be simply counted using `ZCOUNT`.

As an example, requests were registered by the rate limiter as follows:

```
127.0.0.1:6379> ZRANGE 1yp3ic445r:daily 0 -1
 1) "1676895115768:1"
 2) "1676895115768"
 3) "1676895144468:5"
 4) "1676895144468"
 5) "1676895183756:3"
 6) "1676895183756"
 7) "1676895194401:1"
 8) "1676895194401"
 9) "1676895214146:1"
10) "1676895214146"
```

These are the four requests that remain logged after trimming using `ZREMRANGEBYSCORE`, so they were received in the past 24 hours, and the total weights add up to `11`. If we set a threshold of `10000` in a day, there is still room for more operations in our service for that API key. Scores in the Sorted Set are a temporal reference for trimming. This simple algorithm can be executed from the client using a pipeline or stored as a function in the server and adapted at will to size the desired window duration.

In this section, we modeled a rate limiter with the `string` data type and the Sorted Set. In the next section, we will discover another popular use of the Sorted Set in application development for gaming: leaderboards.

Leaderboards

Gaming leaderboards enable players to track performance against each other. They have a social component of encouraging competition but may also contribute to the overall logic of a game for tuning or matching players with similar skill levels.

Leaderboards require every participant's score to be updated and calculated against the overall group. This demands simultaneous updates from thousands/millions of active participants, making this an intensive write-load scenario. The results need to be accurately displayed by thousands/millions of users with periodic polls for updates, making this a high-read scenario.

The Sorted Set can model a leaderboard efficiently and guarantee fast access, even when storing the score of millions of players. The Sorted Set is implemented as a skip list and is optimized for random access, which guarantees efficient range searches. Using a Sorted Set is equivalent to having direct access to a secondary index, without the overhead of the traditional layers of relational databases in front of the storage engine, such as the query parsing and validation stage, the optimizer, fetching data from disk if it's not present in the buffer pool, and so on.

Using the Sorted Set, a collection of members that are automatically ordered by their associated score, is as easy as adding score-member pairs to the data structure:

```
127.0.0.1:6379> ZADD user:score 234 John 232 Tim 1234 Dan 27 Eva 2213
Julia 32 Dylan 898 Molly
(integer) 7
```

The ZRANGE command retrieves the entries in the desired score range:

```
127.0.0.1:6379> ZRANGE user:score 0 100 BYSCORE WITHSCORES
1) "Eva"
2) "27"
3) "Dylan"
4) "32"
```

The ZRANGE command can also be used to retrieve the entries with the highest scores:

```
127.0.0.1:6379> ZRANGE user:score -2 -1 WITHSCORES
1) "Dan"
2) "1234"
3) "Julia"
4) "2213"
```

A rich set of commands to query and manipulate the Sorted Sets helps with addressing many leaderboard-related problems. In addition, the Sorted Set can be used for lexicographic ordering when all the scores are set to an equal number, which helps fetch data in alphabetical order:

```
127.0.0.1:6379> ZADD user:names 234 John 0 Tim 0 Dan 0 Eva 0 Julia 0
Dylan 0 Molly
(integer) 7
127.0.0.1:6379> ZRANGE user:names [D "(D\xff" BYLEX
1) "Dan"
2) "Dylan"
```

Next, we'll look at data deduplication.

Data deduplication

A popular use case for which Redis Stack has multiple solutions is data deduplication. The title may suggest that we would use Redis Stack to remove duplicates in the database; however, the data deduplication functionality (often referred to as dedup) helps resolve questions such as "*Is this email in the database?*", "*Is this user identifier already used by an existing user?*", and "*Has the user already visited this web page?*".

Redis Stack offers several efficient methods to resolve these cases, with the Set and Bloom filters being the most popular options. So, if we would like to know if a user identifier has already been used (or an email address), we may resort to using a Set, as follows:

```
127.0.0.1:6379> SADD users user-id-1 user-id-2 user-id-3
(integer) 3
127.0.0.1:6379> SISMEMBER users user-id-3
(integer) 1
127.0.0.1:6379> SISMEMBER users user-id-4
(integer) 0
```

With the Bloom filters, we have an efficient solution to check if an element is present in a Set by storing only a hashed representation of the data. Given the approximate behavior of the Bloom filter, false positives are possible. However, no false negatives can happen – if an item does not belong to the filter, I can be sure it was not added to it:

```
127.0.0.1:6379> BF.ADD visited www.redis.com
(integer) 1
127.0.0.1:6379> BF.ADD visited www.redis.io
(integer) 1
127.0.0.1:6379> BF.ADD visited www.mortensi.com(integer) 1
127.0.0.1:6379> BF.EXISTS visited www.learn.redis.com
(integer) 0
```

Redis Stack is especially useful for resolving common problems with minimal waste in terms of memory and resources, which makes it an ideal component in any technological stack. We will talk about probabilistic data structures, including Bloom filters, in *Chapter 8*, *Understanding Probabilistic Data Structures.*

Geo-positioning

Using Redis' **geospatial** indexes, you can implement systems that efficiently resolve problems such as the following:

- Searching for restaurants or cabs close to your position
- Calculating the distance between your position and an arbitrary place
- Finding locations contained in a rectangular or circular area of the desired size
- Finding the location of a mobile phone

Redis represents locations as strings using the **Geohash encoding system**, which encodes a location expressed with latitude and longitude as a string. As an example, Redis' headquarters can be expressed using latitude and longitude:

```
37.37778536400017, -122.0645497140350
```

Here's the equivalent Geohash for the same location:

```
9q9hwk7m3u0
```

Using this encoding and the naturally ordered Sorted Set data structure, Redis achieves fast geospatial searches and addresses many **geo-positioning** requirements. As an example, let's say we add cities to a geospatial index, as follows:

```
GEOADD Italy 14.166667 42.349998 Chieti
GEOADD Italy 11.330556 43.318611 Siena
GEOADD Italy 7.783333 43.816666 Sanremo
GEOADD Italy 10.328000 44.801472 Parma 13.45293 43.29789 Macerata
```

Now, we can retrieve the distance between members added to this index:

```
GEODIST Italy Chieti Siena km
"255.1656"
```

We can also find the location within a certain distance from an arbitrary location, expressed using the latitude and longitude pair:

```
127.0.0.1:6379> GEOSEARCH Italy FROMLONLAT 13 43 BYRADIUS 200 km ASC
WITHDIST
1) 1) "Macerata"
   2) "49.4841"
2) 1) "Chieti"
   2) "119.7010"
3) 1) "Siena"
   2) "140.0060"
```

Geospatial capabilities are simple and efficient, and plenty of different applications can leverage this feature to resolve many geo-localization problems.

Message processing and delivery

A typical pattern of distributed architectures is the **messaging pattern**, where several loosely coupled components or services are deployed over the network and need to exchange information. Communicating several distributed services implies resolving problems such as disconnections, ordering of messages, repeated messages (idempotency), and more. A widely accepted solution is to adopt asynchronous messages exchanged over a channel: publishers and consumers are decoupled and manage disconnections and reconnections while guaranteeing that no message will be lost.

Redis core data structures can be adopted to implement the messaging pattern while also allowing the traditional publish/subscribe fire-and-forget type of communication. The suitable data structures for this pattern are as follows:

- **Lists**
- **Sorted Sets**
- **Pub/Sub**
- **Streams**

Let's break these down.

Lists

Redis Lists can be used to implement **FIFO queues**. This data structure maintains the ordering of items pushed to it. Items can be pushed or popped on both ends of a List, using `LPUSH`, `RPUSH`, `LPOP`, and `RPOP`. Lists ensure that the queue of events is persisted and survives a failure of the server. It also guarantees that messages are delivered in order and that at least one consumer pulls a specific message. Lists can be used as an inter-process communication method and are helpful as a means to decouple the processing of a list of items. However, Lists do not offer an acknowledgment mechanism: if a client crashes after pulling an item from a queue implemented as a List, it may lose the information about the item that needs to be processed. The following is one example of using a List as a queue:

```
127.0.0.1:6379> LPUSH queue item1 item2 item3
(integer) 3
127.0.0.1:6379> LRANGE queue 0 -1
1) "item3"
2) "item2"
3) "item1"
127.0.0.1:6379> RPOP queue
"item1"
127.0.0.1:6379> LRANGE queue 0 -1
1) "item3"
2) "item2"
```

This example shows how to add items to the queue on the left-hand side and pop them from the right-hand side.

Sorted Sets

Similarly to Lists, Sorted Sets can be used to implement **priority message queues**. Items can be inserted anywhere in the Sorted Set based on their score using the `ZADD` command, and the consumers can pop the elements with the highest or lowest score using the `ZPOPMAX` and `ZPOPMIN` commands. As for Lists, there is no acknowledgment mechanism and messages can get lost if the client that has just popped the message crashes. Therefore, it is unable to finish processing the item:

```
127.0.0.1:6379> ZADD priority_queue 1 item1 2 item2 4 item4
(integer) 3
127.0.0.1:6379> ZADD priority_queue 3 item3
(integer) 1
127.0.0.1:6379> ZRANGE priority_queue 0 -1 WITHSCORES
1) "item1"
2) "1"
3) "item2"
4) "2"
5) "item3"
6) "3"
7) "item4"
8) "4"
127.0.0.1:6379> ZPOPMAX priority_queue
1) "item4"
2) "4"
127.0.0.1:6379> ZRANGE priority_queue 0 -1
1) "item1"
2) "item2"
3) "item3"
```

Next, we'll look at Pub/Sub.

Pub/Sub

Using Redis **Pub/Sub**, messages can be broadcasted (using the `PUBLISH` command) over a channel and to an arbitrary number of subscribers (subscribers listen on a channel using the `SUBSCRIBE` command). Subscribers can listen on several channels, and multiple subscribers can subscribe to the same channel, so the same message is consumed in parallel. Redis Pub/Sub is characterized by the fire-and-forget delivery method: if subscribers disconnect from the channel, messages that are published while they persist in a disconnected state are lost. Messages are delivered immediately and not saved in a queue or persisted, which makes the Pub/Sub delivery method suitable for use cases such as reporting or alerting, but less suitable when guarantees that a certain message has been received and processed by at least a client are required.

Using Pub/Sub to deliver messages is straightforward. In the following example, we'll consider a kitchen in a restaurant that needs to inform the waiters when a plate is ready to be delivered to a table. The kitchen will publish messages to the waiters so that they can pick up the plates and serve them to the clients sitting at the tables. One or more waiters subscribe to the same channel used by the kitchen:

```
127.0.0.1:6379> SUBSCRIBE lunch_channel
Reading messages... (press Ctrl-C to quit)
1) "subscribe"
2) "lunch_channel"
3) (integer) 1
```

Then, the publisher in the kitchen broadcasts messages:

```
127.0.0.1:6379> PUBLISH lunch_channel "client:34:ready"
(integer) 1
127.0.0.1:6379> PUBLISH lunch_channel "client:12:ready"
(integer) 1
```

All the waiters subscribed to the channel will get the message, go to the kitchen, and serve the dish to the clients:

```
1) "message"
2) "lunch_channel"
3) "client:34:ready"
1) "message"
2) "lunch_channel"
3) "client:12:ready"
```

As mentioned previously, if a waiter disconnects from the `lunch_channel` channel, once reconnected, they won't be able to dig into the history of messages, and the client will be waiting for the food, which is going cold in the kitchen.

Streams

Using Redis **Streams**, messages are pushed (using the `XADD` command) in an append-only log-like data structure where producers add messages to a stream, and consumers pull the messages, which are ordered by the time of insertion. Consumers of a Redis Stream can pull messages out immediately (`XREAD`) or replay messages from the past. Consumers' scalability is also ensured: multiple consumer groups can read from the same stream and will get access to the entire stream of events, while a consumer group can distribute events to several consumers in the same group. Redis Streams are persisted differently from a Pub/Sub channel. Here, events are not lost, even in the case of a disaster causing the Redis Stack Server to be restarted.

Persistence, the capacity to manage disconnections so that consumers can read a Stream starting from the desired event in the past, and the possibility to acknowledge an event when it is processed, turn

Redis Streams into a good option for asynchronous **inter-service communication**. In the following example, we will revisit the example of a kitchen dispatching orders to waiters, already seen using Pub/Sub. Using the following instruction, we can create a common channel called `lunch_channel` to be used by the kitchen and by waiters as well as a consumer group named `waiters`:

```
127.0.0.1:6379> XGROUP CREATE lunch_channel waiters $ MKSTREAM
OK
```

Now, the kitchen can publish messages on the channel using the XADD command:

```
127.0.0.1:6379> XADD lunch_channel * client:34 pasta
"1676982250423-0"
127.0.0.1:6379> XADD lunch_channel * client:12 pizza
"1676982253435-0"
127.0.0.1:6379> XADD lunch_channel * client:5 coffee
"1676982256586-0"
```

The two waiters in our restaurant, Alice and Tom, will get an order from the kitchen using their palm devices and using the > symbol, they will get only messages that have never been delivered to other consumers so far:

```
127.0.0.1:6379> XREADGROUP GROUP waiters Alice COUNT 1 STREAMS lunch_
channel >
1) 1) "lunch_channel"
   2) 1) 1) "1676982250423-0"
         2) 1) "client:34"
            2) "pasta"
```

While Alice delivers the plate, Tom reads the next order that was never delivered, again using the > symbol. So, he's sure that the next dish isn't already managed by Alice:

```
127.0.0.1:6379> XREADGROUP GROUP waiters Tom COUNT 1 STREAMS lunch_
channel >
1) 1) "lunch_channel"
   2) 1) 1) "1676982253435-0"
         2) 1) "client:12"
            2) "pizza"
```

Alice is back from the table and checks her device to see whether there's another plate to deliver:

```
127.0.0.1:6379> XREADGROUP GROUP waiters Alice COUNT 1 STREAMS lunch_
channel >
1) 1) "lunch_channel"
   2) 1) 1) "1676982256586-0"
         2) 1) "client:5"
            2) "coffee"
```

Tom is free again and checks his device and, lucky him, there is no further work to do:

```
127.0.0.1:6379> XREADGROUP GROUP waiters Tom COUNT 1 STREAMS lunch_
channel >
(nil)
```

However, the cook checks the screen and still sees that the dishes haven't been delivered. How is that possible?

```
127.0.0.1:6379> XPENDING lunch_channel waiters
1) (integer) 3
2) "1676982250423-0"
3) "1676982256586-0"
4) 1) 1) "Alice"
      2) "2"
   2) 1) "Tom"
      2) "1"
```

The explanation is that Alice and Tom did not acknowledge in their devices that the tables were served. So, they do this now and mark the pasta and pizza as delivered:

```
127.0.0.1:6379> XACK lunch_channel waiters 1676982253435-0
(integer) 1
127.0.0.1:6379> XACK lunch_channel waiters 1676982250423-0
(integer) 1
```

A further check in the kitchen misses an acknowledgment for coffee:

```
127.0.0.1:6379> XPENDING lunch_channel waiters
1) (integer) 1
2) "1676982256586-0"
3) "1676982256586-0"
4) 1) 1) "Alice"
      2) "1"
```

This is set to completed soon afterward, and the kitchen to-do list is finally empty!

```
127.0.0.1:6379> XACK lunch_channel waiters 1676982256586-0
(integer) 1
127.0.0.1:6379> XPENDING lunch_channel waiters
1) (integer) 0
2) (nil)
3) (nil)
4) (nil)
```

As shown in this example, consumers can read asynchronously from the stream of events as they don't need to stay connected, and the producer can verify that all the events were dispatched, to whom, and if they were completed.

We have concluded this short overview of the traditional use cases for which Redis is popular, but there are many more situations where developers will find the classical data structures useful, such as building distributed locks to grant exclusive access to shared resources or implementing several counting patterns efficiently (and with minimal memory overhead) using Hashes, Bitmaps, or Bitfields. In the next section, we will focus on the new capabilities that will help modernize your applications and open the doors to new and advanced use cases.

Going beyond the real-time cache with Redis Stack

With the addition of new capabilities, Redis Stack pushes Redis forward and meets the expectations of software architects and developers who are having to deal with myriad new requirements. However, it also pushes the old traditional ones to the next step, which means finding new ways to resolve traditional problems with real-time performance, scalability, and high availability easily and inexpensively. Since its inception, Redis' objective has been to provide suitable data structures and algorithms to ensure speed and minimal footprint. As an example, think of the Bitmap data structure, which grants access down to the bit level. With such flexibility, we can flag the days in a given month when a user has authenticated to a certain service:

```
127.0.0.1:6379> SETBIT user:032023 0 1
(integer) 0
127.0.0.1:6379> SETBIT user:032023 5 1
(integer) 0
127.0.0.1:6379> SETBIT user:032023 10 1
(integer) 0
127.0.0.1:6379> SETBIT user:032023 19 1
(integer) 0
127.0.0.1:6379> SETBIT user:032023 30 1
(integer) 0
```

Then, we count the number of authentications in March 2023:

```
127.0.0.1:6379> BITCOUNT user:032023 0 31
(integer) 5
```

We consume only 72 bytes to store this information per month, per user:

```
127.0.0.1:6379> MEMORY USAGE user:032023
(integer) 72
```

While the classical and well-known use cases are consolidated in Redis Stack with continuous improvements and optimization to Redis Server (the core of Redis Stack), new possibilities are around the corner with the capabilities that we will introduce in this chapter and will explore in detail throughout this book. From working with bits to full-text and faceted search in Hash and JSON documents, from fraud detection to recommendation engines, you will likely find a suitable solution to your modeling problems.

Querying, indexing, and search

We explored the search capabilities of Redis Stack in the previous chapter, where we also introduced full-text, tag, and numeric search. In this section, we will introduce further use cases that are based on secondary indexing.

Faceted search

Objects have attributes. Think of an online retail store, and think of the search bar where you can search by a keyword and get results aggregated by an attribute such as the category of the product, its color, or its size. The ability to search by attribute (or **facet**) goes by the name of **faceted search**. Redis Stack implements a multi-dimensional faceted search by defining the desired attributes as tags. Let's see this with an example:

1. First, we will insert a few shirts into our online store, modeled as Hash objects:

```
HSET item:1 Name "Polo Shirt" Color green Brand "Lacoste"
HSET item:2 Name "Polo Shirt" Color blue Brand "Calvin Klein"
HSET item:3 Name "Polo Shirt" Color orange Brand "Calvin Klein"
HSET item:4 Name "Polo Shirt" Color orange Brand "Lacoste"
HSET item:5 Name "Cotton T-Shirt" Color blue Brand "Sergio
Tacchini"
HSET item:6 Name "Cotton T-Shirt" Color orange Brand "Sergio
Tacchini"
```

2. Now, we will create the index as usual and specify the desired attribute that will represent our facets as tags:

```
FT.CREATE product_idx
ON HASH
PREFIX 1 item:
SCHEMA Name AS name TEXT
Color AS color TAG SORTABLE
Size AS size TAG SORTABLE
Brand as brand TAG SORTABLE
```

3. Then, we can experiment with some aggregations. The following command groups the items and returns the cardinality by color:

```
127.0.0.1:6379> FT.AGGREGATE product_idx * GROUPBY 1 @color
REDUCE COUNT 0 AS items SORTBY 2 @items DESC
1) (integer) 3
2) 1) "color"
   2) "orange"
   3) "items"
   4) "3"
3) 1) "color"
   2) "blue"
   3) "items"
   4) "2"
4) 1) "color"
   2) "green"
   3) "items"
   4) "1"
```

4. The following command groups the items and returns the cardinality by brand:

```
127.0.0.1:6379> FT.AGGREGATE product_idx * GROUPBY 1 @brand
REDUCE COUNT 0 AS items SORTBY 2 @items DESC
1) (integer) 3
2) 1) "brand"
   2) "Sergio Tacchini"
   3) "items"
   4) "2"
3) 1) "brand"
   2) "Calvin Klein"
   3) "items"
   4) "2"
4) 1) "brand"
   2) "Lacoste"
   3) "items"
   4) "2"
```

5. Finally, we can perform a full-text search by `name` and aggregate the results by `color`, all at once:

```
FT.AGGREGATE product_idx '@name:polo @brand:{lacoste}' GROUPBY 1
@color REDUCE COUNT 0 AS items SORTBY 2 @items DESC
1) (integer) 2
2) 1) "color"
   2) "green"
   3) "items"
   4) "1"
```

```
3) 1) "color"
   2) "orange"
   3) "items"
   4) "1"
```

Indexing our data using tags for faceted search enables better searches and drives the design of expressive user interfaces, thus boosting the user experience in online retail stores and similar websites, where finding what we are looking for quickly is a must.

Ephemeral search (retail)

Sometimes, it is desirable to index only a subset of data, especially if the data is stored in an external primary database and we are looking into speeding up searches for a small portion of data, such as customer search history, a shopping cart, or any other user-related information. In such cases, it is possible to create an index on demand. This is an effective option compared to massively indexing an entire dataset, which may even include obsolete or, what's worse, archived data. So, it is possible to create a temporary index, which is a standard index in all respects. Let's see an example for the active user, `user:241245`:

```
FT.CREATE user:241245:idx
ON HASH
PREFIX 1 user:241245
SCHEMA Name AS name TEXT
Id AS id TEXT
Quantity AS quantity NUMERIC
```

This command will scan all the existing and future keys prefixed by the `user:241245` string and will index the fields that have been specified. Let's create some data for this user, which may proceed from an external data source or belong to this Redis Stack Server instance:

```
HSET user:241245:89hgw98 Name "Fashion socks" Id "89hgw98" quantity 1
HSET user:241245:28h880f Name "Printer toner" Id "28h880f" quantity 3
```

Now, we can search this user index as usual:

```
127.0.0.1:6379> FT.SEARCH user:241245:idx toner RETURN 1 name
1) (integer) 1
2) "user:241245:28h880f"
3) 1) "name"
   2) "Printer toner"
```

Once the user logs out, the index can be explicitly dropped, and if desired, together with the document using the DD option:

```
127.0.0.1:6379> FT.DROPINDEX user:241245:idx DD
OK
```

Compared to indexing millions of objects for non-active users, this is surely a cost-effective option.

Research portal

Modeling documents and their related metadata using a Hash or JSON data structure is yet another use case:

1. Creating a **knowledge base** of documents, articles, or any kind of textual entry for full-text search against a local database or as an external index of resources available elsewhere is as easy as creating an index, as follows:

```
FT.CREATE docs_idx
ON HASH
PREFIX 1 doc:
SCHEMA Name AS name TEXT
Isbn AS isbn TEXT
Category AS category TAG
Library as library TEXT
Location AS location GEO
```

2. This command creates an index of books available in **public libraries**. Let's consider a couple of copies of a certain book, available in two public libraries in the United Kingdom and Italy:

```
HSET doc:2334 Name "Wuthering Heights" Isbn "978-0141439556"
Category "Novel" Library "The London Library" Location
"-0.058750,51.510899"
HSET doc:3523 Name "Wuthering Heights" Isbn "978-0141439556"
Category "Novel" Library "Biblioteca Mozzi Borgetti" Location
"13.451154,43.298791"
```

3. Searching for the closest copy to a certain location in Italy, specified by a longitude and latitude pair, would return the desired result:

```
127.0.0.1:6379> FT.SEARCH docs_idx "Wuthering @
location:[13.50337 43.5942 100 km]"
1) (integer) 1
2) "doc:3523"
3)  1) "Name"
    2) "Wuthering Heights"
```

```
 3) "Isbn"
 4) "978-0141439556"
 5) "Category"
 6) "Novel"
 7) "Library"
 8) "Biblioteca Mozzi Borgetti"
 9) "Location"
10) "13.451154,43.298791"
```

Using different index types, it is possible to index heterogeneous metadata (including the geographic location of an item, the genre, the year, and so on) and create indexes of content available elsewhere, digitally stored in an external data store or physically available in a location, such as a public library.

Similarity search

With Redis Stack, it is possible to build a recommendation system based on the **similarity search** of **unstructured data**, such as images, audio files, text, graphs, and other types of data modeled as vectors. Typical applications of the **vector similarity search** (**VSS**) feature are as follows:

- E-commerce product recommendations, based on visual similarity
- Time series similarity, to correlate similar patterns and build a trading recommendation engine or study a disease spread pattern
- Detect similar transactions and reveal **fraud attempts** based on historical data
- Music **recommendation systems**, for playlist suggestions based on users' preferences
- Social networks, where users can connect based on similar profiles and interests

The heart of VSS is Redis Stack's ability to compare vectors and find the best matches. For example, building a similarity search engine for voice recordings means implementing the following pipeline:

1. Use a data model that converts unstructured data into its vector representation. A voice recording is converted into a vector of numbers, which is called a feature vector, or **vector embedding**. This conversion is performed by the client application or an external/third-party service.
2. Store the vector embeddings that correspond to a dataset of voice recordings in Redis Stack and index them so that a database of known voice recordings is built.
3. Match a voice recording to similar recordings in the database by finding the most similar vector representations.

This is illustrated in the following diagram:

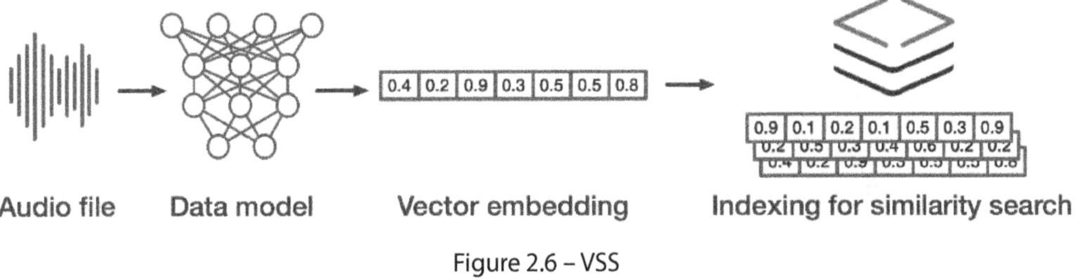

Figure 2.6 – VSS

Many open and available free data models convert data into their corresponding vector representations. By using those models to convert pictures, audio files, or time series data into vector representations, you can build a recommendation system with a few lines of code.

Monitoring and analysis

Many applications can take advantage of time series data modeling to store continuously evolving data, such as climatic data and metrics from monitoring devices. We can try to categorize such use cases:

- **IoT and sensor monitoring**: Devices that emit a stream of events and store data points captured by sensors can help reconstruct a timeline of events (think of flight data captured and stored in a black box) and maximize the health and safety conditions of the crew by creating detailed reports for the equipment manufacturers.
- **Application performance/health monitoring**: Monitor the performance and availability of applications and services such as CPU usage, network latency, memory usage, or I/O pressure. A time series allows us to monitor and react to this data in real time and anticipates any scalability or availability issues.
- **Real-time analytics**: Process, analyze, and react in real time (for example, for selling equities and performing predictive maintenance, product recommendations, or price adjustments).

Beyond storing time series and fetching data from them, Redis Stack can perform aggregated queries for the desired time bucket, or label and index multiple time series and retrieve data points from multiple series at once. Based on data from a master time series, we can create derived and downsampled time series that perform aggregation using options such as `avg`, `sum`, `min`, `max`, `range`, `count`, `first`, `last`, and more. If, for example, we would like to store the CPU usage data points for a certain device, we can create the following time series:

```
TS.CREATE app:34:cpu
```

Then, we can create a new time series to store the maximum CPU usage for every bucket with a duration of 10 seconds:

```
TS.CREATE app:34:cpu:max
TS.CREATERULE app:34:cpu app:34:cpu:max AGGREGATION max 10000
```

We can test this by adding samples that describe the CPU usage, expressed as a percentage:

```
TS.ADD app:34:cpu "*" 67
TS.ADD app:34:cpu "*" 34
TS.ADD app:34:cpu "*" 56
TS.ADD app:34:cpu "*" 32
TS.ADD app:34:cpu "*" 78
TS.ADD app:34:cpu "*" 66
TS.ADD app:34:cpu "*" 65
TS.ADD app:34:cpu "*" 64
TS.ADD app:34:cpu "*" 69
```

We can also check the derived `app:34:cpu:max` time series to get an insight into the maximum CPU usage over time, with a granularity of 10 seconds:

```
127.0.0.1:6379> TS.RANGE app:34:cpu:max - +
1) 1) (integer) 1677061500000
   2) 67
2) 1) (integer) 1677061510000
   2) 78
3) 1) (integer) 1677061520000
   2) 69
```

There are many ways to store, aggregate, and retrieve data points using the time series capability of Redis Stack, without resorting to a specialized time series database and simplifying the development and integration of new use cases to new and existing applications using Redis Stack data modeling.

Fraud detection

By using time series to model the evolution of a system and the relationships between entities together with the VSS feature of Redis Stack, it is possible to design a **fraud detection** system. In addition, probabilistic data structures in Redis let you verify if certain behaviors resemble known fraudulent patterns and raise an alert for suspect user behaviors. Probabilistic data structures help answer questions such as the following:

- Has the user paid from this location before?
- Has the user ever made purchases in this category of products/services?
- Has this credit card been reported as lost/stolen?
- Do I need to skip some security steps when the user is buying?

Using **probabilistic data structures**, we can represent a set of items compactly, with a reasonable approximation and high performance, which helps us manage and verify the massive amount of user data in high load/data scenarios. To illustrate this capability, let's assume that we establish criteria to validate a transaction based on the location from where the user connects and the time of the day an operation is executed (such as authenticating to a bank account or purchasing an expensive item). In the case of the geographic check, we may want to verify whether a certain location is expected – if the location is new and distant from the known locations, we may want to require additional verification. We can also check if the user is authenticating at an unusual hour; if so, we need to record hours of valid logins beforehand and verify subsequent logins. Using Redis Bloom filters, we can verify if an element is present in a set using a small amount of memory of a fixed size. This is because Bloom filters only store a hashed representation of the data.

The implementation of a minimalistic fraud detection system only uses a few commands to profile user activity. Using the Bloom filter approach, we would create a filter per user, and add to it the location and hour that have already been verified. As an example, if a user is connecting from Italy in the morning, we would add the following to the filter:

```
127.0.0.1:6379> BF.MADD usr:1 ITA 11
1) (integer) 1
2) (integer) 1
127.0.0.1:6379> BF.MADD usr:1 ITA 10
1) (integer) 0
2) (integer) 1
127.0.0.1:6379> BF.MADD usr:1 ITA 9
1) (integer) 0
2) (integer) 1
```

Now, we can verify new subsequent operations that happen in Italy in the morning:

```
127.0.0.1:6379> BF.MEXISTS usr:1 ITA 9
1) (integer) 1
2) (integer) 1
127.0.0.1:6379> BF.MEXISTS usr:1 ITA 10
1) (integer) 1
2) (integer) 1
```

As we can see, there is no reason to raise an alert. But if an operation occurs at an unusual time in Canada and is checked for this user against the related filter, `usr:1`, we would get the following output:

```
127.0.0.1:6379> BF.MEXISTS usr:1 CAN 3
1) (integer) 0
2) (integer) 0
```

We would spot suspicious activity and take action to verify the operation or enforce a stronger authentication method.

There are many different checks we may implement in a fraud detection system using probabilistic data structures or the other Redis Stack modeling and search capabilities.

Feature store for machine learning

Looking at the emerging technologies and techniques to resolve the hottest problems in the areas of data classification and predicting events, there is undoubtedly **artificial intelligence** (**AI**) and the ability to create systems that learn from existing data without being specifically programmed. Creating models to generate predictions from data is referred to as **machine learning** (**ML**), a branch of AI.

In addition to the traditional use cases that are becoming innovative and being able to perform more solutions using AI techniques, such as video recommendation, fraud detection, online advertising, spam filtering, and speech and identity recognition, we have new emerging fields where AI has gained relevance and becoming central and irreplaceable, such as medical diagnosis or self-driving cars. Traditional use cases are becoming real time, and emerging use cases natively need real-time responsiveness (a self-driving car) and are fed with freshly captured data as events occur and data is registered and passed through a pipeline. While implementing a real-time pipeline using AI techniques is complex and expensive, it's doubtful that the ability to classify data and make predictions in real time contributes to speeding up the innovation of original solutions when they're used on older and newer problems.

To simplify the workflow, which takes data as input and returns a prediction as output, we can summarize the entire matter in two big branches: training a model and performing a prediction. Both branches are developed around the concept of **features**.

ML model training

ML systems are taught to perform the duty they're designed for by creating a model from existing known data. You can think of a model as a function that takes data in as input, attempts to classify it, and returns an output. Data that will be used to create the model must be transformed and cleaned to extract relevant information, such as IP addresses, locations, emails, timestamps, or unstructured data such as voice recordings and traffic images… anything that defines an event and that is relevant to describe the behaviors that we want our model to recognize. Once the data has been polished and structured using standard criteria, we obtain **features**. As an example, if we have an array of data describing a transaction and we know that such data is describing a fraud attempt that happened in the past, we can use such data to **train a model**. This model will help determine whether a future transaction is classified as fraud or not. A data scientist must build a set of representative and non-redundant features.

Performing predictions

Once we have trained a model to perform a job (for example, classifying transactions as legitimate or fraudulent), we need to understand what use cases our model can serve. If the model is used with data from a data warehouse or offline storage, we can have predictions, but these won't be in real time. We need fast storage to get real-time predictions that will store only fresh and relevant features in an **online feature store**. With a real-time feature store, we can input data into the model as fast as possible and achieve online predictions. In addition, we can stream data (from Redis Streams or Kafka, for example) into a Redis online feature store to serve real-time predictions. This way, we can detect a fraud attempt as it happens.

Redis as an online feature store

An online feature store holds input data that is fed into ML models. Its main features are as follows:

- It acts as the single source of truth for features
- It allows data scientists to find new features and reuse them for different ML use cases
- The features need to be served in real time for real-time predictions; this is where Redis comes into play:

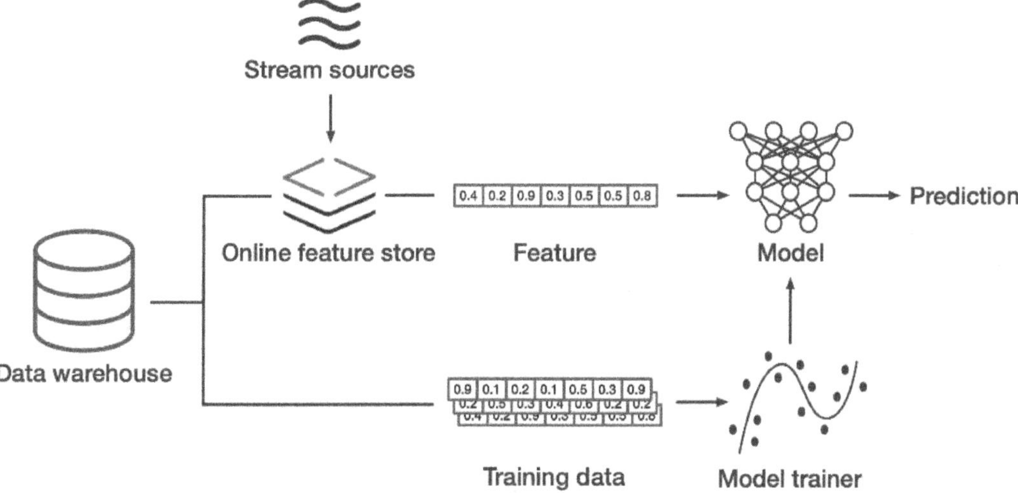

Figure 2.7 – ML pipeline

Online feature stores are used for real-time predictions where the data source is live data, in addition to data from offline stores (such as archives). Offline stores, which usually store historical and consolidated data of some kind, serve different use cases, such as batch predictions, though they can be used to train new models.

With that, we have concluded this overview of the traditional use cases and the new possible scenarios that can be addressed using Redis Stack. In the next section, we will discover how Redis Stack can help implement the design patterns of a microservice architecture.

Designing microservice architectures with Redis Stack

Microservice architecture is a system design pattern that promotes subdividing large services into smaller units by decomposing the business logic into decoupled and independent services, each depending on the preferred technology stack, languages data models, and more. These services take the name of **microservices** and, communicating over a network, deliver the functionality of a larger system.

In this section, we will introduce some of the principal patterns for microservice architectures. These patterns are guidelines for designing, developing, and deploying microservices. We will approach this subject by presenting the value that the capabilities of Redis Stack provide at the time of choosing the suitable technology for the implementation. In this section, we will discuss the following patterns:

- API gateway
- API gateway caching
- Domain-driven design
- Query caching
- Command query responsibility segregation
- Inter-service communication

These patterns can be combined and implement architectures such as the one shown in the following figure, which describes the typical microservices in an online retail store:

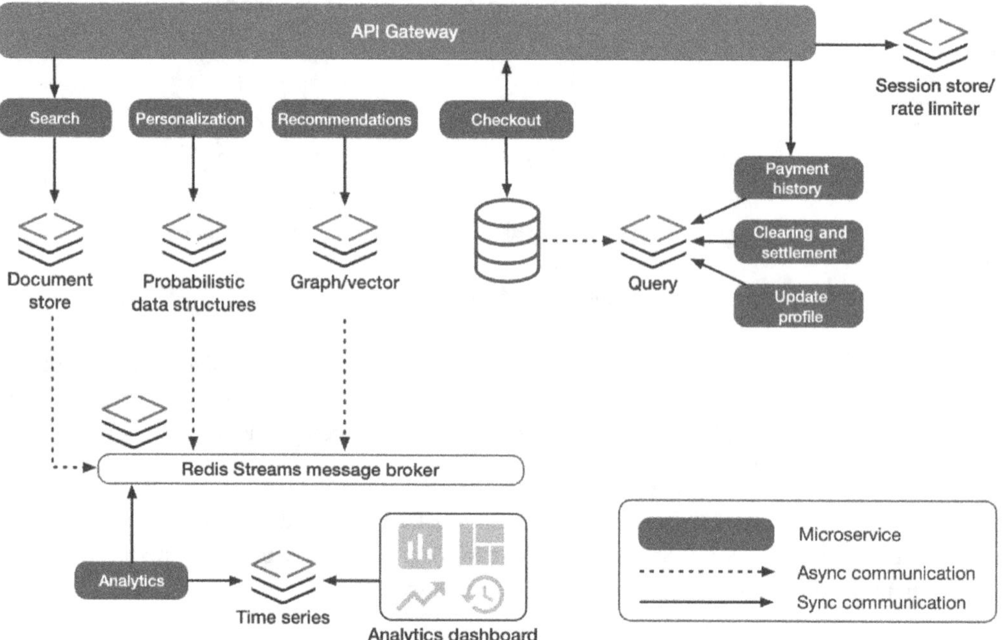

Figure 2.8 – Redis Stack in microservice architectures

Let's break this architecture down and look at each part of it.

API gateway

Clients of a service that have been designed as per the principles of a microservice architecture should not have access to the individual microservices. There are a few good reasons to justify this pattern:

- A frontend client needs to aggregate heterogeneous data and should retrieve it from multiple microservices
- An API endpoint may change (signature, IP, or port)
- A microservice can be split into more microservices
- A microservice may expose a specific protocol

These and other problems increase the complexity from the perspective of the client and their life cycle. This is why we need to simplify the way clients can consume services. We can do this by creating an **abstraction layer**, which exposes a more compact REST API endpoint, implements additional logic, and represents the single entry point to the microservices.

Clients accessing functionality from this layer don't need to know anything about the complexity of the microservices. This abstraction layer is what we call an API gateway, one of the fundamental patterns for microservice architectures.

The **API gateway** is an entry point for external clients, a fundamental component of the microservice architecture that abstracts the multi-domain business logic of the different microservices.

Microservices expose the functionality they implement to other microservices or directly to external clients via a REST API. Having to deal with multiple REST API endpoints for several microservices adds complexity from the perspective of the client:

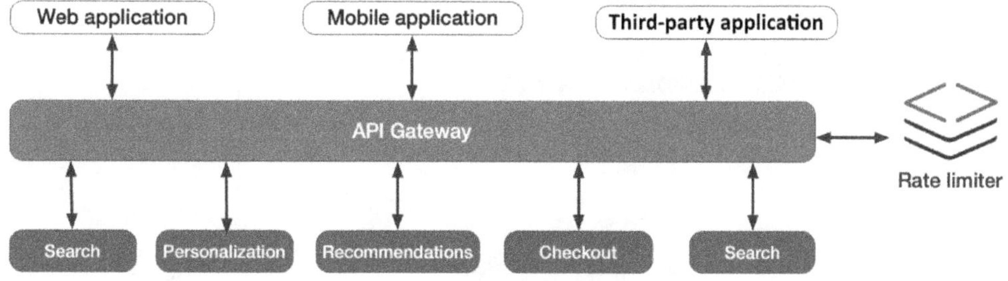

Figure 2.9 – API gateway pattern

The API gateway acts as an entry point for a system that's implemented with the microservice architecture pattern. Every time the client makes requests, the API gateway performs authentication and authorization checks and forwards the request to the correct microservice based on the REST path requested.

In the context of the API gateway, Redis Stack can be adopted as an external and distributed **rate limiter** to enforce rate-limiting policies using the desired method (fixed window, sliding window, and more). Developers can limit requests to a particular service over a given period by identifying users by an API key. The API gateway can limit to a given number of requests in any given timespan, which can prevent the system from being overloaded and mitigate DDoS attacks.

Now that we have introduced the API gateway, it is important to understand the importance of a healthy gateway, and how a real-time caching layer may resolve latency issues. The following section focuses on using Redis Stack as a cache at this layer of the architecture.

API gateway caching

Authenticating millions of users and managing their entitlements can quickly become a significant bottleneck when large volumes of API calls overwhelm the API gateway. This causes unresponsive services, which leads to poor customer experience.

In addition to variable throughput, API gateways usually manage data that must be accessed by all microservices (such as session data or authentication tokens) at the API gateway level.

Caching at the API gateway level alleviates the load on underlying application servers and makes **globally accessed data** available with high performance by all services. Examples of data that is managed by the API gateway include sessions (user ID, preferences, and so on) and authentication data (tokens, authorization status, permissions, and so on). API gateway caching enables frequently needed data available in real time to all services, reducing application latency without breaking the bounds of each microservice business context:

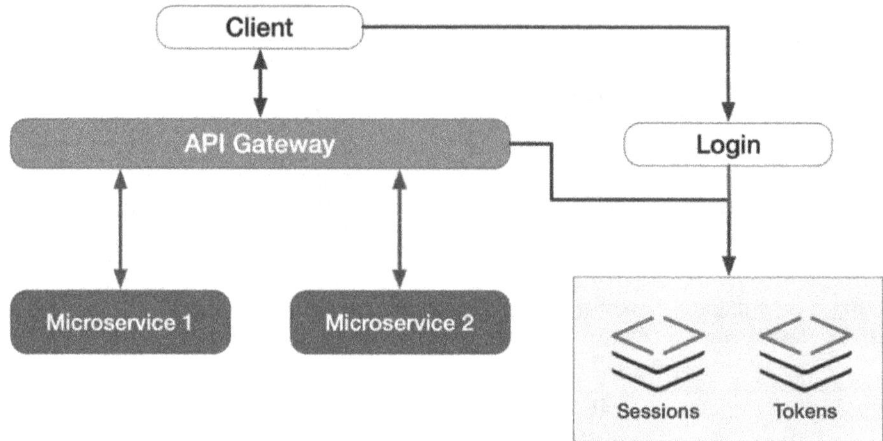

Figure 2.10 – API gateway caching pattern

Redis Stack caches authentication data in a token that can be quickly pulled by the API gateway to authenticate users and relay key session information such as user settings and permissions or user data, such as a shopping cart.

Domain-driven design

Microservice architectures are decentralized and implemented by orchestrating multiple small loosely coupled services: the microservices. Isolated or bounded context is a key characteristic of a microservice architecture. As a result of this strategy, different microservices can adopt many different technology stacks to do a particular job; autonomous teams own one or more microservices and have the right skills in those domains. The consequences of the **domain-driven design** approach extend to the storage layer: each service can have its own unique data model and service level agreement goals, which require a dedicated database. The database must be decentralized: shared data across multiple microservices can cause major scalability or availability issues and is bad practice (so, rather than a pattern, it is referred to as an **anti-pattern**).

To provide loosely coupled services with the ability to manage (and eventually persist) data, the preferred approach is to let every team decide what kind of data store best fits the data model that is managed by the application. **Polyglot persistence**, which shares the same mission as polyglot programming (that is, letting the team choose the right programming languages to design the service), implies the introduction of specialized databases to satisfy specific requirements or use cases. Redis Stack is a multi-model database and can manage heterogeneous data models:

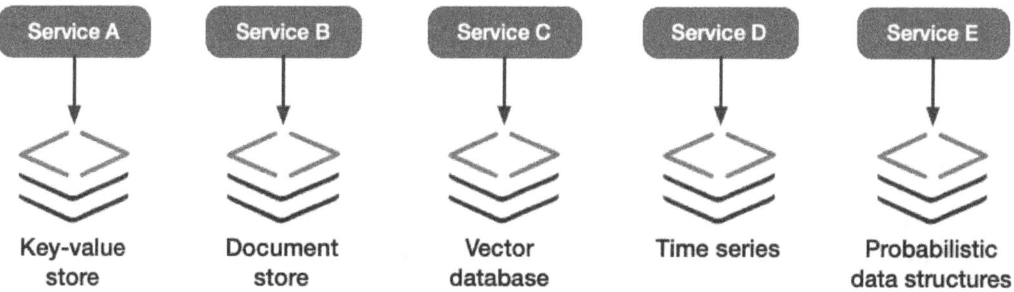

Figure 2.11 – The data layer in the domain-driven design pattern

Managing different data models in the same database has several advantages. Let's mention a few of them:

- It simplifies the paperwork and reduces licensing and maintenance costs
- Developing a competence plan is easier
- Scalability and high availability are addressed at the data layer level
- The ability to combine different data models promotes new approaches to problems
- The semantic data model is abstracted with a unified/compact query language
- Administration and performance-tuning efforts can focus on a single data store

Next, we'll examine query caching.

Query caching

The **query caching** pattern helps improve the performance of a microservice, especially when the database can't serve queries with real-time performance, can't scale the number of concurrent queries beyond a certain degree, or both. Typically, the database that's used and considered the authoritative data source (also referred to as a system of record) is a relational database with **atomicity, consistency, isolation, and durability** (ACID) properties. Introducing a caching layer reduces latency for microservice application performance, but it also presents several challenges.

The **cache-aside** cache pattern can be used to reduce microservices response times. Query caching works by deploying a cache alongside each microservice to deliver **domain-specific** data that is needed within a single business context (it serves only one microservice):

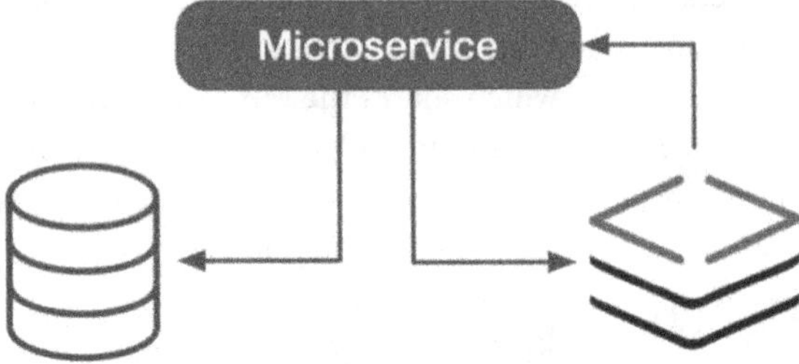

Figure 2.12 – Query caching pattern

Data is cached on demand and returned to the user requesting it using the following algorithm:

1. Queries from the microservice or application are first sent to a Redis Stack database acting as a cache.
2. If data is present (cache hit), it is delivered with real-time performance.
3. If the data does not reside in the cache (cache miss), it is delivered by the slower system of record, and then stored in the cache to reduce the latency of future requests.

Next, we'll look at segregating commands and queries to speed up read operations and alleviate the pressure on the primary database.

Command query responsibility segregation

Not all microservices have the same requirements for the data layer. When durability is an unavoidable requirement, one microservice owns the authoritative copy of data (system of record), while other microservices may require the same information in real time, for different business contexts. If the same database is used for all the microservices, their deployment would be coupled, breaking the isolation principle, and could only be optimized for either write or read operations, but not both. Excessive calls to the system of record database for read-only data will cause performance penalties and higher costs.

Command query responsibility segregation (**CQRS**) is a critical pattern within a microservice architecture that decouples reads (queries) and writes (commands). **Commands** focus on higher durability and consistency, while **queries** focus on performance. This enables a microservice to write data to a slower **system of record** (**SOR**) (the authoritative data source) disk-based database while pre-fetching and caching that data in a cache for reads. This makes that data available in real time to other associated microservices that need it while maintaining isolation between microservices and optimizing both reads and writes:

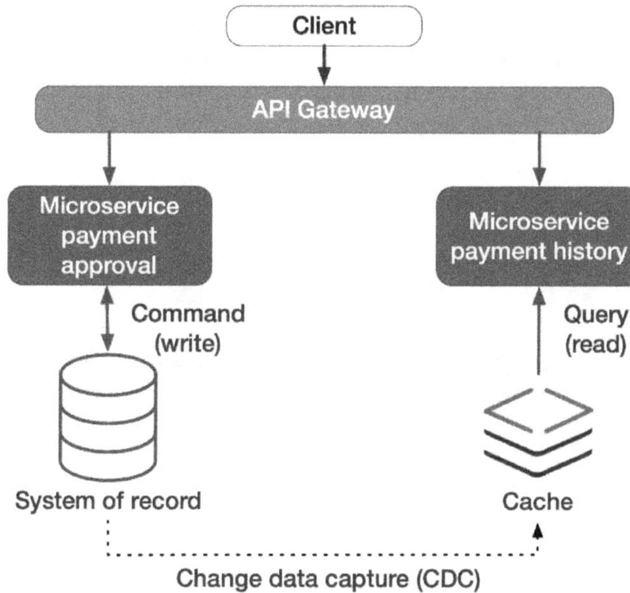

Figure 2.13 – The CQRS pattern

With this pattern, data is written to its original system of record database in a microservice domain, and data is replicated to the cache as it changes in the system of record so that it is available locally or to other microservices for read operations, in a **cross-domain** caching scenario. Other microservices can then read directly from the cache.

Inter-service communication

The microservice architecture is effective at splitting the responsibility of a bigger monolithic system into smaller, loosely coupled microservices. However, the microservices resulting from this functional decomposition must communicate their state, events, and data among one another without breaking isolation, and they must stay decoupled.

Inter-service communication can be implemented via an event-driven asynchronous publish-subscribe message broker. This pattern introduces several advantages, such as decoupling between the producers, which publish events at their own pace to a shared channel, and the consumers, which read asynchronously from it. Another relevant benefit of using message brokers for inter-service communication is the tolerance to disconnections: consumers can reconnect and restart reading from the desired event in the past. Scalability is another strong point: multiple concurrent consumers can assign and process a subset of events from the queue. Additionally, with a **message broker**, producers do not need to know the location (IP and port) of consumers in the network.

Redis Stream is an append-only log data structure with multiple features, such as persistence, random access, read-scalability through consumer groups, data persistence, and more, making this data structure comparable to Apache Kafka topic partitions. Redis Streams provides delivery guarantees, so a single message can only be processed by a single consumer in a consumer group, and a consumer can retrieve messages that were never delivered to other consumers. The state of consumers is observable – it is possible to monitor which messages were never delivered, or the messages that were delivered but not acknowledged:

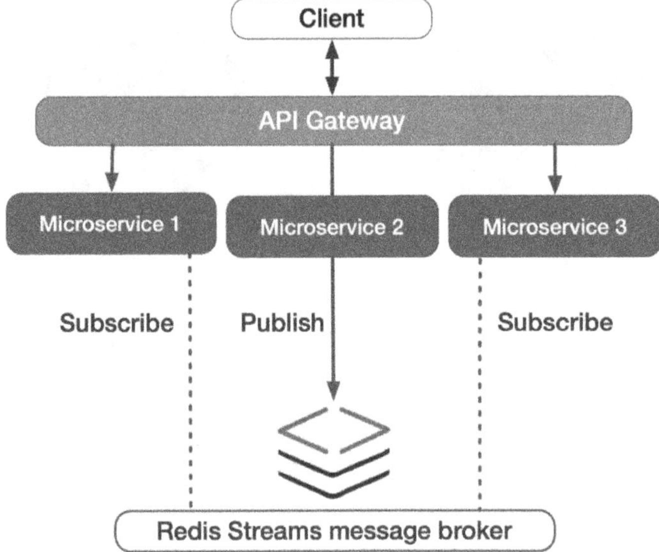

Figure 2.14 – Inter-service communication pattern

Redis Streams can increase the processing throughput with consumer groups. When every service needs to access all the messages in the stream, but it is also desired to process such messages in parallel using several workers, it is possible to provide different messages to the consumers in the same consumer group:

- Multiple consumer groups can read from the same stream
- A consumer group can have multiple consumers
- A typical design where Redis Streams is used as a message broker would use *a consumer group per microservice*

Let's recap what we've discussed in this chapter.

Summary

In this chapter, we reviewed the common scenarios Redis is known for: a real-time store for caching, a compact session store, a flexible message broker, and more. We also introduced modern use cases that can be implemented using the capabilities of Redis Stack. You learned about the indexing features to implement a faceted search in an online retail store and the convenience of indexing a dataset partially. You also discovered how to work with unstructured data to implement a recommendation system based on VSS or to serve an ML pipeline when Redis Stack is used as an online feature store. Finally, you explored microservice architecture patterns and learned how to implement them with Redis Stack.

In *Chapter 3*, *Getting Started with Redis Stack*, you will learn how to install Redis Stack on different environments using binary packages, Docker images, and more. You will also prepare your environment so that you can work with the client libraries for the desired programming language and install RedisInsight, a graphical data management tool.

3

Getting Started with Redis Stack

Redis Stack is a collection of software components that together provide a complete solution for managing data.

As we saw in the previous chapter, Redis Stack is a bundle composed of Redis, plus additional capabilities and data structures. Redis Stack operates under a dual-license framework: the **Redis Source Available License** (**RSALv2**) and the **Server Side Public License** (**SSPL**). Before Redis Stack was released, each additional data structure and functionality needed to be added separately and activated for each Redis database. Now, everything is integrated and activated by default, easing both the developer and the operational experience.

The Redis Stack community has been focusing on improving the **Developer eXperience** (**DX**) for its users. In general, DX refers to the experience of developers as they work with tools, technologies, and platforms to create software. It encompasses everything from the ease of setting up a development environment to the intuitiveness of an API, and the quality of documentation and support available.

Redis Stack aims to provide the best experience possible for your Redis infrastructure and architecture; as such, Redis Stack can be installed using native packages, as a Linux container using the Docker format image, or directly, by downloading the source code.

By the end of this chapter, you will understand how to install Redis Stack for your developer and production-like environments in a few easy steps. You will learn the basics of the Redis Stack architecture to start managing and visualizing your data in a fully integrated environment using RedisInsight.

In this chapter, we are going to cover the following:

- Installing Redis Stack using binary packages
- Installing Redis Stack using native packages
- Using Redis Cloud

- Installing RedisInsight
- Installing the Redis Stack client libraries
- Running health checks

Installing Redis Stack using binary packages

Redis Stack is source-available software, allowing users to freely access and modify its source code. However, executing the software requires first building it, which can occasionally be complex due to hard-to-find dependencies on system libraries. The simplest way to initiate the software is by obtaining its precompiled binary and executing it. This method is the primary focus of the discussion in this section. However, the complete list of installation options can be found at the following site: `https://redis.io/download/#redis-stack-downloads`.

Because most of the server environments, either developer local desktop or production, are based on Linux machines, for our example, I'll use the Ubuntu `Focal x86_64` binary:

1. Let's start by opening your preferred terminal application and navigating in the filesystem to the path that you want your Redis Stack software to be. In my case, I'm creating a folder called `rs` in my `user-home`:

```
root@foogaro-linux:~# mkdir rs
root@foogaro-linux:~# cd rs
root@foogaro-linux:~/rs#
```

2. Now, we can proceed by downloading the Redis Stack binary, as follows:

```
root@foogaro-linux:~/rs# wget  https://packages.redis.io/redis-
stack/redis-stack-server-7.2.0-v3.focal.x86_64.tar.gz
...
 2023-10-08 18:56:39 (18.1 MB/s) - 'redis-stack-server-7.2.0-v3.
focal.x86_64.tar.gz' saved [54926682/54926682]

root@foogaro-linux:~/rs#
```

3. Next, we need to extract the compressed binary, as follows:

```
root@foogaro-linux:~/rs# tar zxvf  redis-stack-server-7.2.0-v3.
focal.x86_64.tar.gz
./
./redis-stack-server-7.2.0-v3/
./redis-stack-server-7.2.0-v3/lib/
./redis-stack-server-7.2.0-v3/lib/libredisgears_v8_plugin.so
./redis-stack-server-7.2.0-v3/lib/redistimeseries.so
./redis-stack-server-7.2.0-v3/lib/redisbloom.so
./redis-stack-server-7.2.0-v3/lib/redisgears.so
```

```
./redis-stack-server-7.2.0-v3/lib/rejson.so
./redis-stack-server-7.2.0-v3/lib/redisearch.so
./redis-stack-server-7.2.0-v3/share/
./redis-stack-server-7.2.0-v3/share/RSAL_LICENSE
./redis-stack-server-7.2.0-v3/share/APACHE_LICENSE
./redis-stack-server-7.2.0-v3/etc/
./redis-stack-server-7.2.0-v3/etc/redis-stack.conf
./redis-stack-server-7.2.0-v3/etc/redis-stack-service.conf
./redis-stack-server-7.2.0-v3/etc/README
./redis-stack-server-7.2.0-v3/bin/
./redis-stack-server-7.2.0-v3/bin/redis-sentinel
./redis-stack-server-7.2.0-v3/bin/redis-server
./redis-stack-server-7.2.0-v3/bin/redis-benchmark
./redis-stack-server-7.2.0-v3/bin/redis-cli
./redis-stack-server-7.2.0-v3/bin/redis-check-rdb
./redis-stack-server-7.2.0-v3/bin/redis-check-aof
./redis-stack-server-7.2.0-v3/bin/redis-stack-server
root@foogaro-linux:~/rs#
```

Let's pause for a second and analyze the content of the Redis Stack bundle.

It has four different folders:

- `share`: This folder stores the licenses related to Redis Stack (`RSAL_LICENSE`) and to the Redis modules (`APACHE_LICENSE`)
- `lib`: This folder stores the modules that come with Redis Stack: `RedisTimeSeries`, `RedisBloom`, `RedisJSON`, `RediSearch`, and triggers and functions
- `etc`: This folder stores the configuration files with its default values
- `bin`: This folder stores the actual binaries that will be used to run Redis Stack

Let's take a closer look at the contents of the `bin` folder. Inside we can find a series of executable files, each with a specific task.

In lexicographic order, the first one is `redis-benchmark`, which is an efficient and valuable method to obtain statistics and assess the performance of a Redis instance on specific hardware.

The program named `redis-check-aof` is a method to check whether the persisted Redis database in the **AOF** format was saved correctly. It also provides a method to fix any eventual issues (for example, data corruption). This implies, and we will see more in the later chapter, that Redis Stack can work as a primary database, thanks to its persistence capabilities.

The program named `redis-check-rdb` provides the same capabilities as the previous program, `redis-check-aof`, but it's specific to a Redis database persisted using the **RDB** format.

The program named `redis-cli` is used to interact with Redis Stack via a **command-line interface (CLI)**. This is one of the most used tools to access a Redis database, browse through its keys, execute queries, and write data.

The program named `redis-sentinel` is a monitoring tool designed for Redis instances, which manages the automatic failover of the Redis master in a replicated topology. In addition to failover management, `redis-sentinel` also facilitates a discovery service by providing a way for clients to find the current Redis master instance. We will discuss `redis-sentinel` in more detail in *Chapter 12, Managing Development and Production Environments*. Last but not least, the program named `redis-server` is the main program of Redis. In addition, the native binary also provides a shell script named `redis-stack-server`, which is used to start the complete Redis Stack environment.

Let's see Redis Stack in action by going back to the terminal and launching the `redis-stack-server` script in the `bin` folder, as follows:

```
./redis-stack-server
 Starting redis-stack-server, database path ../var/db/redis-stack
31502:C 08 Oct 2023 19:24:59.556 * oO0OoO0OoO0Oo Redis is starting
oO0OoO0OoO0Oo
31502:C 08 Oct 2023 19:24:59.557 * Redis version=7.2.1, bits=64,
commit=00000000, modified=0, pid=31502, just started
…
 2753:M 08 Oct 2023 19:37:57.230 * Ready to accept connections tcp
```

Redis Stack Server has been launched successfully, and you can now start managing your data.

During the startup, you might encounter an error related to a system library not being found. This is highly dependent on the OS you choose to use for the examples. I opted for Ubuntu version 20.04 named Focal Fossa and, indeed, faced several issues, such as the one shown here:

```
libgomp.so.1: cannot open shared object file: No such file or
directory
```

If that is the case, it means you are missing that specific library in your system, and it's related to GCC's OpenMP. The GCC OpenMP is a library that enables concurrency and parallelism. To install the GCC OpenMP system library for Linux Debian-based systems, do the following:

```
sudo apt-get install libgomp1
```

And for CentOS-based systems, do the following:

```
yum install libgomp
```

What we have seen so far is the installation process for a Linux Ubuntu environment. For other operating systems, the approach is similar but you may find a few variations. Now, let's try to install Redis Stack using native packages.

Installing Redis Stack using native packages

Different operating systems have their own native package managers that allow you to easily download and install software from a repository of pre-built packages. For example, on Linux, package managers such as APT, YUM, and Pacman are used to manage the installation of software. On macOS, the native package manager is **Homebrew**, and on Windows, it is **Windows Package Manager** (**WinGet**).

To install software using native packages, you simply need to run a command in the command line or use a **graphical user interface** (**GUI**) to search for the desired package and initiate the installation process. The package manager will then download the required files and dependencies and install the software on the system.

Using native packages for installation has several advantages over other methods, such as manual installation or downloading from third-party websites. These advantages include the following:

- **Convenience**: The installation process is typically automated and requires minimal user intervention
- **Security**: Native packages are typically signed and verified to ensure that they are from a trusted source
- **Dependency management**: The package manager automatically handles the installation and management of dependencies required by the software
- **Updates**: The package manager can also be used to manage updates and upgrades for the installed software, ensuring that the system is always up to date with the latest patches and features

Let's see some of the package tools for each OS.

macOS-native package

For macOS users, Homebrew is used, so make sure it is installed.

Open a terminal window and search for Redis Stack, as follows:

```
foogaro@~ # brew search redis-stack/redis-stack
==> Casks
redis-stack/redis-stack/redis-stack
redis-stack/redis-stack/redis-stack-redisinsight
redis-stack/redis-stack/redis-stack-server
foogaro@~ #
```

As you can see from the output of the previous command, there are three casks available:

- `redis-stack-server` contains Redis Stack Server
- `redis-stack-redisinsight` contains the RedisInsight tool
- `redis-stack` contains both `redis-stack-server` and `redis-stack-redisinsight` casks

The natural choice for a development environment is of course the `redis-stack` cask, and to proceed with the installation, do the following:

```
foogaro@~ # brew tap redis-stack/redis-stack
foogaro@~ # brew install redis-stack
```

Next, we'll look at Linux.

Linux-native package

There are many different Linux distributions out there, and each one of them comes with its preferred package manager. In this guide, we will see how to install Redis Stack using the **APT** and **YUM** package managers.

Debian/Ubuntu APT repository

The APT repository supports the following versions:

- Debian Bullseye (11)
- Ubuntu Xenial (16.04)
- Ubuntu Bionic (18.04)
- Ubuntu Focal (20.04)

All of them are supported on the x86 hardware architecture.

Before proceeding with the installation command, we first need to add the repository to the APT index, update the APT index, and finally install it, as follows:

```
curl -fsSL https://packages.redis.io/gpg | sudo gpg -dearmor -o /usr/share/keyrings/redis-archive-keyring.gpg
echo "deb [signed-by=/usr/share/keyrings/redis-archive-keyring.gpg] https://packages.redis.io/deb $(lsb_release -cs) main" | sudo tee /etc/apt/sources.list.d/redis.list
sudo apt-get update
sudo apt-get install redis-stack-server
```

At this point, Redis Stack should now be ready to run on Debian/Ubuntu.

RedHat/CentOS YUM repository

The YUM repository supports the following versions:

- RHEL 7
- CentOS 7

- RHEL 8
- CentOS Stream 8

All of them are supported on the x86 hardware architecture.

Before proceeding with the installation command, we first need to add the repository to the YUM index and install it:

1. Create the `/etc/yum.repos.d/redis.repo` file, and enter the following code:

```
[Redis]
name=Redis
baseurl=http://packages.redis.io/rpm/rhel7
enabled=1
gpgcheck=1
```

2. Now the installation can proceed with the following command:

```
curl -fsSL https://packages.redis.io/gpg > /tmp/redis.key
sudo rpm --import /tmp/redis.key
sudo yum install epel-release
sudo yum install redis-stack-server
```

Now we'll check Windows.

Windows-native package

At the time of writing, the Redis Stack installation relies on Docker, which needs to be already installed on your Windows machine. Once Docker is available, you can follow what is described in the next section, *Running Redis Stack using Docker*.

Running Redis Stack using Docker

If you try to search for the Redis Stack images using the Docker daemon on your machine, you will notice that there is more than one image available, as shown in the following code block:

```
foogaro@~ # docker search redis-stack
NAME                                  DESCRIP-
TION                                          STARS     OFFICIAL    AUTOMAT-
ED
redis/redis-stack                     redis-stack installs a Redis server
with add…    37
redis/redis-stack-server              redis-stack-server installs a Redis
server w…    18
```

Which image name is right for you?

The image named `redis/redis-stack-server` provides Redis Stack Server without any additional tools. On the other hand, the image named `redis/redis-stack` provides Redis Stack Server plus RedisInsight, the official Redis visualization tool.

For a production-like environment based on containers or Kubernetes, the `redis/redis-stack-server` image is definitely the best option. For a development environment, such as your machine, `redis/redis-stack` provides the best developer experience.

So, for a production-like environment, you can run the `redis/redis-stack-server` image, as follows:

```
docker run -d --name redis-stack-server -p 6379:6379 redis/redis-
stack-server:latest
```

And, for a developer environment, you can run the `redis/redis-stack` image, as follows:

```
docker run -d --name redis-stack -p 6379:6379 -p 8001:8001 redis/
redis-stack:latest
```

As you can see, the last `docker run` exposes an additional port, `8001`, that you can use to connect to RedisInsight using a browser, pointing at the following URL: `http://127.0.0.1:8081`.

We will have a closer look at RedisInsight in later sections and chapters.

Using Redis Cloud

In the previous sections, we saw how easy it is to install Redis Stack, but there is another option that is even easier. You can avoid installation entirely, by using Redis Cloud, a service provided by Redis (the company). Redis Cloud can be used as a **Database as a Service** (**DBaaS**) on leading cloud providers such as Google Cloud, Azure, and AWS.

The only prerequisite is registering to the Redis portal, at the following link: `https://app.redislabs.com/`.

Once registered, you can start configuring the size of your Redis Stack database in a few seconds, as follows:

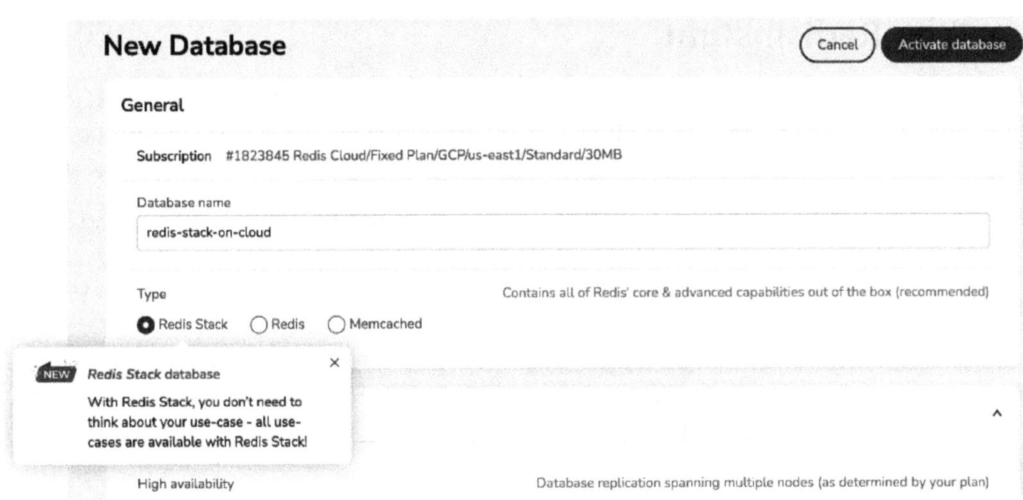

Figure 3.2 – Redis Cloud

Once configured, Redis Cloud will provide the endpoint of your Redis Stack database, which is accessible with the credentials you provided, as depicted in the following figure:

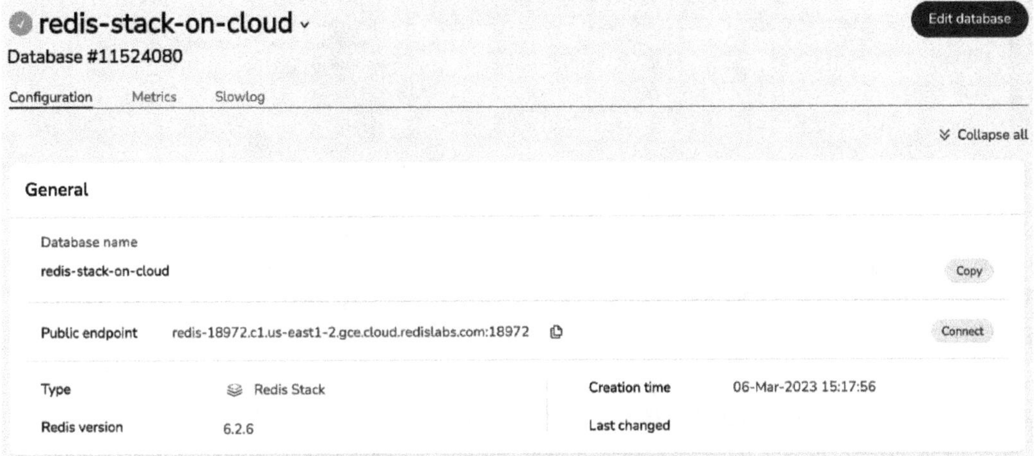

Figure 3.2 – Redis Cloud database endpoint

Overall, the fully managed service offers an easy and convenient way to use Redis Stack without the need for installation and management.

Installing RedisInsight

RedisInsight is designed with a strong focus on developer experience. Its web-based interface is intuitive and user-friendly, providing a visual way for developers and database administrators to interact with Redis instances.

RedisInsight can be downloaded from the following link: `https://redis.com/redis-enterprise/redis-insight/`.

Installation packages are provided for Linux, Windows, and macOS.

The tool provides real-time monitoring and debugging capabilities, allowing developers to quickly identify and resolve issues in Redis databases. It also includes a number of features designed to simplify common Redis tasks, such as adding and modifying Redis keys and executing Redis commands and scripts.

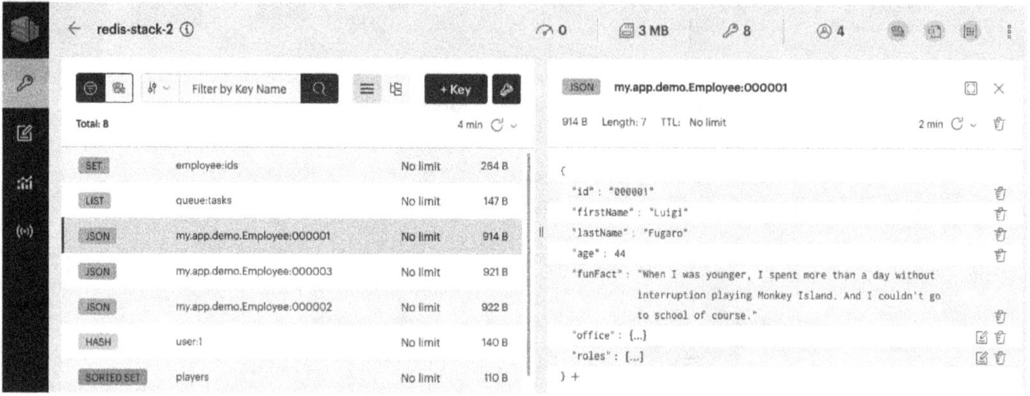

Figure 3.3 – RedisInsight

Overall, RedisInsight's focus on the developer experience makes it a valuable tool for any team working with Redis. By providing a simple and intuitive interface, as well as powerful monitoring and debugging capabilities, RedisInsight helps developers work more efficiently and effectively with Redis databases.

Installing the Redis Stack client libraries

Redis Stack is based on Redis, which means it uses the same protocol, **REdis Serialization Protocol (RESP)**. Therefore, all the Redis client libraries available are also valid for Redis Stack.

Here is a list of the supported client libraries:

- `jedis`: The Java client library supported by Redis and its community
- `node-redis`: The JavaScript client library supported by Redis and its community
- `redis-py`: The Python client library supported by Redis and its community

- `go-redis`: The Golang client library supported by Redis and its community
- `NRedisStack`: The C#/.NET client library supported by Redis and its community

In this section, we will see how to import those libraries into your code.

Java client library

To use the `jedis` library, it has to be imported and declared as a dependency in your code.

For **Maven**-based projects, you can use the following code snippet:

```
<dependency>
    <groupId>redis.clients</groupId>
    <artifactId>jedis</artifactId>
    <version>4.3.1</version>
</dependency>
```

For **Gradle**-based projects, you can use the following code snippet:

```
implementation 'redis.clients:jedis:4.3.1'
```

Additional information can be found in its GitHub repository at the following link: `https://github.com/redis/jedis`.

JavaScript client library

To use the `node-redis` library, it has to be installed in your **Node.js** environment, using the `npm` package manager, as follows:

```
npm install redis
```

Additional information can be found in its GitHub repository at the following link: `https://github.com/redis/node-redis`.

Python client library

To use the `redis-py` library, it has to be installed in your Python environment, using the `pip` package manager, as follows:

```
pip install redis
```

Additional information can be found in its GitHub repository at the following link: `https://github.com/redis/redis-py`.

Golang client library

To use the `go-redis` library, it has to be installed in your Golang environment after you have initialized your module, as follows:

```
go mod init github.com/my/repo
go get github.com/redis/go-redis/v9
```

Additional information can be found in its GitHub repository at the following link: `https://github.com/redis/go-redis`.

C#/.NET client library

To use the `NRedisStack` library, it must be installed in your C#/.NET environment, as follows:

```
dotnet add package NRedisStack
```

Additional information can be found in its GitHub repository at the following link: `https://github.com/redis/NRedisStack`.

Running health checks

Redis is a powerful, yet simple-to-use, open source data structure server that is designed for high performance and scalability. One of the core principles behind Redis is simplicity, which is reflected both in its design and its architecture. And the question "*Is my Redis ready?*" finds its answer in the **redis-cli** tool.

Verifying whether the installation has been completed correctly is as simple as running the following command in a terminal window:

```
redis-cli -h 127.0.0.1 -p 6379 PING
PONG
```

This is the most reliable and secure way to check whether Redis is up and running. If it is, a `PONG` response message will be given. Failing that, an alternative message will be reported, as follows:

```
redis-cli -h 127.0.0.1 -p 6379 PING
LOADING Redis is loading the dataset in memory
```

Automating the health check for Redis is possible using the `redis-cli` executable. This means that scripts can be written to interpret the output message from the executable, enabling additional checks to be executed using other tools. These checks may include examining open ports, sockets, and other relevant factors. In essence, automating the health check process using `redis-cli` provides a flexible and customizable solution that can be tailored to the specific needs of each user.

Summary

In this chapter, we have conducted a comprehensive review of the various techniques for installing Redis Stack, encompassing the use of binaries, native packages, and Docker. Additionally, we delved into the process of optimizing the development experience by installing RedisInsight, a GUI, alongside client libraries suitable for different programming languages. Moreover, we addressed the crucial topic of running Redis health checks in a straightforward and dependable manner. It is our expectation that after studying this chapter, you will possess a sound understanding of the procedures involved in installing Redis, and that you will be equipped with the knowledge and tools necessary for monitoring its health to ensure the smooth and uninterrupted functioning of Redis Stack.

In *Chapter 4, Setting Up Client Libraries*, we will focus on the developer experience by building projects for each Redis-supported client library, and we will start coding some examples using the Redis OM framework.

4

Setting Up Client Libraries

In the previous chapter, we learned that Redis Stack is a powerful and versatile in-memory data structure store that is widely used for caching, message brokering, and real-time data processing. To facilitate seamless interaction between various programming languages and Redis, a variety of client libraries have been developed. These client libraries, also known as Redis clients, provide a convenient interface to access and manipulate Redis data structures through their respective language-specific APIs.

In this chapter, you will learn how to properly initialize and set up your Redis project in your preferred programming language, using Redis-supported client libraries.

First, you will learn the basics of the Redis Stack client libraries, and then you will learn, with hands-on examples, how to use those client libraries for your projects in your preferred programming languages:

- Programming in Python using `redis-py`
- Programming in Java using `Jedis`
- Programming in JavaScript using `node-redis`
- Programming in Go using `go-redis`
- Programming in C#/.NET using `NRedisStack`

Each section is self-contained, so unless you want to try the support for each programming language, you can jump directly to the section that matches your preferred programming language, client libraries, or your day-to-day runtime environment.

Technical requirements

In this chapter, we will begin the hands-on part of the book by exploring various programming languages and their individual configurations. We will provide a comprehensive overview of the required resources for each Redis Stack client library variant with details laid out in their respective sections.

Redis Stack client libraries

Redis Stack client libraries enable you to easily integrate Redis into your applications, regardless of your preferred programming language. By using the appropriate Redis Stack client library, you can significantly improve the performance, scalability, and reliability of your applications, while also benefiting from the extensive features and capabilities of Redis.

The supported Redis Stack client libraries are as follows:

- `redis-py` (Python): A widely used and well-maintained Python client library that supports various Redis features and offers thread-safe and robust connection handling.
- `Jedis` (Java): A popular Java client library with high performance and comprehensive support for Redis commands. It provides both synchronous and asynchronous command execution, as well as connection pooling for efficient resource management.
- `node-redis` (Node.js): A robust and feature-rich Redis client for Node.js, offering complete support for Redis commands, and an asynchronous, non-blocking design.
- `go-redis` (Go): A powerful and efficient Go client library that supports a wide range of Redis features, including pipelining, transactions, and custom command creation.
- `NRedisStack` (C#/.NET): A new client library that provides Redis Stack support to the .NET ecosystem.

In addition to the Redis client libraries, there is also an **object mapping** (**OM**) framework called **Redis OM**.

Redis OM is a framework that simplifies interaction with Redis by providing an object-oriented approach to managing Redis data structures. With Redis OM, developers can work with Redis data structures as if they were native objects of your preferred programming language. This enables a more intuitive way to interact with Redis, reducing the complexity of handling raw Redis commands and improving the development experience.

Some key features of Redis OM include the following:

- **Object mapping**: Redis OM maps objects to Redis data structures, allowing developers to interact with these structures using familiar syntax and idioms. It supports the JSON and Hash Redis data structures.
- **Schema definition**: Developers can define objects that represent Redis data structures, providing structure and validation to the data stored in Redis. This makes it easier to enforce data consistency and integrity.
- **Querying**: Redis OM offers a simple yet powerful querying interface to retrieve and manipulate data stored in Redis. It supports operations such as filtering, sorting, and pagination, enabling developers to perform complex queries with minimal effort.

- **Indexing**: Redis OM provides support for indexing, allowing developers to create and manage secondary indexes on Redis JSON and Hash data structures. This enables more efficient and flexible querying capabilities.
- **Transactions**: Redis OM supports transactions, enabling developers to perform multiple Redis operations atomically. This ensures data consistency and integrity when executing complex operations involving multiple data structures.
- **Pipeline**: Redis OM allows developers to use pipelining for batch execution of Redis commands, improving performance by reducing the number of round-trip calls to the server.

By abstracting away the lower-level details of Redis, Redis OM enables you to focus on your application logic and write cleaner, more maintainable code. This makes it a valuable tool when working with Redis on your projects.

Programming in Python using redis-py

Python is a versatile, high-level, and easy-to-learn programming language that has gained immense popularity among developers, data scientists, and software engineers alike. Created by Guido van Rossum and first released in 1991, Python emphasizes readability and simplicity, making it an excellent choice for beginners and experienced programmers.

Python is available on various platforms, such as Windows, macOS, Linux, and Unix, allowing developers to write code that can run on different operating systems. Python supports various programming paradigms, such as object-oriented, procedural, and functional programming, allowing developers to choose the most suitable approach for their projects.

Python's simplicity and power have made it an essential tool in a wide range of industries, including web development, scientific computing, data analysis, artificial intelligence, and automation. With an ever-growing community and a plethora of resources available, learning Python can open doors to numerous opportunities in the world of programming and technology.

As we learned in the previous chapter, the Redis client library for Python can be installed very easily, using the **pip** package manager.

However, since Python version 3.3, a tool named **virtualenv** was integrated into Python's standard library. A Python virtualenv (virtual environment) is an isolated environment that enables developers to work with different Python projects without interfering with each other's dependencies, settings, and configurations. Virtual environments are particularly useful when dealing with multiple projects that require different versions of Python libraries or even different Python interpreter versions.

Using virtual environments has several benefits:

- **Dependency management**: Each virtual environment can have its own set of installed packages, which helps prevent conflicts between different projects with varying requirements

- **Consistency**: Virtual environments ensure a consistent environment for development, testing, and deployment, reducing the risk of issues caused by varying package versions or configurations across different systems
- **Simplified collaboration**: By using virtual environments and specifying project dependencies, developers can easily share their work with others, who can recreate the same environment without any hassle

To create and use virtual environments in Python, you can use tools such as `venv` (included in the Python 3.3+ standard library) or `virtualenv` (a separate package for earlier Python versions).

To install the virtual environment tool for Python, enter the following into a terminal or command prompt:

```
apt install python3.9-venv
```

Here's a basic example of how to create and activate a virtual environment using the `venv` option:

1. First, open a terminal or command prompt and navigate to your project directory.
2. Create a new virtual environment using the following command:

   ```
   python -m venv redis-stack-venv
   ```

   This will create a new directory named `redis-stack-venv` in your project folder, containing the virtual environment's files.

3. To activate the virtual environment, use the appropriate command for your operating system:
   - For Windows, use the following:

     ```
     redis-stack-venv\Scripts\activate.bat
     ```

   - For macOS/Linux, use the following:

     ```
     source redis-stack-venv/bin/activate
     ```

   After activating the virtual environment, your terminal or command prompt should show the environment name (in this example, **redis-stack-venv**), indicating that you're now working within the virtual environment.

4. With the virtual environment active, you can now install packages using `pip` without affecting the global Python environment. To install the Redis client library, do as follows:

   ```
   pip install redis
   ```

5. To deactivate the virtual environment and return to the global Python environment, simply run the following command:

   ```
   deactivate
   ```

By using virtual environments, you can maintain clean and organized Python projects, ensuring that each project has its own isolated environment with specific dependencies, settings, and configurations.

Now it's time to code a bit in Python by implementing a connection to Redis Stack and storing some data in it.

Storing information in Redis Stack using Python

Before you begin, pick the integrated developer environment of your choice and create a new Python file named `example.py`:

1. The first line we are going to insert is the import of the Redis library, as follows:

   ```
   import redis
   ```

2. Next, we are going to connect to a Redis Stack instance. In the previous chapter, you learned how to install Redis Stack in different ways, using binaries, using Docker, and through Redis Cloud, which is still the easiest and fastest way to get a Redis Stack instance.

   Having said that, to connect to your Redis Stack instance you need the hostname or IP of your server, the port Redis Stack is exposed on, and the credentials to authenticate.

   For convention, the hostname will be mapped to `localhost` and the port to `6379`.

   In our `example.py` file, add the following content:

   ```
   client = redis.Redis(host='127.0.0.1', port=6379,
   username='<YOUR_USERNAME>', password='<YOUR_PASSWORD>')
   client.set("Redis", "Stack")
   print(client.get("Redis"))
   ```

   Make sure you replace `<YOUR_USERNAME>` and `<YOUR_PASSWORD>` accordingly with the ones you set when you created and configured your Redis Stack database.

3. To execute this script, just run the following commands in the terminal:

   ```
   (redis-stack-venv) root@foogaro-linux:~/redis-stack-py# python
   example.py
   b'Stack'
   ```

Hurray! You just learned how to use the Redis Stack client library for Python and how to connect to Redis Stack. However, one of the advantages of Redis Stack is its data structures, and those can be mapped one to one with objects in programming languages such as Python.

Nonetheless, storing a simple string is not a big deal, however, the same simplicity can be applied to other Redis data types such as Lists, Sets, Sorted Sets, and Hashes, where for each of them, Python provides a corresponding structure.

Lists

The **List** data structure in Redis Stack bears a striking resemblance to its Python counterpart, which are also called Lists. These collections of elements allow for efficient manipulation and storage in their respective environments, highlighting the similarity in functionality between the two.

Let us now enhance the earlier `example.py` script to generate a Python list and subsequently save it as a Redis List for seamless integration and usage:

```
departmentList = ['Sales','Solution Architects','Technical Enablement Managers']
client.lpush("redis:departments", *departmentList)
print(client.lrange("redis:departments", 0, -1))
print(client.rpop("redis:departments"))
print(client.lrange("redis:departments", 0, -1))
```

When the script is executed, we get the following output:

```
[b'Technical Enablement Managers', b'Solution Architects', b'Sales']
b'Sales'
[b'Technical Enablement Managers', b'Solution Architects']
```

Next, we will look at Sets.

Sets

The **Set** data structure in Redis Stack is analogous to a Python Set, serving the same purpose in both systems. A Set is a collection of distinct, unordered elements, ensuring that no duplicates are present.

Again, let's update the Python script to generate a Python Set and store it as a Redis Set:

```
favouriteCitySet = {'Macerata','Roma','Atlantis'}
print(favouriteCitySet)
client.sadd("city:favourites", *favouriteCitySet)
print(client.smembers("city:favourites"))
```

When the script is executed, it leads to the following output:

```
{'Macerata', 'Atlantis', 'Roma'}
{b'Macerata', b'Atlantis', b'Roma'}
```

The `redis-py` client offers easy integration for the Set data type.

Sorted Sets

The **Sorted Sets** data type in Redis differs from Sets due to the ordering of its elements based on a corresponding score value. In Python, the closest data structure to Sorted Sets is the Dictionary.

Let's update our `example.py` script to create a Python Dictionary, store it as a Redis Sorted Set, and query it in different ways:

```
cityPopulation = {"city:italy:roma": 2748109, "city:italy:macerata":
40820, "city:italy:catania": 298762}
print(cityPopulation)
print(client.zadd("city:italy", cityPopulation))
res = client.zrange("city:italy", 0, -1, withscores=True)
print(res)
cnt = client.zcard("city:italy")
print(cnt)
```

And when the script is executed, we get the following:

```
{'city:italy:roma': 2748109, 'city:italy:macerata': 40820,
'city:italy:catania': 298762}
3
[(b'city:italy:macerata', 40820.0), (b'city:italy:catania', 298762.0),
(b'city:italy:roma', 2748109.0)]
3
```

The integration for the Sorted Set is straightforward and no additional mapping is needed.

Hashes

The Hash data type in Redis is comparable to a Python Dictionary. Both essentially behave as maps of elements. Let's update our `example.py` script to create a Python Dictionary, store it as a Redis Hash, and query it in different ways.

Let's update our Python file to write and read a Dictionary object into a Hash data type, as follows:

```
employee = {"firstname":"Luigi",
      "lastname":"Fugaro",
      "company":"Redis",
      "role":"Solutions Architect",
      "note":"No matter what, we are all in sales!"}
print(employee)
client.hset("employee:1", mapping=employee)
print(client.hgetall("employee:1"))
```

And when the script is executed, we get the following:

```
{'firstname': 'Luigi', 'lastname': 'Fugaro', 'company': 'Redis',
'department': 'Solutions Architect', 'note': 'No matter what, we are
all in sales!'}
```

```
{b'firstname': b'Luigi', b'lastname': b'Fugaro', b'company': b'Redis',
b'department': b'Solutions Architect', b'note': b'No matter what, we
are all in sales!'}
```

In conclusion, while storing a basic string may not pose a significant challenge, the same ease of use can be extended to other Redis data types, including Lists, Sets, Sorted Sets, and Hashes. For each of these data structures, Python offers a corresponding structure, facilitating seamless interaction between the data modeled in Python and stored in Redis Stack, and enhancing the overall functionality and flexibility of data manipulation. Additionally, Redis provides other data types such as **Streams**, **Geospatial**, and **Pub/Sub**, which also have valuable use cases. We will delve deeper into these data types and explore their functionality later, in *Chapter 9, The Programmability of Redis Stack*.

Redis OM for Python

As previously stated, Redis OM is a framework created by Redis to further enhance the **Developer Experience** (**DX**). This framework aims to provide seamless integration for two primary objectives: facilitating document management for both JSON and Hash while offering search capabilities for the latter.

Let's see Redis OM in action.

In order to utilize Redis OM with Python, your project needs the **Pydantic** library, as it relies on it to function properly. To ensure that your project has access to this library, you should include it in your project's `requirements.txt` file, which is a list of dependencies your project requires. By adding `pydantic` to the `requirements.txt` file, you ensure that anyone using your project will install the correct dependencies.

Your project should have the following dependencies:

- `redis==4.1.4`
- `pydantic==1.9.0`
- `redis-om==0.2.1`

We will be modeling an `Employee` object that consists of various attributes, including another custom object called `Office`. This naturally leads to the question: should we use the Hash or JSON data type for this purpose?

A Hash is a flat map consisting of attribute-value pairs, with values restricted to the String data type (string, number, or binary value). In contrast, a JSON can also be viewed as a map, but it supports a broader range of value types, including strings, numbers, arrays, and nested JSONs.

Given these characteristics, the JSON data type is the most suitable choice for modeling the `Employee` object:

1. Create a new Python project in your preferred IDE, and put the following lines in your `requirements.txt` file:

   ```
   redis==4.1.4
   redis-om==0.0.20
   ```

2. Then, create a new file called `model.py`, with the following content:

   ```
   class Office:
           address: str
           address_number: int
           city: str
           state: str
           postal_code: str
           country: str

   class Employee:
           firstname: str
           lastname: str
           age: int
           roles: List[str]
           fun_fact: str
           office: Office
   ```

   And so far, it's just standard Python.

3. Now, to transform these objects into things that can be stored and managed as JSON documents, we need to enrich their constructors with specific directives, such as `JsonModel` and `EmbeddedJsonModel` from the `redis_om` library:

   ```
   class Office(EmbeddedJsonModel):
   ...
   class Employee(JsonModel):
   ...
   ```

   Both `JsonModel` and `EmbeddedJsonModel` objects inherit from the base `RedisModel` class, which supplies extra methods for persisting objects according to their data types. Consequently, if an object is designated as JSON, it will be persisted using the Redis Stack JSON data type; if it is designated as a Hash, the Redis Stack Hash data type will be used for persistence.

4. If a Hash data type is suitable for modeling objects, the corresponding directive would be `HashModel`, as demonstrated in the following example:

   ```
   class User(HashModel):
         firstname: str
         lastname: str
         email: str
         username: str
   ```

To harness the indexing capabilities provided by Redis Stack, two options are considered:

- Create indexes using Redis Stack syntax with `redis-cli`, as outlined in *Chapter 1, Introducing Redis Stack*
- Create indexes using Redis OM commands directly on the object class

In this case, Redis OM directives will be employed to define and declare the indexing approach for the objects programmatically.

Indexes are used to enhance query performance; in fact, they should be designed to align with how you search and query your data, considering your preferred aggregation methods and sorting.

For instance, with the `Employee` entity, it might be beneficial to search for employees based on their names and surnames. Additionally, grouping employees by attributes such as role, age, or office, or even concentrating on a particular office, could be insightful. There are countless ways to obtain value from data, and no universal solution exists. The most effective approach is the one that corresponds to specific business requirements.

Here is what our `model.py` file looks like after adding Redis OM directives for connection, JSON, and querying capabilities:

```
from typing import List

from redis_om import EmbeddedJsonModel, Field, JsonModel, get_redis_
connection, Migrator

redisClient = get_redis_connection(
      host='<YOUR_HOSTNAME>',
      port=<YOUR_PORT>,
      username='<YOUR_USERNAME>',
      password='<YOUR_PASSWORD>',
      decode_responses=True
)

class Office(EmbeddedJsonModel):
```

```
    address: str = Field(index=True)
    address_number: int = Field(index=True)
    city: str = Field(index=True)
    state: str = Field(index=True)
    postal_code: str = Field(index=True)
    country: str = Field(index=True, default="Remote")

    class Meta:
        database = redisClient

class Employee(JsonModel):
    firstname: str = Field(index=True)
    lastname: str = Field(index=True)
    age: int = Field(index=True)
    office: Office
    roles: List[str] = Field(index=True)
    fun_fact: str = Field(index=True, full_text_search=True)

    class Meta:
        database = redisClient

Migrator().run()
```

The primary purpose of the `JsonModel` parent class is to identify entities as JSON documents. Additionally, it offers methods for saving, finding, updating, and deleting these entities. Additionally, Redis OM requires a distinct approach for defining connections compared to the `redis-py` library. The connection must then be associated with the `JsonModel` entities. Finally, to facilitate the creation of indexes, the `run` method of the `Migrator` helper class must be called.

For instance, to save our `Employee` entity, we can use its `save` method, as follows:

```
new_office = Office(
    address="Via Italia",
    address_number=1,
    city="Roma",
    state="Roma",
    postal_code="00100",
    country="Italy"
)
new_employee = Employee(
    firstname="Luigi",
    lastname="Fugaro",
    age=44,
```

```
        office=new_office,
        roles=["Solution Architect"],
        fun_fact="No matter what, we are all in sales!"
)
new_employee.save()
```

To update it, do as follows:

```
emp.age = 45
emp.save()
```

To delete it, do the following:

```
Employee.delete(1)
```

And to find it, apart from its ID, which would be the most common way in any key-value store such as Redis Stack, Redis OM provides the capability to combine different criteria:

- Here's how you find by ID:

  ```
  employee = Employee.get(1)
  ```

- To find by matching first name and last name, do the following:

  ```
  employees = Employee.find(
          (Employee.first_name == "Luigi") &
          (Employee.last_name == "Fugaro")
     ).all()
  ```

- You can also find by age range:

  ```
  employees = Employee.find(
          (Employee.age >= 35) &
          (Employee.age <= 45)
     ).sort_by("age").all()
  ```

- The following will let you find by role and office:

  ```
  employees = Employee.find(
          (Employee.roles << "Solution Architect") &
          (Employee.office.city == "Rome")
     ).all()
  ```

- You can find by "fun fact" using a full-text search:

  ```
  employees = Employee.find(Employee.fun_fact % "monkey island").
  all()
  ```

Utilizing Python and Redis Stack together forms a potent environment for swiftly developing applications, catering to both frontend and backend services.

Next, we'll look at one of the alternatives to using Python.

Programming in Java using Jedis

Java is a robust, high-level, and widely used programming language that has become a staple for developers, software engineers, and IT professionals across various industries. Developed by James Gosling at Sun Microsystems and released in 1995, Java prioritizes portability, scalability, and maintainability, making it a popular choice for both novice and experienced programmers.

Java is platform-independent, thanks to its "write once, run anywhere" philosophy, which allows developers to create code that can be executed on different operating systems, such as Windows, Macintosh, Solaris, Linux, and Unix. This is made possible by the **Java Virtual Machine** (**JVM**), which translates Java bytecode into machine code for the specific platform.

Java supports object-oriented programming principles, encouraging modular, reusable, and maintainable code. Its extensive standard library, known as the **Java Development Kit** (**JDK**), provides developers with a wide array of tools and resources to create powerful applications.

Java's versatility and robustness have made it an integral part of various industries, including web development, enterprise software, mobile app development, embedded systems, and big data processing. With a thriving community, numerous resources, and a strong focus on enterprise solutions, learning Java can unlock a wealth of opportunities in the ever-evolving world of technology and programming.

As covered in the previous chapter, installing the Redis client library for Java is a straightforward process, thanks to widely used project management tools such as **Maven** and **Gradle**. This section will not delve deeply into Maven and Gradle, nor discuss which tool is superior or how to create a new project using either of these tools. Instead, the focus will be on properly setting up your project dependencies for the Redis Stack Java client library, Jedis, in a courteous manner.

In order to significantly enhance developer productivity and facilitate readability without introducing excessive technical detail, the implementation of Java code will be carried out using Spring Boot applications, and then its structure will be generated using the **Spring Initializr** site.

Therefore, according to individual preferences, choose the appropriate option, as demonstrated in this example:

- **Project**: `Maven`
- **Language**: `Java`
- **Spring Boot**: `3.0.5`

- **Project Metadata**:
  - **Group**: `my.app`
  - **Artifact**: `demo`
  - **Name**: `demo`
  - **Description**: `Demo project for Spring Boot using Redis Stack`
  - **Package name**: `my.app.demo`
  - **Packaging**: `Jar`
  - **Java**: `17`
- **Dependencies**:
  - Spring Web
  - Spring Boot DevTools
  - Lombok

Those options can be easily loaded by constructing a URL that looks like the following: `https://start.spring.io/#!type=maven-project&language=java&platformVersion=3.0.5&packaging=jar&jvmVersion=17&groupId=my.app&artifactId=demo&name=demo&description=Demo%20project%20for%20Spring%20Boot%20using%20Redis%20Stack&packageName=my.app.demo&dependencies=web,devtools,lombok`

On the aforementioned website, if you click the button labeled **GENERATE** located in the bottom-left corner, a file named `demo.zip` will be created and downloaded to your workstation. This file contains the structure of your Java project, tailored for the selected project management tool.

Unzip the content of the file and open your project with your favorite IDE. Once done, open your project file descriptor and add the `Jedis` dependency:

- For a Maven-based project, open the `pom.xml` file and add the following code snippet:

```
<dependency>
      <groupId>redis.clients</groupId>
      <artifactId>jedis</artifactId>
      <version>5.0.0</version>
</dependency>
```

- For a Gradle-based project, open the `build.gradle` file and add the following code snippet:

```
implementation 'redis.clients:jedis:5.0.0'
```

Let's start some coding.

Storing information in Redis Stack using Java

Before storing information in Redis, it is necessary to establish a connection by utilizing a connection pool. Although not strictly required, using a connection pool is highly recommended, particularly for production environments. In `Jedis`, a connection pool is known as a **JedisPool** and can be instantiated as follows:

```
JedisPool pool = new JedisPool("localhost", 6379, "<YOUR_USERNAME>",
"<YOUR_PASSWORD>");
```

The `localhost` and `6379` items represent the hostname and port of an active Redis Stack instance, respectively. As noted in the previous chapter, the most convenient method for running Redis Stack is by utilizing Redis Cloud, a comprehensive DBaaS environment for Redis Stack. Other alternatives are detailed in *Chapter 3, Getting Started with Redis Stack*. For the example provided in this chapter, it is assumed that a Redis Stack instance is already set up and operational.

Make sure you replace `"<YOUR_USERNAME>"` and `"<YOUR_PASSWORD>"` accordingly with the ones you set when you created and configured your Redis Stack database.

Once the pool is created, a connection can be requested, as follows:

```
try (Jedis jedis = pool.getResource()) {
  jedis.set("client", "Jedis");
  String val = jedis.get("client");
  log.info("Retrieved value {}, for key \"client\".", val)
} catch (Exception ex) {
  log.error("Exception caught in set", ex);
}
```

The Jedis resource implements the `java.lang.AutoCloseable` interface. As such, it can be used with a `try-with-resources` statement, and there is no need to close the resource and return it to the pool. This process is done automatically at the end of the statement.

Both `JedisPool` and `Jedis` classes belong to the `redis.clients.jedis` Java package, so the following imports need to be set:

```
import redis.clients.jedis.Jedis;
import redis.clients.jedis.JedisPool;
```

Running the application will output the following:

```
2023-03-26T23:56:25.623+02:00  INFO 27401 --- [           main]
my.app.demo.DemoApplication                  : Retrieved value Luigi
for key name
```

You are now acquainted with using the Redis Stack client library for Java and connecting to Redis Stack. A significant benefit of Redis Stack lies in its data structures, which can be directly mapped to objects in programming languages such as Java.

Storing a simple string may not be a challenging task, but the same ease can be extended to other Redis data types, including Lists, Sets, Sorted Sets, and Hashes. Jedis offers seamless integration for these data types as well.

Lists

Redis Lists are data structures that store ordered collections of strings, arranged according to the order in which they are inserted. This property of maintaining the insertion order makes them an excellent choice for a range of applications, including the implementation of message queues.

As ordered collections, Redis Lists allow for efficient manipulation of elements at both the beginning and the end of the list. They provide a variety of commands for adding, removing, and querying elements, as well as for trimming and modifying the list based on specific requirements.

The following code is an example:

```
long numberOfTasks = client.lpush("queue:tasks", "Task-1");
log.info("numberOfTasks {}", numberOfTasks);
numberOfTasks = client.lpush("queue:tasks", "Task-2");
log.info("numberOfTasks {}", numberOfTasks);
String task = client.rpop("queue:tasks");
log.info("Retrieved task {}", task);
```

The output is as follows:

```
2023-03-27T00:20:47.673+02:00  INFO 28100 --- [            main]
my.app.demo.DemoApplication                 : numberOfTasks 1
2023-03-27T00:20:47.802+02:00  INFO 28100 --- [            main]
my.app.demo.DemoApplication                 : numberOfTasks 2
2023-03-27T00:20:47.934+02:00  INFO 28100 --- [            main]
my.app.demo.DemoApplication                 : Retrieved task Task-1
```

Next, we'll look at sets.

Sets

Redis Sets are data structures that store unordered collections of unique strings, making them particularly valuable when it is essential to ensure that duplicate elements are not present within the collection. These sets provide an efficient way to represent, store, and manipulate distinct pieces of data, such as user IDs, unique tokens, or IP addresses.

The following code is an example:

```
client.sadd("employee:ids", "00000001");
client.sadd("employee:ids", "00000002");
client.sadd("employee:ids", "00000001");
Set<String> employeeIds = client.smembers("employee:ids");
```

```
log.info("Employee IDs {}", employeeIds);
employeeIds.forEach(s -> log.info("Employee: {}", s));
boolean exists = client.sismember("employee:ids", "00000001");
log.info("Employee id \"00000001\" exists {}", exists);
```

You should see the following output:

```
2023-03-27T00:33:48.126+02:00  INFO 28508 --- [           main]
my.app.demo.DemoApplication                    : Employee IDs
[00000002, 00000001]
2023-03-27T00:33:48.127+02:00  INFO 28508 --- [           main]
my.app.demo.DemoApplication                    : Employee: 00000002
2023-03-27T00:33:48.127+02:00  INFO 28508 --- [           main]
my.app.demo.DemoApplication                    : Employee: 00000001
2023-03-27T00:33:48.254+02:00  INFO 28508 --- [           main]
my.app.demo.DemoApplication                    : Employee id
"00000001" exists true
```

Next, we'll look at Sorted Sets.

Sorted Sets

Sorted Sets are a specialized type of Set in Redis, with the key difference being that each member in a Sorted Set has an associated score, or ranking, which dictates its position within the collection. This additional attribute allows Sorted Sets to maintain a consistent order based on the scores assigned to each member.

For an example, see the following code:

```
Map<String, Double> scores = new HashMap<>();
scores.put("PlayerOne", 22.0);
scores.put("PlayerTwo", 10.0);
scores.put("PlayerThree", 78.0);
log.info("Scores map {}", scores);
Long addedScores = client.zadd("players", scores);
log.info("Added scores {}", addedScores);
List<String> players = client.zrangeByScore("players", 0, 50);
log.info("Players with score in range 0-50 {}", players);
Double score = client.zscore("players", "PlayerTwo");
log.info("Score for \"PlayerTwo\" {}", score);
```

The output is as follows:

```
2023-03-27T01:06:17.125+02:00  INFO 29367 --- [           main]
my.app.demo.DemoApplication                    : Scores map
{PlayerThree=78.0, PlayerTwo=10.0, PlayerOne=22.0}
2023-03-27T01:06:17.257+02:00  INFO 29367 --- [           main]
my.app.demo.DemoApplication                    : Added scores 3
```

```
2023-03-27T01:06:17.384+02:00  INFO 29367 --- [           main]
my.app.demo.DemoApplication                  : Players with score in
range 0-50 [PlayerTwo, PlayerOne]
2023-03-27T01:06:17.511+02:00  INFO 29367 --- [           main]
my.app.demo.DemoApplication                  : Score for "PlayerTwo"
10.0
```

Next, we'll look at Hashes.

Hashes

Redis Hashes are data structures that establish relationships between string fields and their associated string values. These mappings allow for efficient storage and retrieval of key-value pairs, making them particularly useful for organizing and managing data within a Redis database. In essence, Redis Hashes enable users to store, access, and manipulate data as a collection of field-value pairs, where both fields and values are strings.

For an example, see the following:

```
Map<String,String> user = new HashMap<>();
user.put("firstname", "Luigi");
user.put("lastname", "Fugaro");
user.put("username", "foogaro");
log.info("User {}", user);

Long numberOfFields = client.hset("user:1", user);
log.info("numberOfFields {}", numberOfFields);
numberOfFields = client.hset("user:1", "email", "luigi@foogaro.com");
log.info("numberOfFields {}", numberOfFields);
String firstname = client.hget("user:1", "firstname");
log.info("User firstname {}", firstname);
Map<String, String> fields = client.hgetAll("user:1");
log.info("All fields {}", fields);
```

This produces the following output:

```
2023-03-27T01:25:02.048+02:00  INFO 29862 --- [           main]
my.app.demo.DemoApplication                  : User
{firstname=Luigi, lastname=Fugaro, username=foogaro}
2023-03-27T01:25:02.181+02:00  INFO 29862 --- [           main]
my.app.demo.DemoApplication                  : numberOfFields 3
2023-03-27T01:25:02.317+02:00  INFO 29862 --- [           main]
my.app.demo.DemoApplication                  : numberOfFields 1
2023-03-27T01:25:02.458+02:00  INFO 29862 --- [           main]
my.app.demo.DemoApplication                  : User firstname Luigi
```

```
2023-03-27T01:25:02.594+02:00  INFO 29862 --- [           main]
my.app.demo.DemoApplication                   : All fields
{firstname=Luigi, email=luigi@foogaro.com, lastname=Fugaro,
username=foogaro}
```

Finally, we'll set up Redis OM for Java.

Redis OM for Java

Redis OM for Spring not only streamlines the process of mapping Java objects to Redis data structures but also provides robust support for managing JSON documents and creating indexes. This added functionality makes it even more convenient for developers to work with Redis databases in their Spring applications.

Utilizing Redis OM for Spring, developers can easily store, retrieve, and manipulate JSON documents within Redis, taking advantage of the flexibility and performance that JSON data types offer. Additionally, the library allows for the creation and management of indexes, which facilitates efficient querying and searching of data stored in Redis.

By combining the powerful features of Spring Data for Redis with the enhanced capabilities of Redis OM, such as JSON document management and indexing, developers can build more sophisticated and performant Spring applications that interact seamlessly with Redis databases:

1. To use the Redis OM framework, your Java project needs an additional dependency, which belongs to a custom repository, as described in the following code block:

   ```
   <repositories>
     <repository>
        <id>snapshots-repo</id>
   <url>https://s01.oss.sonatype.org/content/repositories/
   snapshots/</url>
     </repository>
   </repositories>

   <dependency>
     <groupId>com.redis.om</groupId>
     <artifactId>redis-om-spring</artifactId>
     <version>0.8.0-SNAPSHOT</version>
   </dependency>
   ```

   Because Redis OM is an extension of Spring Data for Redis, which already uses the `Jedis` client, there is no need to include `Jedis` as a separate dependency, so it can be removed from the previous declaration.

   The next task involves modeling an `Employee` object that comprises several attributes, one of which is a custom object called `Office`. This raises the question of whether to employ the Hash or the JSON data type for this purpose.

A Hash is a flat map composed of attribute-value pairs, where values are limited to the String data type (string, number, or binary value). Conversely, a JSON functions as a map but accommodates a wider variety of value types, such as strings, numbers, arrays, and nested JSONs. Based on these properties, the JSON data type emerges as the optimal choice for modeling the `Employee` object.

2. Create a new class called `Employee.java`, with the following content:

```
package my.app.demo;

import com.redis.om.spring.annotations.Document;
import com.redis.om.spring.annotations.Indexed;
import com.redis.om.spring.annotations.Searchable;
import lombok.*;
import org.springframework.data.annotation.Id;

import java.util.Set;

@RequiredArgsConstructor(staticName = "of")
@AllArgsConstructor(access = AccessLevel.PROTECTED)
@Data
@Document
public class Employee {

    @Id
    @Indexed
    private String id;

    @Indexed @NonNull
    private String firstName;

    @Indexed @NonNull
    private String lastName;

    @Indexed @NonNull
    private Integer age;

    @Searchable @NonNull
    private String funFact;

    @Indexed @NonNull
    private Office office;
```

```
        @Indexed @NonNull
        private Set<String> roles;
    }
```

The `Employee` class is marked with the `@Document` annotation, designating it as a JSON document. Moreover, additional annotations are employed to establish the necessary indexes for querying, searching, and aggregating data.

3. Next, the `Office` class should be created, which will be maintained as a nested JSON document within the `Employee` structure:

```
package my.app.demo;

import com.redis.om.spring.annotations.Indexed;
import com.redis.om.spring.annotations.Searchable;
import lombok.Data;
import lombok.NonNull;
import lombok.RequiredArgsConstructor;

@Data
@RequiredArgsConstructor(staticName = "of")
public class Office {

    @NonNull
    @Searchable(nostem = true)
    private String address;

    @NonNull
    @Indexed
    private String addressNumber;

    @NonNull
    @Indexed
    private String city;

    @NonNull
    @Indexed
    private String state;

    @NonNull
    @Indexed
    private String postalCode;

    @NonNull
```

```
    @Indexed
    private String country;
}
```

The integration of Redis OM with Spring simplifies the development process for domain models, allowing them to benefit from standard annotations such as `@Id`, `@NotNull`, and others for data modeling purposes. Another outstanding feature is the ability to utilize a Spring repository with Redis Stack as the target data store.

4. Create a Redis repository called `EmployeeRepository.java`, with the following content:

```
package my.app.demo;

import com.redis.om.spring.repository.RedisDocumentRepository;

import java.util.List;

public interface EmployeeRepository extends
RedisDocumentRepository<Employee,String> {
    List<Employee> findByLastNameAndFirstName(String lastName,
String firstName);
}
```

Now we are ready to save and retrieve the information to and from Redis Stack. To facilitate this process, we rely on the concept of `CommandLineRunner` to load some data and execute our queries on it.

5. Add the following `Bean` declarations to your code:

```
@Bean @Order(1)
CommandLineRunner loadTestData() {
   return args -> {
        employeeRepository.deleteAll();
        Office romeOffice = Office.of("Via Roma", "1", "Roma",
"Roma", "00100", "Italy");
        Office macerataOffice = Office.of("Via Macerata", "1",
"Macerata", "Macerata", "62100", "Italy");

        Employee luigi = Employee.of("Luigi", "Fugaro",
44, "When I was younger, I spent more than a day without
interruption playing Monkey Island. And I couldn't go to school
of course.", romeOffice, Set.of("Solution Architect"));
        Employee mirko = Employee.of("Mirko", "Ortensi",
44, "When I was younger, I spent more than a day without
interruption playing Pac-Man. And I couldn't go to school of
course.", macerataOffice, Set.of("Technical Architect"));

        employeeRepository.save(luigi);
```

```
            employeeRepository.save(mirko);
        };
    }

    @Bean @Order(2)
    CommandLineRunner findAll() {
        return args -> {
            List<Employee> employees = employeeRepository.findAll();
            employees.forEach(employee -> log.info("Find all 
Employee: {}", employee));
        };
    }

    @Bean @Order(3)
    CommandLineRunner findById() {
        return args -> {
            Optional<Employee> employee = employeeRepository.
findById("000001");
            log.info("Find by ID '000001' Employee: {}", employee.
orElseThrow());
        };
    }

    @Bean @Order(4)
    CommandLineRunner findByLastNameAndFirstName() {
        return args -> {
            List<Employee> employees = employeeRepository.
findByLastNameAndFirstName("Ortensi", "Mirko");
            employees.forEach(employee -> log.info("Find by 
firstnale and lastname - Employee: {}", employee));
        };
    }
```

This is the output collected when this Spring application is executed:

```
2023-03-27T12:47:19.691+02:00  INFO 46533 --- [  restartedMain]
my.app.demo.DemoApplication                      : Find all
Employee: Employee(id=000001, firstName=Luigi, lastName=Fugaro,
age=44, funFact=When I was younger, I spent more than a day
without interruption playing Monkey Island. And I couldn't
go to school of course., office=Office(address=Via Roma,
addressNumber=1, city=Roma, state=Roma, postalCode=00100,
country=Italy), roles=[Solution Architect])
2023-03-27T12:47:19.692+02:00  INFO 46533 --- [  restartedMain]
my.app.demo.DemoApplication                      : Find
all Employee: Employee(id=000002, firstName=Mirko,
lastName=Ortensi, age=44, funFact=When I was younger, I spent
more than a day without interruption playing Pac-Man. And I
```

```
couldn't go to school of course., office=Office(address=Via
Macerata, addressNumber=1, city=Macerata, state=Macerata,
postalCode=62100, country=Italy), roles=[Technical Architect])
2023-03-27T12:47:19.692+02:00  INFO 46533 --- [  restartedMain]
my.app.demo.DemoApplication                     : Find all
Employee: Employee(id=000003, firstName=Luigi, lastName=Fugaro,
age=44, funFact=When I was younger, I spent more than a day
without interruption playing Monkey Island. And I couldn't
go to school of course., office=Office(address=Via Roma,
addressNumber=1, city=Roma, state=Roma, postalCode=00100,
country=Italy), roles=[Senior Solution Architect])
2023-03-27T12:47:19.833+02:00  INFO 46533 --- [  restartedMain]
my.app.demo.DemoApplication                     : Find by
ID '000001' Employee: Employee(id=000001, firstName=Luigi,
lastName=Fugaro, age=44, funFact=When I was younger, I spent
more than a day without interruption playing Monkey Island. And
I couldn't go to school of course., office=Office(address=Via
Roma, addressNumber=1, city=Roma, state=Roma, postalCode=00100,
country=Italy), roles=[Solution Architect])
2023-03-27T12:47:19.976+02:00  INFO 46533 --- [  restartedMain]
my.app.demo.DemoApplication                     : Find by
firstnale and lastname - Employee: Employee(id=000002,
firstName=Mirko, lastName=Ortensi, age=44, funFact=When I
was younger, I spent more than a day without interruption
playing Pac-Man. And I couldn't go to school of course.,
office=Office(address=Via Macerata, addressNumber=1,
city=Macerata, state=Macerata, postalCode=62100, country=Italy),
roles=[Technical Architect])
```

By making use of a Spring repository, developers can benefit from a standardized method for declaring information requests, which simplifies the process of accessing and managing data in their applications. Additionally, the `@Query` annotation plays a significant role in enhancing data retrieval capabilities, offering more flexibility and control over the way data is searched for, filtered, and retrieved from the underlying data source.

In essence, the combination of a Spring repository and the `@Query` annotation allows developers to create more efficient and maintainable data access layers in their applications, contributing to an overall improvement in application performance and code quality.

With Java's role in the programming world established, let's now turn our attention to another influential language, JavaScript, which has made a significant impact on web development and user experiences.

Programming in JavaScript using node-redis

Node.js is an excellent choice for various types of applications, particularly those that require real-time communication, scalability, and high performance. One of its main strengths is its non-blocking, event-driven architecture. This means that Node.js can handle multiple requests simultaneously without waiting for any single request to complete. As a result, it is especially suitable for applications that require real-time communication, such as chat applications and online gaming.

Another advantage of Node.js is that it allows you to use JavaScript on the server side. By using the same language for both frontend and backend development, you can streamline your workflow and reduce the learning curve for your development team. This consistency between the frontend and backend can lead to faster development times and improved maintainability.

Node.js also boasts a large and active community of developers, which means you'll have access to a wealth of resources, tutorials, and libraries to help you get started and build your applications. The **Node Package Manager (npm)** is the largest ecosystem of open source libraries, providing a wide range of pre-built modules to help you with anything from handling HTTP requests to working with databases.

Scalability is another key reason to choose Node.js for your projects. Its lightweight architecture and ability to handle a large number of simultaneous connections make it ideal for applications that need to scale as they grow. With support for both horizontal and vertical scaling, Node.js can be easily adapted to meet the demands of your growing user base.

As discussed in the previous section, the installation of the Redis client library for JavaScript is a simple procedure, assuming that your workstation already has the Node.js runtime up and running. At the time this content was created, the version used was 18.14.0.

The installation of the Redis Stack client library for Node.js requires the invocation of the following command:

```
npm install redis
```

And that's all that is needed to start programming in JavaScript, targeting Redis Stack as a data store.

Let's create a folder for your project and edit the `app.js` file, with the following content:

```
import { createClient } from 'redis';

const client = createClient({
    password: '<PASSWORD>',
    socket: {
        host: 'localhost',
        port: 6379
    }
});

(async () => {
    console.log('Connecting...');
    await client.connect();
})();

client.on('error', (err) => {
    console.log('Could not establish a connection with redis. ' +
err);
```

```
});

client.on('connect', function (err) {
     console.log('Connected to Redis Stack successfully');
});


const resp = await client.set('client', 'node-redis', (err, reply) =>
{
    console.log(err);
    console.log(reply);
});
console.log('Set: ' + resp);

const val = await client.get('client', (err, reply) => {
    console.log(err);
    console.log(reply);
});
console.log('Val: ' + val);

await client.quit();
```

Upon running the application, the output will be the following:

```
Connecting...
Connected to Redis Stack successfully
Set: OK
Val: redis
```

The terms `localhost` and `6379` denote the hostname and port of a running Redis Stack instance, respectively. As mentioned earlier, the easiest way to operate Redis Stack is through Redis Cloud, a fully featured DBaaS platform for Redis Stack. *Chapter 3, Getting Started with Redis Stack* elaborates on other options. It is assumed in this chapter's example that a Redis Stack instance has already been established and is functioning.

Ensure that you substitute `<PASSWORD>` with the appropriate password that you assigned when creating and configuring your Redis Stack database.

By now, you have familiarized yourself with the Redis Stack client library for JavaScript and how to connect to Redis Stack. One of the key advantages of Redis Stack is its data structures, which can be easily mapped to objects in programming languages such as JavaScript, especially when it comes to JSON, which is natively supported by the language.

While storing a simple string might not pose many difficulties, the same level of simplicity can be applied to other Redis data types such as Lists, Sets, Sorted Sets, and Hashes. The `node-redis` client library provides smooth integration for these data types too.

Lists

Redis Lists are data structures that hold ordered collections of strings, organized based on the sequence of their insertion. This attribute of preserving the insertion order makes them a superb choice for numerous applications, such as implementing message queues.

Being ordered collections, Redis Lists enable efficient handling of elements at the List's start and end. They offer an array of commands for inserting, deleting, and retrieving elements, along with trimming and modifying the list according to particular needs.

The following is some example code:

```
let result = await client.lPush("queue:tasks", "Task-1");
console.log("numberOfTasks {}"+ result);
result = await client.lPush("queue:tasks", "Task-2");
console.log("numberOfTasks {}"+ result);
result = await client.rPop("queue:tasks");
console.log("Retrieved task {}"+ result);
```

The output should be as follows:

```
Connecting...
Connected to Redis Stack successfully
Set: OK
Val: redis
numberOfTasks {}1
numberOfTasks {}2
Retrieved task {}Task-1
```

Next, we'll look at Sets.

Sets

Redis Sets are data structures that hold unordered collections of distinct strings, which makes them especially useful when preventing duplicate elements in the collection is crucial. These sets offer an effective method for representing, storing, and managing unique data items, such as user IDs, one-of-a-kind tokens, or IP addresses.

For an example, see the following code:

```
result = await client.sAdd('employee:ids', '00000001');
console.log('Added employee:00000001' + result);
result = await client.sAdd('employee:ids', '00000002');
console.log('Added employee:00000002' + result);
result = await client.sAdd('employee:ids', '00000001');
console.log('Added employee:00000001' + result);
```

```
let employeeIds = await client.sMembers('employee:ids');
console.log('Employee IDs: ' + employeeIds);
employeeIds.forEach(employee => {
    console.log('Employee ID: ' + employee);
});
let exists = await client.sIsMember('employee:ids', '00000001');
console.log('Employee ID-00000001 exists? ' + exists);
```

The output should be as follows:

```
Added employee:00000001 - 1
Added employee:00000002 - 1
Added employee:00000001 - 0
Employee IDs: 00000002,00000001
Employee ID: 00000002
Employee ID: 00000001
Employee ID-00000001 exists? True
```

Next, we'll look at Sorted Sets.

Sorted Sets

Sorted Sets in Redis represent a unique variant of Sets, characterized by the fact that every member in a Sorted Set possesses a related score or ranking, determining its placement within the collection. This supplementary characteristic enables Sorted Sets to preserve a stable order based on the scores allocated to each member.

The following is some example code:

```
const players = [
    {
        score: 22.0,
        value: "PlayerOne"
    },
    {
        score: 10.0,
        value: "PlayerTwo"
    },
    {
        score: 78.0,
        value: "PlayerThree"
    }
];
console.log('Players map:' + players);
let added = await client.zAdd('players', players);
```

```
console.log('Added players: ' + added);
let playersWithScores = await client.zRangeByScore("players", 0, 50);
console.log('Players with score in range 0-50: ' + playersWithScores);
playersWithScores.forEach(element => {
    console.log('Player with score: ' + element);
});
let score = await client.zScore("players", "PlayerTwo");
console.log('Player PlayerTwo with score: ' + score);
```

You should see the following output:

```
Players map:[object Object],[object Object],[object Object]
Added players: 3
Players with score in range 0-50: PlayerTwo,PlayerOne
Player with score: PlayerTwo
Player with score: PlayerOne
Player PlayerTwo with score: 10
```

We will look at Hashes next.

Hashes

Redis Hashes are data structures that create connections between string fields and their corresponding string values. These associations facilitate effective storage and retrieval of key-value pairs, making them especially advantageous for organizing and handling data within a Redis database. Fundamentally, Redis Hashes allow users to store, access, and modify data as an assembly of field-value pairs, with both fields and values being strings.

Here is some example code:

```
let user =
{'firstname':'Luigi','lastname':'Fugaro','username':'foogaro'}
console.log('User: ' + user);
let fieldValuePairs = await client.hSet('user:1', user);
console.log('User fields added in Hash: ' + fieldValuePairs);
let email = await client.hSet('user:1', 'email', 'luigi@foogaro.com');
console.log('Email added: ' + email);
let firstname = await client.hGet('user:1', 'firstname');
console.log('User firstname: ', firstname);
let fields = await client.hGetAll('user:1');
console.log('All fields: ', JSON.parse(JSON.stringify(fields)));
```

And here is the expected output:

```
User: [object Object]
User fields added in Hash: 3
```

```
Email added: 1
User firstname:  Luigi
All fields:  {
  firstname: 'Luigi',
  lastname: 'Fugaro',
  username: 'foogaro',
  email: 'luigi@foogaro.com'
}
```

Let's go through Redis OM for JavaScript.

Redis OM for JavaScript

Redis OM for Node.js not only simplifies working with Redis data structures but also provides the ability to manage JSON documents and create secondary indexes for performing full-text search queries. This feature further enhances the versatility of Redis OM for Node.js, as it allows you to work with JSON data in a more efficient manner and perform powerful search operations on your dataset.

By using secondary indexes, you can optimize the search performance of your Node.js applications and quickly retrieve relevant information based on specific criteria. This makes Redis OM for Node.js an even more powerful tool for building feature-rich applications that require sophisticated data management and search capabilities.

The Redis OM integration for Node.js applications involves adding the Redis OM package to the project, using NPM, or editing the `package.json` file with the following content:

```
{
  "name": "app",
  "version": "1.0.0",
  "description": "",
  "main": "app.js",
  "type": "module",
  "scripts": {
    "test": "echo \"Error: no test specified\" && exit 1"
  },
  "dependencies": {
    "redis": "^4.6.5",
    "redis-om": "^0.4.2"
  },
  "author": "Luigi Fugaro",
  "license": "ISC"
}
```

The following task requires creating an `Employee` object containing various attributes, and this leads to the consideration of whether to use the Hash or JSON Redis data type for this purpose.

A Hash is a flat map consisting of attribute-value pairs, with values restricted to the String data type (string, number, or binary value). On the other hand, a JSON data type serves as a map but supports a broader range of value types, such as strings, numbers, arrays, and geospatial objects. Given these characteristics, the JSON data type appears to be the most suitable option for modeling the `Employee` object.

Let's create a new Node.js application by editing a new file named `redis-om.js`, starting with the statements needed to establish a connection to Redis Stack, as follows:

```
import { createClient } from 'redis';
import {EntityId, EntityKeyName, Schema} from 'redis-om'
import { Repository } from 'redis-om'

const redisClient = createClient({
      password: '<PASSWORD>',
      socket: {
            host: 'localhost',
            port: 6379
      }
});
(async () => {
      console.log('Connecting...');
      await redisClient.connect();
})();
redisClient.on('error', (err) => {
      console.log('Could not establish a connection with Redis
Stack.');
      console.log(err);
});
redisClient.on('connect', function (err) {
      console.log('Connected to Redis Stack successfully');
});
```

Next, we will define our schema for the `Employee` model and we will initialize its repository, as follows:

```
const employeeSchema = new Schema('Employee', {
      firstName: { type: 'string' },
      lastName: { type: 'string' },
      age: { type: 'number' },
      roles: { type: 'string[]' },
      office: { type: 'text' },
      funFact: { type: 'text' }
},{
```

```
    dataStructure: 'JSON'
});
export const employeeRepository = new Repository(employeeSchema, redisClient);

await employeeRepository.createIndex();
```

Last, but not least, we can define two `Employee` instances and save them into Redis Stack using the previously declared repository, as follows:

```
let luigi = {
    'firstName': 'Luigi',
    'lastName': 'Fugaro',
    'age': 45,
    'roles': ['Solution Architect'],
    'office': 'Roma',
    'funFact': 'I still play PAC-MAN.'
}
console.log('Luigi: ' + luigi);
let mirko = {
    'firstName': 'Mirko',
    'lastName': 'Ortensi',
    'age': 46,
    'roles': ['Technical Architect'],
    'office': 'Macerata',
    'funFact': I still play Arkanoid.'
}
console.log('Mirko: ' + mirko);

const luigiEmployee = await employeeRepository.save(luigi)
const mirkoEmployee = await employeeRepository.save(mirko)
```

And for debugging purposes, we will print to the console the values of our newly created and stored `Employee` objects, as follows:

```
console.log('luigiEmployee.EntityId: ' + luigiEmployee[EntityId]);
console.log('luigiEmployee.EntityKeyName: ' +
luigiEmployee[EntityKeyName]);
console.log('mirkoEmployee.EntityId: ' + mirkoEmployee[EntityId]);
console.log('mirkoEmployee.EntityKeyName: ' +
mirkoEmployee[EntityKeyName]);

let employees = await employeeRepository.search().return.all();
console.log('employees: ' + employees);
```

```
employees.forEach(employee => {
     console.log('Employee: ' + employee);
});

await redisClient.quit();
```

From the preceding code, there are two main concepts that deserve special mention: **schema**, **repository**, and **entity**.

A schema in Redis OM is defined using JavaScript classes and decorators. The decorators are used to associate class properties with corresponding Redis data structures, such as Strings, Lists, Sets, Sorted Sets, and Hashes. These decorators help to define the structure and constraints of the data model, enabling Redis OM to map JavaScript objects to Redis data structures accurately. By defining a schema for your entities, you can ensure data consistency and validation when working with Redis data. Additionally, it provides a clear representation of your data models, making it easier to understand and maintain the code base in your Node.js application.

A repository is a design pattern that provides a higher-level, abstract interface for managing entities and their persistence in the Redis database. It encapsulates the operations associated with querying, storing, updating, and deleting data, allowing you to interact with the Redis data structures in a more object-oriented and consistent manner.

Repositories in Redis OM help separate the concerns of data access and manipulation from the rest of your application logic. This separation makes your code base more maintainable, testable, and easier to understand.

To implement a repository in your Node.js application using Redis OM, you would typically create a custom class that encapsulates the Redis OM client operations for a specific entity type. This class would contain methods for common data access and manipulation tasks, such as creating, updating, fetching, and deleting instances of the entity.

An entity represents the domain object you intend to store via the repository. Upon saving the entity into the repository, an `EntityID` is created. This ID is a unique, randomly generated identifier that acts as the primary key for the entity.

After running the Node.js application, this is the output:

```
Connecting...
Connected to Redis Stack successfully.
Luigi: [object Object]
Mirko: [object Object]
luigiEmployee.EntityId: 01GWKJ094J538KQ2XD2MJ8DRWZ
luigiEmployee.EntityKeyName: Employee:01GWKJ094J538KQ2XD2MJ8DRWZ
mirkoEmployee.EntityId: 01GWKJ098HTM49C6W7XXE0CPF0
mirkoEmployee.EntityKeyName: Employee:01GWKJ098HTM49C6W7XXE0CPF0
```

For the sake of brevity, I have kept the output log that identifies our `Employee` models, and I removed the output log typically used for debugging purposes.

With Redis OM for Node.js, you can further streamline your data management code and create a more organized and maintainable application structure.

Having discussed JavaScript, let's shift our focus to the next programming language in line, Golang, which has been gaining traction for its unique features and performance capabilities.

Programming in Go using go-redis

Golang, more commonly known as **Go**, is an open source programming language that has grown in popularity due to its many advantages. One of the most significant benefits of using Go is its simplicity and minimalistic design. This aspect makes it easy to learn and understand for developers of varying experience levels, from beginners to seasoned professionals.

The Go community is another reason to consider using the language. It is an active and growing group of developers that contributes to an ever-expanding ecosystem of libraries and frameworks. This evolving ecosystem offers resources and support to help you learn about and use the language effectively.

In order to install the Golang Redis library, you need to utilize the widely used `go-redis/redis` package, which is a thoroughly maintained and feature-packed Redis client for Go. Before installing the package, ensure that Go is already set up on your system. At the time this content was created, the version used was `go version go1.20.2 darwin/amd64`.

To install the Golang Redis client library, follow these steps:

1. Initialize the Go module for your project:

   ```
   go mod init <PROJECT_MODULE>
   ```

   The output should be similar to the following:

   ```
   go: creating new go.mod: module <PROJECT_MODULE>
   ```

2. Install the `go-redis/v9` module as follows:

   ```
   go get github.com/redis/go-redis/v9
   ```

   The output should be similar to the following:

   ```
   go: downloading github.com/redis/go-redis/v9 v9.0.2
   go: downloading github.com/redis/go-redis v6.15.9+incompatible
   go: downloading github.com/cespare/xxhash/v2 v2.2.0
   go: added github.com/cespare/xxhash/v2 v2.2.0
   go: added github.com/dgryski/go-rendezvous v0.0.0-
   20200823014737-9f7001d12a5f
   go: added github.com/redis/go-redis/v9 v9.0.2
   ```

Now it's time to code a bit in Go by implementing a connection to Redis Stack and storing some data in it.

Storing information in Redis Stack using Go

Before you begin, pick the integrated developer environment of your choice and create a new Go file named `main.go`:

1. The first line we are going to insert is the import of the Redis library, as follows:

   ```
   import (
     "github.com/redis/go-redis/v9"
   )
   ```

   Next, we are going to connect to a Redis Stack instance. In the previous chapter, you learned how to install Redis Stack in different ways, using binaries, using Docker, and through Redis Cloud, which is still the easiest and fastest way to get a Redis Stack instance. Having said that, to connect to your Redis Stack instance, you need the hostname or IP of your server, the port Redis Stack is exposed on, and the credentials to authenticate.

2. For convention, the hostname will be mapped to `localhost` and the port to `6379`. In our `main.go` file, add the following content:

   ```
   func main() {
     rdb := redis.NewClient(&redis.Options{
       Addr:       "localhost:6379",
       Username: "<USERNAME>",
       Password: "<PASSWORD>",
     })

     ctx := context.Background()
     err := rdb.Set(ctx, "client", "go-redis", 0).Err()
     if err != nil {
       panic(err)
     }

     val, err := rdb.Get(ctx, "client").Result()
     if err != nil {
       panic(err)
     }
     fmt.Printf("The value of key 'client' is: %s\n", val)
   }
   ```

   Make sure you replace `"<USERNAME>"` and `"<PASSWORD>"` accordingly with the ones you set when you created and configured your Redis Stack database.

3. To compile and launch the application, just run the following commands from the terminal:

   ```
   go run main.go
   The value of key 'client' is: go-redis
   ```

Congratulations! You've now learned how to utilize the Redis Stack client library for Golang and establish a connection to Redis Stack. One of the key benefits of Redis Stack lies in its data structures, which can be mapped one to one with objects in programming languages such as Go.

While storing a simple string is straightforward, the same ease of use can be extended to other Redis data types such as Lists, Sets, Sorted Sets, and Hashes. For each of these data types, Golang offers a corresponding structure.

Lists

Redis Lists serve as data structures that maintain ordered collections of strings, arranged according to the order in which they were added. Their ability to preserve the insertion order makes them an excellent option for various applications, including the implementation of message queues.

As ordered collections, Redis Lists facilitate effective management of elements at the beginning and end of the list. They provide a range of commands for adding, removing, and fetching elements, as well as trimming and altering the list based on specific requirements.

For instance, see the following:

```
cities := []string{"Roma", "Macerata", "Atlantis"}
err = rdb.RPush(ctx, "cities", cities).Err()
if err != nil {
  panic(err)
}
err = rdb.LPush(ctx, "queue:tasks", "Task-1").Err()
if err != nil {
  panic(err)
}
err = rdb.LPush(ctx, "queue:tasks", "Task-2").Err()
if err != nil {
  panic(err)
}
task, err := rdb.RPop(ctx, "queue:tasks").Result()
if err != nil {
  panic(err)
}
fmt.Printf("The task retrieved from the list 'queue:tasks' is: %s\n",
task)
```

You should see the following output:

```
The value of key 'client' is: go-redis
The task retrieved from the list 'queue:tasks' is: Task-1
```

Let's now see how to manage the Sets data type.

Sets

Redis Sets are data structures containing unordered collections of unique strings, making them particularly valuable when ensuring no duplicate elements exist within the collection. These sets provide an efficient approach to represent, store, and handle distinct data items, such as user IDs, unique tokens, or IP addresses.

For example, see the following:

```
resp, err := rdb.SAdd(ctx, "employee:ids", "00000001", "00000002").
Result()
if err != nil {
  panic(err)
}
fmt.Printf("Added %d employees\n", resp)
resp, err = rdb.SAdd(ctx, "employee:ids", "00000001").Result()
if err != nil {
  panic(err)
}
fmt.Printf("Added %d employees\n", resp)
emps, err := rdb.SMembers(ctx, "employee:ids").Result()
if err != nil {
  panic(err)
}
for index, emp := range emps {
  fmt.Printf("All employees[%d]: %s\n", index, emp)
}
emp, err := rdb.SIsMember(ctx, "employee:ids", "00000001").Result()
if err != nil {
  panic(err)
}
fmt.Printf("Employee '00000001' exists %t\n", emp)
```

The output would be as follows:

```
Added 2 employees
Added 0 employees
All employees[0]: 00000002
All employees[1]: 00000001
Employee '00000001' exists true
```

Let's see now how to manage the Sorted Sets data type.

Sorted Sets

Redis Sorted Sets are a specialized version of Sets, distinguished by each member having an associated score or rank that determines its position in the collection. This additional feature allows Sorted Sets to maintain a consistent order based on the scores assigned to each member.

For example, see the following:

```
const players = [
        {
                score: 22.0,
                value: "PlayerOne"
        },
        {
                score: 10.0,
                value: "PlayerTwo"
        },
        {
                score: 78.0,
                value: "PlayerThree"
        }
];
console.log('Players map:' + players);
let added = await client.zAdd('players', players);
console.log('Added players: ' + added);
let playersWithScores = await client.zRangeByScore("players", 0, 50);
console.log('Players with score in range 0-50: ' + playersWithScores);
playersWithScores.forEach(element => {
    console.log('Player with score: ' + element);
});
let score = await client.zScore("players", "PlayerTwo");
console.log('Player PlayerTwo with score: ' + score);
```

You should see the following output:

```
Players map:[object Object],[object Object],[object Object]
Added players: 3
Players with score in range 0-50: PlayerTwo,PlayerOne
Player with score: PlayerTwo
Player with score: PlayerOne
Player PlayerTwo with score: 10
```

Let's see now how to manage the Hash data type.

Hashes

Redis Hashes are data structures that establish relationships between string fields and their respective string values. These connections enable efficient storage and retrieval of key-value pairs, making them particularly useful for organizing and managing data within a Redis database. Essentially, Redis Hashes permit users to store, access, and modify data as a collection of field-value pairs, where both fields and values are strings.

The following is some example code:

```
user := map[string]interface{}{
  "firstname": "Luigi",
  "lastname":  "Fugaro",
  "username":  "foogaro",
}
fmt.Printf("User %s:\n", user)
err = rdb.HMSet(ctx, "user:1", user).Err()
if err != nil {
  panic(err)
}
fmt.Println("Hash saved to Redis successfully")
resp, err = rdb.HSet(ctx, "user:1", "email", "luigi@foogaro.com").
Result()
if err != nil {
  panic(err)
}
fmt.Println("Email field added to the Hash user:1")
firstname, err := rdb.HGet(ctx, "user:1", "firstname").Result()
if err != nil {
  panic(err)
}
fmt.Printf("User Firstname %s\n", firstname)
allFields, err := rdb.HGetAll(ctx, "user:1").Result()
if err != nil {
  panic(err)
}
fmt.Printf("User all fileds %s\n", allFields)
```

You should see the following output:

```
User map[firstname:Luigi lastname:Fugaro username:foogaro]:
Hash saved to Redis successfully
Email field added to the Hash user:1
User Firstname Luigi
```

```
User all fileds map[email:luigi@foogaro.com firstname:Luigi
lastname:Fugaro username:foogaro]
```

As of the time of writing, the Redis OM framework for Go and full support for the Redis Stack capabilities have not been released yet. However, the Redis community is continuously working on developing new tools and libraries to enhance the experience of working with Redis in various programming languages. In the meantime, you can continue to use existing libraries such as `go-redis/redis` for your Redis operations in Go.

Programming in C#/.NET using NRedisStack

.NET Framework boasts a comprehensive standard library, streamlining many development tasks. It provides a myriad of built-in functionalities, reducing the need for external libraries and helping you to build applications more efficiently.

While .NET Framework has traditionally been Windows-centric, the introduction of **.NET Core** extends support to macOS and Linux. This ensures your applications can reach a broader audience without significant code changes.

To work with Redis Stack in a C#/.NET environment, you would typically use the `StackExchange.Redis` package. It's a high-performance, fully featured client dedicated to Redis for .NET. Before incorporating the package, ensure that .NET is properly configured on your system. As of the time this content was crafted, the version referenced was .NET 7.0.

To install the C#/.NET Redis client library, follow these steps:

```
Install-Package StackExchange.Redis
```

Let's dive into some C# coding by establishing a connection to Redis Stack and saving some data within it.

Storing information in Redis Stack using C#/.NET

Before you begin, pick the integrated developer environment of your choice and create a new console application project, targeting .NET Core 7.0 and the C# programming language.

The first line we are going to insert is the import of the Redis library, as follows:

```
using NRedisStack;
using NRedisStack.RedisStackCommands;
using StackExchange.Redis;
```

Next, we are going to connect to a Redis Stack instance. In the previous chapter, you learned how to install Redis Stack in different ways, using binaries, using Docker, and through Redis Cloud, which is still the easiest and fastest way to get a Redis Stack instance. Having that said, to connect to your Redis Stack instance you need the hostname or IP of your server, the port Redis Stack is exposed on, and the credentials to authenticate.

For convention, the hostname will be mapped to localhost and the port to `6379`. In our `Program.cs` file, add the following content:

```
ConnectionMultiplexer redis = ConnectionMultiplexer.
Connect("localhost:6379,username=<USERNAME>,password=<PASSWORD>");
IDatabase db = redis.GetDatabase();
db.StringSet("client", "NRedisStack");
Console.WriteLine("Retrieved value {0} for key client",
db.StringGet("client"));
```

Make sure you replace `<USERNAME>` and `<PASSWORD>` accordingly with the ones you set when you created and configured your Redis Stack database.

Compile and start the application from your IDE, and observe the following message displayed in the console output:

```
Retrieved value NRedisStack for key client
```

Congratulations! You've now learned how to utilize the Redis Stack client library for C#/.NET and establish a connection to Redis Stack.

While storing a simple string is straightforward, the same ease of use can be extended to other Redis data types such as Lists, Sets, Sorted Sets, and Hashes.

Lists

Redis Lists act as data structures that hold ordered sequences of strings, organized by their insertion sequence. This inherent ordering capability renders them ideal for multiple uses, notably for setting up message queues. Being ordered lists, Redis Lists enable efficient handling of items at both the head and tail of the list. They come equipped with a suite of commands to insert, delete, and retrieve elements, and also to modify and trim the list as per distinct needs. For an example, see the following:

```
long numberOfTasks = db.ListLeftPush("queue:tasks", "Task-1");
Console.WriteLine("Number of tasks: {0}", numberOfTasks);
numberOfTasks = db.ListLeftPush("queue:tasks", "Task-2");
Console.WriteLine("Number of tasks: {0}", numberOfTasks);
string task = db.ListRightPop("queue:tasks").ToString();
Console.WriteLine("Retrieved task: {0}", task);
```

You should see the following output:

```
Number of tasks: 1
Number of tasks: 2
Retrieved task: Task-1
```

Next, we'll look at Sets.

Sets

Redis Sets are data structures that house unordered groupings of distinct strings. Their intrinsic nature ensures the exclusion of any repeated elements within the collection. These sets offer a streamlined method for representing, preserving, and managing unique data pieces, such as user IDs, exclusive tokens, or IP addresses.

For example, see the following:

```
db.SetAdd("employee:ids", "00000001");
db.SetAdd("employee:ids", "00000002");
db.SetAdd("employee:ids", "00000001");
RedisValue[] employeeIds = db.SetMembers("employee:ids");
Console.WriteLine("Employee IDs {0}", employeeIds);
Array.ForEach(employeeIds, employeeId => Console.WriteLine("Employee:
{0}", employeeId));
bool exists = db.SetContains("employee:ids", "00000001");
Console.WriteLine("Employee id \"00000001\" exists {0}", exists);
```

You should see the following output:

```
Employee IDs StackExchange.Redis.RedisValue[]
Employee: 00000001
Employee: 00000002
Employee id "00000001" exists True
```

Next, we'll look at Sorted Sets.

Sorted Sets

Redis Sorted Sets are a specialized version of Sets, distinguished by each member having an associated score or rank that determines its position in the collection. This additional feature allows Sorted Sets to maintain a consistent order based on the scores assigned to each member.

For example, see the following code:

```
SortedSetEntry[] scores = new SortedSetEntry[3];
scores[0] = new SortedSetEntry("PlayerOne", 22.0);
scores[1] = new SortedSetEntry("PlayerTwo", 10.0);
scores[2] = new SortedSetEntry("PlayerThree", 78.0);
Console.WriteLine("Scores map {0}", scores);
long addedScores = db.SortedSetAdd("players", scores);
Console.WriteLine("Added scores {0}", addedScores);
RedisValue[] players = db.SortedSetRangeByScore("players", 0, 50);
Console.WriteLine("Players with score in range 0-50:");
Array.ForEach(players, player => Console.WriteLine(player));
```

```
double score = db.SortedSetScore("players", "PlayerTwo").Value;
Console.WriteLine("Score for \"PlayerTwo\" {0}", score);
```

You should see the following output:

```
Scores map StackExchange.Redis.SortedSetEntry[]
Added scores 3
Players with score in range 0-50:
PlayerTwo
PlayerOne
Score for "PlayerTwo" 10
```

We will look at Hashes next.

Hashes

Redis Hashes are data constructs linking string fields to their corresponding string values. This association facilitates swift storage and fetching of key-value duos, rendering them exceptionally useful for structuring and handling data in a Redis database. In essence, Redis Hashes allow users to manage data as sets of field-value pairings, with both the fields and values being strings.

The code shown here is an example:

```
HashEntry[] user = new HashEntry[3];
user[0] = new HashEntry("FirstName", "Luigi");
user[1] = new HashEntry("LastName", "Fugaro");
user[2] = new HashEntry("UserName", "foogaro");
db.HashSet("user:1", user);
string firstName = db.HashGet("user:1", "FirstName").ToString();
Console.WriteLine("User firstname {0}", firstName);
HashEntry[] userFields = db.HashGetAll("user:1");
Array.ForEach(userFields, userField => Console.WriteLine("Field {0}:
{1}", userField.Name, userField.Value));
```

You should see the following output:

```
User firstname Luigi
Field FirstName: Luigi
Field LastName: Fugaro
Field UserName: foogaro
```

Let's go through the OM for C#/.NET.

Redis OM for C#/.NET

Redis OM serves as a powerful interface for .NET developers, offering elevated abstractions tailored for Redis usage.

In this latest release, the enhancements and features provided include the following:

- Intuitive object mapping for Redis objects, allowing for a declarative approach
- The ability to automatically generate secondary indices in a declarative manner, enhancing data retrieval efficiency
- A fluent API system designed for more streamlined querying within Redis
- Another set of fluent APIs dedicated to executing aggregation operations in Redis, providing more versatility in data operations

Redis OM simplifies the task of modeling and querying your domain objects within Redis, ensuring a more intuitive experience for developers:

1. To use the Redis OM framework, your .NET project needs to load an additional package, by invoking the following command:

   ```
   dotnet add package Redis.OM
   ```

2. The upcoming task is to design an `Employee` object containing multiple attributes, including a specialized object named `Office`. This prompts the consideration of whether to use the Hash or the JSON data type for this endeavor.

   A Hash essentially represents a simple map consisting of attribute-value pairs, with the caveat that values can only be of the String data type, be it a string, number, or binary value. On the other hand, JSON operates similarly to a map but is more versatile, supporting a broader array of value types such as strings, numbers, arrays, and even embedded JSONs. Given these characteristics, the JSON data type stands out as the more suitable option for representing the `Employee` object:

   ```
   using Redis.OM.Modeling;

   namespace dotnet;

   [Document(StorageType = StorageType.Json, Prefixes = new []
   {"Employee"})]
   public class Employee
   {
       [RedisIdField] [Indexed] public string? Id { get; set; }
       [Indexed] public string? FirstName { get; set; }
       [Indexed] public string? LastName { get; set; }
       [Indexed] public int? Age { get; set; }
       [Searchable] public string? FunFact { get; set; }
   ```

```
        [Indexed(CascadeDepth = 1)] public Office? Office { get;
set; }
        [Indexed] public string[] Roles { get; set; } = Array.
Empty<string>();
}
```

The `Employee` class is decorated as `Document`, meaning its role as a JSON document. Furthermore, supplementary decorators are utilized to define the essential indexes for data querying, searching, and aggregation.

3. Next, the `Office` class should be created, which will be maintained as a nested JSON document within the `Employee` structure:

```
using Redis.OM.Modeling;

namespace dotnet;

public class Office
{
        [Searchable] public string? Address { get; set; }
        [Indexed] public string? AddressNumber { get; set; }
        [Indexed] public string? City { get; set; }
        [Indexed] public string? State { get; set; }
        [Indexed] public string? PostalCode { get; set; }
        [Indexed] public string? Country { get; set; }
}
```

In this setup, you'll observe that all fields have the `Indexed` attribute, except for `Address`, which is specifically tagged as `Searchable`. These designations, `Indexed` and `Searchable`, clearly instruct Redis OM as to which fields to consider during queries within Redis Stack. `Address` isn't set up as an independent document, so no overarching attributes are applied to the main class. Instead, the `Office` model is neatly nested within the `Employee` model.

4. To begin, we'll generate load test data by setting up two `Employee` objects, each with its associated `Office`, as described in the following code.

The following initializes the first employee:

```
Employee luigi = new Employee();
luigi.FirstName = "Luigi";
luigi.LastName = "Fugaro";
luigi.Age = 44;
luigi.FunFact = "What goes around, comes around!";
luigi.Roles = new[] { "Solution Architect" };

Office romeOffice = new Office();
romeOffice.Address = "Via Roma";
```

```
romeOffice.AddressNumber = "1";
romeOffice.PostalCode = "00100";
romeOffice.City = "Rome";
romeOffice.Country = "Italy";
romeOffice.State = "Italy";

luigi.Office = romeOffice;
```

This is for the second employee:

```
Employee mirko = new Employee();
mirko.FirstName = "Mirko";
mirko.LastName = "Ortensi";
mirko.Age = 44;
mirko.FunFact = "Sing a song and jump around!";
mirko.Roles = new[] { "Technical Enablement Architect" };

Office macerataOffice = new Office();
romeOffice.Address = "Via Macerata";
romeOffice.AddressNumber = "1";
romeOffice.PostalCode = "62100";
romeOffice.City = "Macerata";
romeOffice.Country = "Italy";
romeOffice.State = "Italy";

mirko.Office = macerataOffice;
```

5. Now, we'll establish a connection to Redis using the steps outlined here:

```
var provider = new RedisConnectionProvider("redis://<USER-
NAME>:<PASSWORD>@<HOSTNAME>:<PORT>");
```

Replace the placeholders with the values related to your environment.

6. Now, we'll set up the handler class responsible for managing `Employee` entities, as outlined here:

```
var employees = provider.RedisCollection<Employee>();
```

7. Now, we'll proceed to save our entities in Redis using the steps provided here:

```
var employeeLuigi = employees.InsertAsync(luigi);
Console.WriteLine("Employee ID: {0}", employeeLuigi.Result);
var employeeMirko = employees.InsertAsync(mirko);
Console.WriteLine("Employee ID: {0}", employeeMirko.Result);
```

By executing the preceding code, the output should be similar to the following:

```
Employee ID: Employee:01HCD2SYHEKK6STHZBRK70J0VH
Employee ID: Employee:01HCD2SYS3B4PSJ0HH7CM98VMF
```

The ID won't match exactly since it's generated randomly.

8. Having saved our entities, we'll now set up the Index to search and query our data using the following steps:

   ```
   var connection = provider.Connection;
   var indexCreated = connection.CreateIndex(typeof(Employee));
   ```

   Even if the database is empty, you can still create the Index. It will update automatically as new data comes in.

9. To locate our entities by ID, we have two options: using the general Redis connection handler or the specific `employees` handler for `Employee` entities.

   We'll explore both approaches:

   ```
   var loo = connection.GetAsync<Employee>(employeeLuigi.Result);
   Console.WriteLine("GetAsync Employee LastName: {0}", loo.
   Result?.LastName);
   var mee = employees.FindByIdAsync(employeeMirko.Result);
   Console.WriteLine("FindByIdAsync Employee LastName: {0}", mee.
   Result?.LastName);
   ```

   By executing the preceding code, the output should look like the following:

   ```
   GetAsync Employee LastName: Fugaro
   FindByIdAsync Employee LastName: Ortensi
   ```

10. To search our data, we'll use the handler specific to `Employee`. Depending on the attribute in the search criteria, it will either use the exact-match or the full-text search method.

    We'll experiment with both approaches:

    ```
    var empsByExactMatch = employees.Where(x => x.FirstName ==
    "Luigi");
    foreach (var emp in empsByExactMatch)
    {
         Console.WriteLine($"{emp.FirstName} is {emp.Age} years old
    and works as {emp.Roles[0]}!");
    }

    var empsByFullText = employees.Where(e => e.FunFact ==
    "around");
    foreach (var emp in empsByFullText)
    {
    ```

```
        Console.WriteLine($"{emp.FirstName} is {emp.Age} years old
    and works as {emp.Roles[0]}!");
    }
```

By executing the code, the output should look like the following:

```
Luigi is 44 years old and works as Solution Architect!
Mirko is 44 years old and works as Technical Enablement
Architect!
```

As you've likely observed, the code is remarkably intuitive and direct. The Redis OM framework not only streamlines your development process but also elevates your applications. Its inherent flexibility combined with its user-friendly design ensures that developers can harness the full potential of Redis without steep learning curves, enabling rapid development and robust application performance.

Summary

In this chapter, we have explored various Redis client libraries and OM solutions across five popular programming languages: Python, Java, JavaScript, C#, and Go..

For Python, we learned about `redis-py`, a widely used Redis client library that provides an easy-to-use interface for interacting with Redis data structures and commands. To simplify working with Redis data structures in Python applications, Redis OM allows us to map Redis data to Python objects, offering a more intuitive, object-oriented approach to data management.

In the Java programming language, `Jedis` is a popular client library that enables developers to work seamlessly with Redis data structures. With Redis OM for Java, developers can further enhance their experience by mapping Java objects to Redis data structures, improving code organization and maintainability.

For JavaScript, we discussed `node-redis`, a widely used Redis client library designed to work efficiently with Node.js, offering a straightforward way to interact with Redis data structures. By utilizing Redis OM for JavaScript, we can map Redis data structures to JavaScript objects, providing a more natural, object-oriented approach to data management in Node.js applications.

In C#, NRedisStack is a widely-used client library that simplifies working with Redis data structures. Redis OM for .NET enhances this by allowing developers to link their domain objects to Redis data structures, making the code more organized and easier to maintain.

Lastly, we have explored programming in Golang using `go-redis`, a robust Redis client tailored for Go. This client boasts a comprehensive set of features, making it a versatile tool for handling various Redis operations in your Go projects. The `go-redis` library provides an idiomatic API that adheres to Go's conventions and best practices, ensuring a seamless experience for developers familiar with the language.

By understanding these libraries and OM solutions, we can effectively work with Redis across Python, Java, JavaScript, and Go, harnessing their respective features to build efficient and maintainable applications.

In *Chapter 5, Redis Stack as a Document Store*, we will delve much deeper into how data modeling techniques can be achieved using the core data types, focusing on Redis Stack's ability to execute real-time queries and searches for Hashes and JSON types. From full-text searching and tagging to aggregation, auto-completion, and the novel Vector Similarity Search, Redis Stack can serve as a document store equipped with sophisticated features.

Part 2: Data Modeling

Redis Stack extends the capabilities of Redis, allowing for real-time queries and searches on Hashes and JSON types. It encompasses a variety of functionalities, including full-text search, tagging, aggregation, and notably, vector search, which is ideal for recommendation engines.

The focus is on data modeling techniques within Redis Stack, particularly the application of vector search. As a multi-model, real-time data server, Redis Stack efficiently manages time-series data, where each point can be augmented with metadata labels, facilitating advanced filtering, searching, and aggregation.

Another significant aspect of Redis Stack is its incorporation of probabilistic data structures. These structures provide fast, approximate answers using minimal time and memory, and are well-suited for queries such as verifying user locations, identifying top players in games, or tracking unique user activities. The content in this part aims to convey the advanced features of Redis Stack and their practical applications in various scenarios.

This part contains the following chapters:

- *Chapter 5, Redis Stack as a Document Store*
- *Chapter 6, Redis Stack as a Vector Database*
- *Chapter 7, Redis Stack as a Time Series Database*
- *Chapter 8, Understanding Probabilistic Data Structures*

5

Redis Stack as a Document Store

The traditional data modeling technique of using Redis' core data types is possible with Redis Stack, which means that we can model an object using the popular Hash data structure, for example. This chapter presents Redis Stack's capability to perform real-time queries and searches against the Hash data type, with the advantages of secondary indexing and additional search features. After that, we will discover how data modeling can be addressed using the JSON data structure. We will present different search and query features, from full-text to tagging, from aggregation to auto-completion, so that you understand how to use Redis Stack as a document store with advanced features.

By the end of this chapter, you will know how to rethink the data model of your application and use Redis Stack data structures to perform real-time queries and searches. You will also know how to use Hash and JSON data structures to store, query, and search documents through practical real-life examples.

In this chapter, we are going to cover the following topics:

- Storing and querying documents in Redis Stack
- Working with Hashes
- Working with JSON
- Redis Stack as a recommendation engine
- Redis Stack as a session store

Technical requirements

To follow along with the examples in this chapter, you will need the following:

- Install Redis Stack Server 7.2 or a later version on your development environment. Alternatively, you can create a free Redis Cloud subscription to achieve a free plan and use a managed Redis Stack database.

- The dataset that will be used in the examples is a conversion of the popular MySQL **World** database to Redis Hashes.
- We will introduce data modeling through Hash and JSON data structures with examples that can be tested using a simple *KnowledgeBase* dataset.
- Find and download all the datasets from this book's repository if you'd like to test the examples that we'll propose in this chapter: `https://github.com/PacktPublishing/Redis-Stack-for-Application-Modernization`.

Storing and querying documents in Redis Stack

The usual approach to organizing information that helps to describe a system is to identify the entities in the specific business domain and the relationships interconnecting them. Examples of entities could be companies and employees, and the relationship interconnecting them would describe the employee as part of the headcount. Other examples include universities and students, cars and their components, and so on. This high-level description is referred to as the **conceptual data model**, where we describe the things that are interesting for the domain we are considering.

Once this synthetic description has been completed, we refine it into a **logical data model** by describing all the elements in detail. Here, the entities and relationships are defined more specifically, with attributes, keys, and data types (for example, strings or integers). Finally, when the domain description is completed and we need a concrete implementation to manage the information in the domain under analysis, the conclusive phase of the data model design is to implement the **physical data model**. Such a model uses the low-level description provided by the logical data model, and entities and relationships are mapped to a concrete database instance, with the data structures and the features that the specific storage technology offers.

Jumping back in time for a second, the relational database was theorized in 1970 by Ted Codd, a computer scientist at IBM, and first implemented in 1973 (Ingress), while the entity-relationship model was formulated in 1976 by computer scientist Peter Chen (*The Entity-Relationship Model - Toward a Unified View of Data*, MIT). It is easy to anticipate the logical consequence, which saw the physical data model implementation based on relational databases, where data is stored in tables of related information and manipulated using a **Structured Query Language** (**SQL**).

Back in our days, limitations of relational databases to answer scalability, performance, and other requirements cleared the way for the popularity of the **NoSQL** movement. The main idea behind a NoSQL database is that data is not stored in tables as the relational model dictates but structured in different ways and aggregated and optimized for scalability over multiple machines. Hence, there are four main NoSQL databases:

- Document stores
- Key-value stores

- Columnar databases
- Graph databases

Among the main features of a NoSQL database, we find the simplicity and flexibility to store, organize, access, and modify the data. The data model is not strictly defined by a schema, so it is easy to modify the objects, for example, by adding additional fields without limitations on their number or size. Horizontal scalability is another important capability that differentiates NoSQL databases from relational databases as they support reorganizing the dataset into multiple partitions, thus turning a NoSQL database into a distributed system.

In this chapter, we will focus on Redis Stack's ability to manage Hash-encoded and JSON-encoded documents, and the rich set of features to design a data model using its indexing features, so that it is possible to either retrieve (query) a document by known criteria or get a list of documents (search) based on a search. Let's continue looking at database interactions:

- **Real-time querying**: Queries are deterministic – you know precisely what you're going to get. Retrieving data via tags or numerical ranges are examples of queries.
- **Real-time searching**: Searches are not deterministic – you ignore the data that will be searched, and there is no formal categorization or taxonomy for it. Results are filtered and returned based on their relevance, which is calculated using scores and the frequency of the terms in the documents that are indexed, for example.

Storing documents while having the flexibility to choose between the Hash and JSON formats and the ability to index the documents is a great asset not just for storing and serving data with real-time speed and efficiency but also for performing complex queries and aggregation. Users will be satisfied with their decision to choose Redis as their primary data store, migrate from a relational database, or pair it with an authoritative data source to achieve real-time performance.

These search capabilities extend Redis with specialized data structures and algorithms that index the data transparently and compute queries and complex searches while maintaining high throughput. Data is stored using core data structures (Hash and JSON), while indexes live out of the keyspace, are detached from data, and follow data changes so that the index is updated as soon as updates happen.

In the following subsections, we will learn how to index the data that's stored in a Redis Stack database and understand how to write elegant queries to implement query and search operations. Concrete examples will be presented so that you can reproduce the syntax and verify the results.

The dialect and other configuration parameters

Before we start exploring the modeling, indexing, and search features of Redis Stack, let's anticipate a few notes about search-related configuration parameters. Parameters can be set at load time or runtime. In particular, parameters that are set at runtime can influence the behavior of the search features and determine how the query executes. The configuration at runtime can be managed by the

`FT.CONFIG` command, which will set and get the configuration parameters. So, you would read the entire configuration parameters as follows:

```
FT.CONFIG GET *
```

You can get a specific parameter:

```
FT.CONFIG GET CONCURRENT_WRITE_MODE
1) 1) CONCURRENT_WRITE_MODE
   2) false
```

You can also set a parameter:

```
FT.CONFIG SET DEFAULT_DIALECT 2
OK
```

Of all the parameters, dialect is worth mentioning because, in some cases, it influences the results that are returned by certain queries. As an example, the following query, when executed with `DIALECT 1` (which is the default), returns 234 results:

```
FT.SEARCH country_idx @region:"-North America" RETURN 0
 1) (integer) 234
 2) "country:abw"
 3) "country:afg"
...
```

This query retrieves all the results that do not contain either "North" or "America" in the region. Note the use of `RETURN 0`, which omits the field-value pairs in the results; it just returns the key name matching the clauses in the query. Now, let's change the default dialect to `DIALECT 2`:

```
FT.CONFIG SET DEFAULT_DIALECT 2
```

Here, the number of returned results is quite different:

```
FT.SEARCH country_idx @region:"-North America" RETURN 0
 1) (integer) 22
 2) "country:bra"
 3) "country:guf"
...
```

The reason for this is that when using `DIALECT 2`, only the negation on "North" applies, while "America" is still valid as a match. We can override the default `DIALECT` using the inline specification:

```
FT.SEARCH country_idx @region:"-North America" RETURN 0 DIALECT 1
 1) (integer) 234
 2) "country:abw"
```

```
 3) "country:uga"
...
```

It is also possible to rewrite the query using parentheses:

```
FT.SEARCH country_idx @region:"-(North America)" RETURN 0
 1) (integer) 234
 2) "country:abw"
 3) "country:uga"
...
```

To wrap up, if your query does not behave as expected, make sure you are using the correct `DIALECT`; refer to the documentation available at `https://redis.io/docs/stack/search/reference/query_syntax/` to learn more about the available dialects (there are three in total) and to discover the rest of configuration parameters.

In this chapter, we will execute the examples using the default `DIALECT 1`.

The query language

We introduced the syntax to create an index in *Chapter 1, Introducing Redis Stack*:

```
FT.CREATE city_idx
ON HASH
PREFIX 1 city:
SCHEMA Name AS name TEXT
CountryCode AS countrycode TAG SORTABLE
Population AS population NUMERIC SORTABLE
```

Using this syntax, we have chosen the index name and defined a **schema** and the **fields** – that is, `Name`, `CountryCode`, and `Population`.

We have also queried the index and understood how to specify the query to retrieve results, filtering on the country and the population:

```
FT.SEARCH city_idx '@countrycode:{ESP}' FILTER population 2000000 +inf
RETURN 1 name
```

We can introduce a **query term** and search by the city's `name` while excluding a country using the `-` symbol, as well as a numeric range match so that we can filter by population:

```
FT.SEARCH city_idx "London @population:[300000 +inf] -@
countrycode:{GBR}" RETURN 1 District
1) (integer) 1
2) "city:1820"
```

```
3) 1) "District"
   2) "Ontario"
```

In this example, we used a search term, introduced a negative tag clause to remove results, and filtered by a numeric range. Using a relational database, we can achieve the result using the following SQL statement:

```
ALTER TABLE city ADD FULLTEXT(Name);

mysql> SELECT District FROM city WHERE MATCH(Name) AGAINST("London" IN
NATURAL LANGUAGE MODE) AND Population>=300000 AND CountryCode!="GBR";

+----------+
| District |
+----------+
| Ontario  |
+----------+

1 row in set (0.00 sec)
```

Most of the usual SQL statements can be mapped using the Redis Stack query syntax, which is executed in real time, including aggregations with the `FT.AGGREGATE` command. Furthermore, Redis Stack goes beyond the traditional keyword-based search, as we will see in the next chapter when we discuss semantic search with vector similarity search. Let's consider additional examples of the query search syntax in Redis Stack. Let's create an additional and more detailed index that we will use in the subsequent examples for more complex queries:

```
FT.CREATE country_idx
ON HASH
PREFIX 1 country:
SCHEMA Name AS name TEXT
LocalName AS localname TEXT
Region AS region TEXT
Continent AS continent TAG
HeadOfState AS headofstate TEXT
SurfaceArea as surfacearea NUMERIC SORTABLE
Population AS population NUMERIC SORTABLE
GovernmentForm AS governmentform TAG SORTABLE
```

In the next few sections, we will learn how to write queries and leverage all the search features. A query can be decomposed as follows:

- **The index**: The index name is required and must be specified as the first parameter when executing the `FT.SEARCH` command.
- **The query**: This is required and specifies what we are looking for and in what fields. It can be composed of multiple clauses and their intersection, union, or negation.
- **Optional arguments**: Arguments help format the results and extend them with the numerous available features. You can find a comprehensive list of such arguments in the documentation at `https://redis.io/commands/ft.search/`; we'll see a few examples later in this chapter.

If you'd like to test the examples in this section, import the *World* dataset as follows (assuming Redis Stack is running locally and on the default port, `6379`; otherwise, specify the connectivity parameters):

```
cat world.txt | redis-cli
```

Then, make sure you have created the `city_idx` and `country_idx` indexes and verify their existence with the following command:

```
FT._LIST
```

You are now ready to dive into querying and searching using Redis Stack!

Simple terms

You can search for a term in *all the fields* of the schema that are indexed as `TEXT`. Then, you can specify both the index and the query, which is the required argument of `FT.SEARCH`:

```
FT.SEARCH country_idx Italy
```

This command will return all the objects that contain the search term in any of the `TEXT` fields.

Using field modifiers

If you'd like to specify that the search should be only on a *specific field* indexed as `TEXT`, you must specify the field using the @ symbol. For simplicity, in these examples, we will skip the returned field often and get the key name only using the `NOCONTENT` argument (or `RETURN 0`):

```
FT.SEARCH country_idx '@name:Italy' NOCONTENT
1) (integer) 1
2) "country:ita"
```

Intersection of results (AND)

You can use quotes if you're searching for results that contain multiple terms. It is equivalent to the AND (intersection) logical operator, regardless of the order. For the country named "United Arab Emirates," you would get the following result:

```
FT.SEARCH country_idx 'United Emirates Arab' RETURN 0
1) (integer) 1
2) "country:are"
```

If the order of the terms is important, you can add the `INORDER` argument:

```
FT.SEARCH country_idx 'United Emirates Arab' RETURN 0 INORDER
1) (integer) 0
```

And if you want no intermediate or a maximum number of terms between the terms to be matched in the query, you can set `SLOP` accordingly to indicate this:

```
FT.SEARCH country_idx 'United Emirates' RETURN 0 INORDER SLOP 0
1) (integer) 0
FT.SEARCH country_idx 'United Emirates' RETURN 0 INORDER SLOP 1
1) (integer) 1
2) "country:are"
```

To compose a query that will retrieve those results with the desired terms, you can use multiple modifiers:

```
FT.SEARCH country_idx "@region:europe @headofstate:carlo" RETURN 2
name headofstate
```

Union of results (OR)

Using the pipe (|) symbol, it is possible to perform the union of the results. So, we can research the results that contain at least one of the terms:

```
FT.SEARCH country_idx "@region:europe | @region:america" NOCONTENT
LIMIT 0 100
```

We can use the equivalent and more compact syntax:

```
FT.SEARCH country_idx "@region:(europe|america)" NOCONTENT LIMIT 0 100
```

We can also compose a query with an AND operator to filter the results further:

```
FT.SEARCH country_idx "@name:(Spain|Italy) @region:'Southern Europe'"
RETURN 2 name region
```

Searching for the same term in multiple fields is also possible using the pipe symbol. A valid example would be performing a search in the title and the content of a document. Sticking to the country examples, it would look something like this:

```
FT.SEARCH country_idx "@name|localname:Ital*" RETURN 2 name localname
```

Exact query matches

You can also add additional quotation marks if you're looking for an exact query match:

```
FT.SEARCH country_idx 'United Emirates' RETURN 0
1) (integer) 1
2) "country:are"
FT.SEARCH country_idx '"United Emirates"' RETURN 0
1) (integer) 0
```

As you can see, if the country is stored as "United Arab Emirates," then it is not returned if we introduce the quotes to get an exact match.

Stop words

If we would like to look for "Trinidad and Tobago" by specifying the terms "Trinidad and Tobago," the exact match would return an error:

```
FT.SEARCH country_idx '"Trinidad and Tobago"' RETURN 0
(error) Syntax error at offset 10 near and
```

The reason is that the term "and" is excluded from indexing. This is the default configuration of an index: the following terms are not indexed because they don't provide relevant information to an index and a search, and the query should not include them. These terms are referred to as stop words. By default, they are as follows:

```
a,     is,    the,    an,    and,  are, as,  at,   be,   but,  by,   for,
if,    in,    into,   it,    no,   not, of,  on,   or,   such, that,
their, then,  there,  these, they, this, to,  was, will, with
```

You can configure your desired stop words or exclude them all at once by recreating the index with the `STOPWORDS 0` argument. The former search without stop words would return the following:

```
FT.SEARCH country_idx '"Trinidad and Tobago"' RETURN 0
1) (integer) 1
2) "country:tto"
```

Negation and purely negative queries

You can exclude results from your search by using the - symbol on the desired modifier:

```
FT.SEARCH country_idx "@region:europe -@region:'Southern Europe'"
RETURN 1 name LIMIT 0 100
```

You can also perform purely negative queries:

```
FT.SEARCH country_idx "-@region:'Southern Europe'" RETURN 1 name LIMIT
0 100
```

Prefix, infix, and suffix queries

Case-insensitive prefix, infix, and suffix queries can be executed by using the * symbol:

```
FT.SEARCH country_idx "@name:'hond*'" RETURN 2 name headofstate

FT.SEARCH country_idx "@name:'*dura*'" RETURN 2 name headofstate

FT.SEARCH country_idx "@name:'*uras'" RETURN 2 name headofstate
```

Wildcard matching

Wildcard matching is possible using the ? symbol, matching a single character, or *, for any character that repeats 0 or more times:

```
FT.SEARCH country_idx "@name:'*ndura?'" RETURN 2 name headofstate
```

> **Note**
>
> Note that when using `DIALECT 2`, the wildcard pattern is expressed as follows (forcing `DIALECT 2` inline for demonstrative purposes):
>
> ```
> FT.SEARCH country_idx "@name:w'*ndura?'" RETURN 2 name headofstate
> DIALECT 2
> ```

Fuzzy matching

Redis Stack supports fuzzy matching, which permits approximate matching of search terms based on the Levenshtein distance, which measures the difference between terms. Oversimplifying the theory, the Levenshtein distance is equivalent to the number of single-character edits to turn one string into another. Here are some examples:

- The distance between *back* and *black* is `1`

- The distance between *understanding* and *undestandig* is 2
- The distance between *crystal* and *ctal* is 3

Fuzzy matching in Redis Stack is based on the Levenshtein distance and is executed by surrounding the search term with the % symbol several times equal to the maximum distance of the resulting terms. Here are some examples of fuzzy matching:

```
FT.SEARCH country_idx "@name:%hondras%" RETURN 1 name
1) (integer) 1
2) "country:hnd"
3) 1) "name"
   2) "Honduras"
FT.SEARCH country_idx "@name:%%hondur%%" RETURN 1 name
1) (integer) 1
2) "country:hnd"
3) 1) "name"
   2) "Honduras"
```

Numeric filters

With Redis Stack, it is possible to create indexes to perform numeric-based filtering or range searches. Continuing with the series of examples to extract relevant data from our World dataset, we can write either a modifier-based syntax or use the `FILTER` argument, so the following two queries are equivalent:

```
FT.SEARCH country_idx "@region:'Southern Europe' @population:[50000000
+inf]" RETURN 1 name
FT.SEARCH country_idx "@region:'Southern Europe'" FILTER population
50000000 +inf RETURN 1 name
```

You can use `-inf` and `+inf` to specify unbounded limits, and you can exclude the boundaries (by default, they are included) using parenthesis, as shown in the following example:

```
FT.SEARCH country_idx "@region:'Southern Europe'" FILTER population
(39441700 +inf RETURN 1 population
```

Tag filters

It is possible to classify and search documents with labels, categories, versions, serial numbers/identifiers, genre, style, color, features, and more. Tag filters come to the rescue here:

```
FT.SEARCH country_idx '@governmentform:{monarchy}' RETURN 1 name LIMIT
0 100
```

We can specify that we desire the intersection or the union as usual:

```
FT.SEARCH country_idx '@governmentform:{monarchy|republic}' RETURN 1
name LIMIT 0 100
```

We can compose the query with several modifiers and filters:

```
FT.SEARCH country_idx '@governmentform:{republic} @population:[-inf
100000]' RETURN 2 name surfacearea LIMIT 0 3 SORTBY surfacearea ASC
```

Using the examples proposed so far, you will be able to address the majority of query and search problems to extract the relevant information from your data. Let's use this simple World dataset once more by feeding query results to a pipeline of operations for aggregation, sorting, and transformation using the `FT.AGGREGATE` command.

Geospatial filters

Real-time tracking systems, which require real-time geographical positions to be processed and displayed, have long been supported by the `GEO` field in indexed Hash and JSON documents.

Redis Stack 7.2 enhances **geospatial capabilities** and introduces the ability to model polygons while maintaining compatibility with the `GEO` type. At the time of writing, the new `GEOSHAPE` index field type can model points and polygons. In particular, you can decide whether to model geometries as geographical entities or not using the corresponding coordinates:

- `SPHERICAL`, to specify longitude and latitude coordinates
- `FLAT`, to specify the *X* and *Y* coordinates on a Cartesian plane

Using the `FLAT` coordinate systems, we can model geometries on a Cartesian plane and store them in the database. The index can be created as follows:

```
FT.CREATE polygon_idx PREFIX 1 shape: SCHEMA g GEOSHAPE FLAT t TEXT
```

Once the index has been created, we can model and store geometries. The currently supported format to describe the geometries is the **Well-Known Text** (**WKT**) format, a text markup language format. As an example, a point in the WKT format has the following syntax:

```
POINT (-73.9857 40.7484)
```

The two following commands create two shapes: a triangle and a square. Note that the polygons must be closed – the first and the last point must match:

```
HSET shape:1 t "this is a triangle" g "POLYGON((2 2, 6 8, 10 2, 2 2))"
HSET shape:2 t "this is a square" g "POLYGON((3 3, 3 7, 7 7, 7 3, 3
3))"
```

Points can be modeled with the POINT keyword:

```
HSET shape:point:1 g 'POINT(3 3)'
HSET shape:point:2 g 'POINT(14 14)'
```

Having inserted a few geometries into the database, we can now test relations. Currently, the CONTAINS and WITHIN relations are supported, and more are under development.

In this example, the CONTAINS clause returns the documents containing the query geometry:

```
127.0.0.1:6379> FT.SEARCH polygon_idx "@g:[CONTAINS $poly]" PARAMS 2
poly 'POLYGON((6 6, 6 7, 7 7, 7 6, 6 6))' DIALECT 3
1) (integer) 1
2) "shape:2"
3) 1) "t"
   2) "this is a square"
   3) "g"
   4) "POLYGON((3 3, 3 7, 7 7, 7 3, 3 3))"
```

WITHIN, on the other hand, returns all the geometries within a certain area, which is a point in the following example:

```
127.0.0.1:6379> FT.SEARCH polygon_idx "@g:[WITHIN $poly]" PARAMS 2
poly 'POLYGON((13 13, 13 15, 15 15, 15 13, 13 13))' DIALECT 3
1) (integer) 1
2) "shape:point:2"
3) 1) "g"
   2) "POINT(14 14)"
```

New and powerful use cases can be implemented with these new geospatial capabilities thanks to the combined searches and queries on multiple fields that are defined in the index.

Aggregation and transformation

Using Redis Stack, you can query the database as usual and manipulate the results that are returned by your queries by aggregating, transforming, filtering, and sorting them in cascade, in a pipeline fashion. For example, to group countries by continent, we would use the GROUPBY clause to group the results based on the corresponding property (in the same way as the "GROUP BY" SQL statement does). In addition to grouping the results, we need to represent the groups with a single record that's been computed using the desired reducer, introduced by the REDUCE clause.

Then, to discover the flexibility of **data aggregation** in Redis Stack, we can compute the total population per continent and return the most populated one. You can write such a query and aggregate the results using an `FT.AGGREGATE` request that has the following syntax:

```
FT.AGGREGATE country_idx *
GROUPBY 1 @continent
REDUCE SUM 1 @population AS population
SORTBY 2 @population DESC
LIMIT 0 1
1) (integer) 7
2) 1) "continent"
   2) "Asia"
   3) "population"
   4) "3705025700"
```

Taking this example a step further, if we would like to compute the population density by continent and sort the results, we would execute a transformation that uses the `APPLY` argument and the desired expression or function:

```
FT.AGGREGATE country_idx *
GROUPBY 1 @continent
REDUCE SUM 1 @population AS tot_pop
REDUCE SUM 1 @surfacearea AS tot_sur
APPLY "floor(@tot_pop/@tot_sur)" AS people_per_km2
SORTBY 2 @people_per_km2 DESC
LIMIT 0 1
1) (integer) 7
2) 1) "continent"
   2) "Asia"
   3) "tot_pop"
   4) "3705025700"
   5) "tot_sur"
   6) "31881005"
   7) "people_per_km2"
   8) "116"
```

Finally, we can filter the results using a `FILTER` expression, which is evaluated at the end of the pipeline and can be used to retain the desired results:

```
FT.AGGREGATE country_idx *
GROUPBY 1 @continent
REDUCE SUM 1 @population AS tot_pop
REDUCE SUM 1 @surfacearea AS tot_sur
APPLY "floor(@tot_pop/@tot_sur)" AS people_per_km2
```

```
SORTBY 2 @people_per_km2 DESC
FILTER "@continent=='Europe'"
1) (integer) 7
2) 1) "continent"
   2) "Europe"
   3) "tot_pop"
   4) "730074600"
   5) "tot_sur"
   6) "23049133.9"
   7) "people_per_km2"
   8) "31"
```

Cursor-based requests

Another feature of aggregations is their support for cursor-based `FT.AGGREGATE` requests, enabling users to consume only a part of the results. The advantage of using cursors compared to requesting partial results with the `LIMIT` sub-command is that with cursors, the query is computed only once, and the results are stored on the server and consumed by the client in iterations. As an example, let's aggregate cities by country and return batches of five countries:

```
FT.AGGREGATE city_idx * WITHCURSOR COUNT 5 GROUPBY 1 @countrycode
1) 1) (integer) 232
   2) 1) "countrycode"
      2) "swz"
   3) 1) "countrycode"
      2) "are"
   4) 1) "countrycode"
      2) "blr"
   5) 1) "countrycode"
      2) "kna"
   6) 1) "countrycode"
      2) "shn"
2) (integer) 1032568724
```

This command reports the total number of results (`232`), some results (`5`, as indicated by the `COUNT` argument), and the next cursor to be invoked. We can read from the existing cursor using the `FT.CURSOR` command. By default, the number of results returned by `FT.CURSOR` is the same as indicated in `FT.AGGREGATE`, which originated at the cursor – 5, in this example:

```
FT.CURSOR READ city_idx 1032568724
1) 1) (integer) 0
   2) 1) "countrycode"
      2) "syc"
   3) 1) "countrycode"
```

```
      2) "tkm"
   4) 1) "countrycode"
      2) "mkd"
   5) 1) "countrycode"
      2) "pse"
   6) 1) "countrycode"
      2) "plw"
2) (integer) 1032568724
```

We can override the value of COUNT when reading from the cursor:

```
FT.CURSOR READ city_idx 1032568724 COUNT 3
1) 1) (integer) 0
   2) 1) "countrycode"
      2) "mys"
   3) 1) "countrycode"
      2) "msr"
   4) 1) "countrycode"
      2) "myt"
2) (integer) 1032568724
```

Repeating the read operation will return different results until we fetch all of them, and the cursor will indicate that the iteration has concluded, reporting a value of 0:

```
FT.CURSOR READ city_idx 1032568724
1) 1) (integer) 0
   2) 1) "countrycode"
      2) "ner"
   3) 1) "countrycode"
      2) "irq"
2) (integer) 0
```

The cursor uses resources on the database, and it is removed in one of the following situations:

- If not consumed, the cursor will time out after 300 seconds. This timeout can be configured with MAXIDLE.
- When the results are entirely consumed, the cursor is deleted automatically and resources are freed.
- On demand with the FT.CURSOR DEL command.

Faceted search using aggregations

We have considered the capability to perform searches and obtain results that have been aggregated by an attribute of a certain item, such as shirts in a retail store, aggregated by color or brand, and returning the cardinality for the products in the store. In addition to modeling one attribute per TAG, we can perform a **faceted search** by modeling multiple categories using a flat string with all the categories (such as cotton, wool, spandex, polyester, flannel, and more) separated by a comma or other separator.

We could also specify some laundry recommendations, such as handwash, no bleach, machine wash, and no iron. If we would like to get clothes classified by individual categories, we can use the `FT.AGGREGATE` command on the dataset and the `split` function on this flat comma-separated list of categories indexed as TAG. Let's create a new index to see an example:

```
FT.CREATE product_idx
PREFIX 1 item:
SCHEMA laundry TAG SEPARATOR "," SORTABLE
```

Let's add some shirts to our store, including laundry recommendations as a single comma-separated list of values:

```
HSET item:1 Name "Cotton Shirt" laundry "handwash,iron"
HSET item:2 Name "Polo Shirt" laundry "machinewash,handwash,nobleach"
HSET item:3 Name "Cotton T-Shirt" laundry "machinewash,nobleach"
HSET item:4 Name "Polo Shirt" laundry "machinewash,iron"
```

The desired aggregation will get the clothes grouped by laundry recommendation; this should include the cardinality of the items per category. Resolving this requirement is as easy and efficient as running the following statement to classify and count the shirts per laundry recommendation:

```
FT.AGGREGATE product_idx *
APPLY "split(@laundry)" AS laundry_recommend
GROUPBY 1 @laundry_recommend
REDUCE COUNT 0 AS num_per_ctg
SORTBY 2 @num_per_ctg ASC
1) (integer) 4
2) 1) "laundry_recommend"
   2) "handwash"
   3) "num_per_ctg"
   4) "2"
3) 1) "laundry_recommend"
   2) "iron"
   3) "num_per_ctg"
   4) "2"
4) 1) "laundry_recommend"
   2) "nobleach"
   3) "num_per_ctg"
   4) "2"
5) 1) "laundry_recommend"
   2) "machinewash"
```

```
   3) "num_per_ctg"
   4) "3"
```

The ability to group, reduce, transform, and filter the data offers flexibility and real-time performance to present results in the desired format and enables several use cases, ranging from **faceted search** to reporting. In the documentation, you will find the list of supported GROUPBY reducers, as well as the functions that can be used in APPLY expressions.

The documentation also specifies additional examples, including **optional terms**, **query attributes** (to customize the behavior of only certain clauses of a query), and more alternatives to address specific data retrieval requirements, such as vector similarity search, which will be discussed in the next chapter. Refer to the *Query syntax* document at https://redis.io/docs/stack/search/reference/query_syntax.

Updating an index in production

Sometimes, you need to update the data model of your application, which means you have to modify the schema of your physical data model. This translates into adding, removing, or modifying attributes in the database, and recalculating the indexes. This is nothing too infrequent, but like all changes, this comes with a price. While modifying the clients to manage the changed data model is in the hands of the developer, the database must support a smooth transition to the newer data model, where a new schema comes into play and indexes are updated. Redis Stack allows you to work with schema-less data structures, so if all of a sudden you require new field-value pairs to be added to a Hash, or new properties injected into a JSON object, you can go ahead and make the change. However, the index related to the data structure may need to be updated if the new attribute needs to be searchable. Redis Stack supports two methods to reconfigure indexes.

FT.ALTER

Using the FT.ALTER command, we can add new attributes to the index, causing the existing documents in the index to be scanned to add the new attribute. Referring to the World dataset we've considered so far, let's support an additional search by district, not included in the former city_idx index. You can verify that a search by an arbitrary district does not return any result because districts are not indexed:

```
FT.SEARCH city_idx @district:{Marche}
1) (integer) 0
```

Using the FT.ALTER command, we will add the attribute to the index:

```
FT.ALTER city_idx SCHEMA ADD District AS district TAG
OK
```

Finally, we can verify that the document has been indexed correctly:

```
FT.SEARCH city_idx @district:{Marche} NOCONTENT
1) (integer) 2
2) "city:1506"
3) "city:1521"
```

This command does not support deleting or updating attributes, so if you want to do that, you should drop and recreate the index using a new index definition. Note that this may not be desired in a production environment. If you need the flexibility to change the index at will without disruption, you may want to use the `FT.ALIAS` command, as explained in the next section.

FT.ALIAS

You can connect your index to an alias and use the alias in your applications. This allows you to create a new index with the desired schema, where this new index is meant to replace an older version of the index. Once you're ready, you can point the alias to the new index so that the application can use it transparently. Let's consider an example. First, let's associate our current index (if you are following on from the previous example, drop it and recreate it) with an alias:

```
FT.ALIASADD city_alias_idx city_idx
```

Then, let's verify that the alias can be used but does not return the desired result:

```
FT.SEARCH city_alias_idx @district:{Marche} NOCONTENT
1) (integer) 0
```

Now, we will create a brand-new index called `city_new_idx` that includes the new `District` attribute in the schema:

```
FT.CREATE city_new_idx
ON HASH
PREFIX 1 city:
SCHEMA Name AS name TEXT
CountryCode AS countrycode TAG SORTABLE
District AS district TAG
Population AS population NUMERIC SORTABLE
```

Now, we can reconnect the alias to the new index using the `FT.ALIASUPDATE` command:

```
FT.ALIASUPDATE city_alias_idx city_new_idx
```

Finally, we can verify that the search operation now returns the expected result:

```
FT.SEARCH city_alias_idx @district:{Marche} NOCONTENT

1) (integer) 2
2) "city:1506"
3) "city:1521"
```

This method applies changes to indexes transparently and does not cause any client disruption.

Temporary indexes

If you would like to perform search operations on temporary data, you can create a temporary index using the `TEMPORARY` keyword. A temporary index will expire after the desired number of seconds of inactivity. We have discussed ephemeral search, and we have seen that the index can be created and dismissed together with the documents by using the `FT.DROPINDEX` command and the `DD` option. A `TEMPORARY` index automates index and related document removal. Create the index as follows:

```
FT.CREATE user:241245:idx
ON HASH
PREFIX 1 user:241245
TEMPORARY 5
SCHEMA Name AS name TEXT
Id AS id TEXT
Quantity AS quantity NUMERIC
```

If you check the information for this index after more than 5 seconds, you will see that the index has disappeared:

```
FT.INFO user:241245:idx

(error) Unknown Index name
```

Additional commands

In this section, we discovered several features we can use to write queries against a basic database, but you can do more using additional commands. If you would like to get the entire list of indexed tags that are stored in the index for an attribute, you can do that easily:

```
FT.TAGVALS city_idx countrycode

   1) "abw"
   2) "afg"
   3) "ago"
...
```

You can also list the existing indexes that Redis Stack is managing:

```
FT._LIST

1) "country_idx"
2) "city_idx"
```

You can also understand the execution plan of a complex query:

```
FT.EXPLAINCLI country_idx '@governmentform:{republic} @population:[-
inf 100000]' RETURN 2 name surfacearea

1) INTERSECT {
2)   TAG:@governmentform {
3)  republic
4)   }
5)   NUMERIC {-inf <= @population <= 100000.000000}
6) }
7)
```

Refer to the documentation to consult the full list of `FT.*` commands.

We'll conclude this section by reminding you that Redis Stack is built on top of Redis, and it extends the classic key-value data modeling capability with support for real-time document querying and searching. Now, let's dive into the Hash and JSON data structures to learn how to put the features we've covered so far into practice and create powerful applications with them.

Working with Hashes

The capabilities we've introduced so far have been explored through concise examples using cities and countries from the World dataset. In this section, we'll consider a full-fledged use case, such as an application that stores and searches documents: a **knowledge base** (along the same lines, we could think of a learning management system, a blogging platform, or a generic and extensible **content management system** (**CMS**) or even a **customer relationship management** (**CRM**) tool). This kind of application works pretty well to present a walk-through of Redis Stack when used as a **document store** as we need solid classification and search capabilities to provide the best user experience, together with friendly user flows and, as usual, the real-time performance that is only possible when all the data is stored in the main memory. Let's proceed to imagine what data we would store in our knowledge base to model a document:

- The title.
- The content of the document, whatever the format is: HTML, Markdown, and unformatted text, to name a few.

- Document creation and update specified as Unix timestamps (so, the number of seconds since January 1, 1970). This is a popular format for storing timestamps, provided it is easily sortable and does not leave room for misleading time zone interpretations.
- The author of the document, or whoever introduced the document in the database.
- The owner of the document – that is, an accountable person that is maintaining the document.
- Comma-separated tags (the comma is the default separator, but this can be changed depending on the index definition).
- The state of the document: draft, review, published, archived, or deleted.
- The privacy setting of the document, either internal or public, or any other label to define who should see the document. This can be a single person, a team, or a custom permission.

You can import the simple KnowledgeBase dataset with 20 documents as follows:

```
cat kb.txt | redis-cli
```

Verify that the dataset has been imported by getting the entire content for a single document:

```
HGETALL kb:aasd999vod
 1) "update"
 2) "1634121118"
 3) "content"
 4) "It is always recommended to use connection pooling, otherwise,
each request will open a new connection. This exposes you to many
possible momentary problems that could prevent the opening of the
connection. In addition, if you make many requests, you will be
frequently opening and closing connections, operations that might fail
from time to time."
 5) "type"
 6) "q&a"
 7) "privacy"
 8) "public"
 9) "owner"
10) "73kd94jh5v2p9dh583ld"
11) "title"
12) "Should connection pooling be used?"
13) "creation"
14) "1627474864"
15) "tags"
16) "connectivity, client, connection, pooling"
17) "author"
18) "73kd94jh5v2p9dh583ld"
19) "state"
20) "published"
```

The dataset includes the statement to create the `kb_idx` index and is written as follows:

```
FT.CREATE kb_idx
ON HASH
PREFIX 1 kb:
SCHEMA title AS title TEXT
content AS content TEXT
creation AS creation NUMERIC SORTABLE
update AS update NUMERIC SORTABLE
tags AS tags TAG SORTABLE
privacy AS privacy TAG
state AS state TAG
author AS author TAG
owner AS owner TAG
type AS type TAG
```

The `kb_idx` index enables the following:

- **Full-text search** on the title and the content
- **Tag search** to filter the documents based on the tags, privacy, state, type, author, and owner
- **Numeric searches** based on the creation and last update timestamp

An example of searching for the desired documents in our database would be by a search term:

```
FT.SEARCH kb_idx "scalability" RETURN 1 title
1) (integer) 1
2) "kb:vvnoino242"
3) 1) "title"
   2) "Scalability Configuration for Redis Cloud Databases"
```

We could search for the most recently updated document using the following code:

```
FT.SEARCH kb_idx * RETURN 1 update SORTBY update DESC LIMIT 0 1
1) (integer) 20
2) "kb:243oifoiff"
3) 1) "update"
   2) "1672339442"
```

While the `FT.AGGREGATE` command is usually adopted to perform aggregations, we can take advantage of the transformation functions, as shown in the following example, and get the latest update timestamp. To format the timestamp as desired, we can use `APPLY` with the standard `strftime` formatting options:

```
FT.AGGREGATE kb_idx * APPLY "timefmt(@update, '%c')" AS human_readable
SORTBY 2 @update DESC LIMIT 0 1
1) (integer) 20
```

```
2) 1) "update"
   2) "1672339442"
   3) "human_readable"
   4) "Thu Dec 29 18:44:02 2022"
```

In this example, the timestamp is formatted with the `%c` code, which provides a date and time representation using the current locale. Another handy feature offered by `FT.AGGREGATE` is the ability to perform numeric sorts on multiple fields. This can be seen in the following example, where we specify a search term and sort by the two numeric indexes, `creation` and `update`:

```
FT.AGGREGATE kb_idx "delete" APPLY "timefmt(@update, '%c')" AS human_
readable SORTBY 4 @update DESC @creation DESC LIMIT 0 2
1) (integer) 4
2) 1) "update"
   2) "1668789612"
   3) "human_readable"
   4) "Fri Nov 18 16:40:12 2022"
   5) "creation"
   6) "1639641925"
3) 1) "update"
   2) "1645323476"
   3) "human_readable"
   4) "Sun Feb 20 02:17:56 2022"
   5) "creation"
   6) "1582566809"
```

Going back to using `FT.AGGREGATE` with `GROUPBY`, we can find the two authors who made the last updates to their documents:

```
FT.AGGREGATE kb_idx * GROUPBY 1 @author REDUCE MAX 1 @update as last_
updated APPLY "timefmt(@last_updated, '%c')" AS human_readable LIMIT 0
2 SORTBY 2 @last_updated DESC
1) (integer) 3
2) 1) "author"
   2) "73kd94jh5v2p9dh583ld"
   3) "last_updated"
   4) "1672339442"
   5) "human_readable"
   6) "Thu Dec 29 18:44:02 2022"
3) 1) "author"
   2) "74uvk593odt6g9h5fukv"
   3) "last_updated"
   4) "1671674172"
   5) "human_readable"
   6) "Thu Dec 22 01:56:12 2022"
```

The strength of the FT.AGGREGATE command is in (mind the repetition!) aggregations, so we could use it to provide an overview of the types of documents, as follows:

```
FT.AGGREGATE kb_idx * GROUPBY 1 @type REDUCE COUNT 0 AS docs
1) (integer) 3
2) 1) "type"
   2) "troubleshooting"
   3) "docs"
   4) "2"
3) 1) "type"
   2) "how-to"
   3) "docs"
   4) "12"
4) 1) "type"
   2) "q&a"
   3) "docs"
   4) "6"
```

Aggregating results using the document type attribute (or facet) is a useful option for users to refine the search and is finalized by retrieving the desired content in the shortest time possible. In the next few sections, we will dive into the optional features we can use to customize the queries using the related arguments and showcase some use cases with practical examples.

Highlighting and summarizing

Sometimes, you would like to propose a series of results to the users, in which you present an excerpt of the documents returned by the search operation with the search terms highlighted in some way (typically boldened), much like an internet search engine. Using the HIGHLIGHT argument of the FT.SEARCH command, you can instruct the database to highlight the search terms using the desired text format, such as the HTML bold tags, <b> and </b>, if the text must be rendered by a web browser or any other format, depending on the rendering engine. A simple example would be using the following syntax:

```
FT.SEARCH kb_idx "delete keys" RETURN 1 content HIGHLIGHT TAGS "<b>"
"</b>" LIMIT 0 1
1) (integer) 4
2) "kb:2axgd318xp"
3) 1) "content"
   2) "Check the slow log looking for EVALSHA, HGETALL, HMGET,
MGET, and all types of SCAN commands. Lower the slow log threshold
to capture more slow commands. Verify the size of <b>keys</b>
using redis-cli --bigkeys. <b>Delete</b> huge <b>keys</b> using
the asynchronous UNLINK rather than <b>deleting</b> keys using the
synchronous DEL. Verify that LUA scripts do not keep the state machine
busy with long executions."
```

Note how the desired tags enclose the relevant search terms. Also, note that variations of the search terms, such as "deleting," are highlighted. The reason is that Redis Stack supports **stemming** – that is, base forms for the words are added to the index, so in this example, both "delete" and "deleting" are good matches and the related documents are returned. Redis Stack uses the Snowball stemmer library, which includes most European languages. You can learn more from Snowball's website at `https://snowballstem.org/`.

If you would like to perform an exact `FT.SEARCH` search, you can discard variants by disabling **stemming** using the optional `VERBATIM` argument. You can entirely disable stemming for an attribute in an index using the `NOSTEM` argument when creating the index with `FT.CREATE`, so no variants will be considered when indexing a term.

In addition to highlighting results, you can request the database to summarize them and configure the results by number of fragments, number of fields to summarize, and more:

```
FT.SEARCH kb_idx "delete keys" RETURN 1 content SUMMARIZE HIGHLIGHT
TAGS "<b>" "</b>" LIMIT 0 2
1) (integer) 4
2) "kb:2axgd318xp"
3) 1) "content"
   2) "commands. Verify the size of <b>keys</b> using redis-cli
--bigkeys. <b>Delete</b> huge <b>keys</b> using the asynchronous
UNLINK rather than <b>deleting</b> keys using the synchronous... "
4) "kb:uiuu43hib7"
5) 1) "content"
   2) "using DEL to <b>delete</b> large <b>keys</b>, it is possible
to increase the latency when the target is a huge <b>key</b>. Try
replacing DEL with UNLINK... this command is very similar to DEL: it
<b>deletes</b> the specified <b>keys</b>. Just like DEL, a <b>key</b>
is ignored if it does not exist. However, the... "
```

Using the highlighting and summarizing features will allow you to present results so that users can see whether their search was good enough. If not, the user can decide to refine the search by specifying additional filters on tags, type of document, or other custom attributes.

Synonyms support

We cannot anticipate what search terms will be employed by users to locate the desired documents in our database. Imagine a scenario where a user wants to know how to perform a delete operation but specifies the "removal" search term. This term is not included in either the titles or the contents of the indexed documents, and because of this, no result is returned:

```
127.0.0.1:6379> FT.SEARCH kb_idx removal NOCONTENT
1) (integer) 0
```

However, if the user uses the right (and indexed) "delete" search term, four documents will be returned:

```
127.0.0.1:6379> FT.SEARCH kb_idx delete NOCONTENT
1) (integer) 4
2) "kb:2axgd318xp"
3) "kb:uiuu43hib7"
4) "kb:fworouwiuv"
5) "kb:vuu7887877"
```

We want to avoid such situations and be able to improve the user experience when a user is browsing our website to retrieve useful content. Redis Stack offers the option to create a dictionary of synonyms by complementing the index with synonyms. So, in this example, if we estimate that a user would use similar but different terms to find out how to perform a deletion, we can create a group of terms:

```
127.0.0.1:6379> FT.SYNUPDATE kb_idx del_group delete deletion remove
removal purge
OK
```

As soon as the group is created, the search is successful:

```
127.0.0.1:6379> FT.SEARCH kb_idx removal NOCONTENT
1) (integer) 3
2) "kb:2axgd318xp"
3) "kb:vuu7887877"
4) "kb:uiuu43hib7"
```

Improving the user experience is crucial to the success of your service. You can start collecting those search terms that return no results, store them (in a Redis Set, List, or a Sorted Set to count the repetitions of the failed searches caused by a certain term), and create synonym groups after a review. This iterative process will lead you to better engagement and increase the chances of users returning to the portal.

Spellchecking

Increasing the chances of users retrieving what they are looking for will also require you to manage the discrepancy between what users would like to search and what users type in your input form. Typos are frequent, and an innocent oversight by the user can compromise the experience when they're using your application. The **spellchecking** feature is yet another useful asset for guessing the desired search terms in the presence of misspellings and providing feedback to the users in the usual form – that is, "You have searched for… did you mean…?" You can even automate the decision and present results based on the most likely terms, as suggested by the spellchecker. An example of introducing spellchecking in the search pipeline could be to test the terms as follows:

```
FT.SPELLCHECK kb_idx "Redis Stack" DISTANCE 1
(empty array)
```

And if they are good, go ahead with the `FT.SEARCH` command. If the spellchecker returns suggestions, you may replace words and try the search with the corrected words:

```
FT.SPELLCHECK kb_idx "Reds Stak" DISTANCE 1
1) 1) "TERM"
   2) "reds"
   3) 1) 1) "0.80000000000000004"
         2) "redis"
2) 1) "TERM"
   2) "stak"
   3) 1) 1) "0.14999999999999999"
         2) "stack"
```

Based on the previous example, we could just get the suggested search terms and go ahead with the search operation, transparently, and maybe inform the user that the terms were rectified. You can refine the precision of the spellchecker by managing the desired dictionary via the `FT.DICTADD`, `FT.DICTDEL`, and `FT.DICTDUMP` commands, which add, remove, and dump the desired terms from the spellchecking dictionary, respectively.

Auto-completion

If you would like to propose results, anticipating the input by the user on a form input field, you don't need to develop a complex frontend implementation of auto-completion – you can use Redis Stack's **auto-completion** feature. You would use auto-completion when, for example, the user expects a concrete option out of a discrete number of results (this could be an airline, a color, a brand, a label, and so on). To use this feature, you need to create a dictionary of auto-complete suggestions:

```
FT.SUGADD tag_suggestions "oss" 1
(integer) 1
FT.SUGADD tag_suggestions "enterprise" 1
(integer) 2
FT.SUGADD tag_suggestions "scalability" 1
(integer) 3
FT.SUGADD tag_suggestions "connection" 1
(integer) 4
FT.SUGADD tag_suggestions "pooling" 1
(integer) 5
```

Once you've done this, you can query the auto-complete dictionary and get a proposal for the user:

```
FT.SUGGET tag_suggestions "scala"
1) "scalability"
FT.SUGGET tag_suggestions "conn"
1) "connection"
```

As you know, typos are around the corner. So, if you would like to prevent no auto-complete suggestions from being returned because of user mistakes when typing a term, as in this example, you could resort to fuzzy suggestions and get results even in the case of typos in the prefix:

```
FT.SUGGET tag_suggestions "scalbi"
(empty array)
```

Here's an example of using fuzzy suggestions:

```
FT.SUGGET tag_suggestions "scalbi" FUZZY
1) "scalability"
```

Using fuzzy suggestions may be expensive with dictionaries of considerable size because of the performance penalty introduced by dictionary traversal. This overhead becomes negligible when dictionaries are limited in size, and the feature will contribute to maximizing the responsiveness and usability of your application.

Phonetic matching

Another useful feature when searching for phonetically similar terms, such as names of entities (you are storing and making a list of employees or cities searchable), is **phonetic matching**. When a `TEXT` field in the index is defined with the `PHONETIC` attribute, both the term and its phonetic approximation will be indexed. This contributes to finding results when the spelling is not correct, so the search is performed based on how a word sounds rather than how it is written. This helps with retrieving results, even in the presence of typing errors.

For example, using the dataset we've considered so far, we may define another index to include phonetic variations of the city name, as follows:

```
FT.CREATE city_phonetic_idx
ON HASH PREFIX 1 "city:"
SCHEMA Name AS name TEXT PHONETIC "dm:en"
```

Then, we can search the index with an intentional misspelling and still be able to retrieve results:

```
FT.SEARCH city_phonetic_idx Rawma RETURN 1 Name
1) (integer) 2
2) "city:1464"
3) 1) "Name"
   2) "Roma"
4) "city:3388"
5) 1) "Name"
   2) "\xc3\x87orum"
```

Such results would have been omitted by the former index:

```
FT.SEARCH city_idx Rawma
1) (integer) 0
```

Managing documents in Redis Stack together with the advanced search capabilities we've explored so far means bringing legacy applications running on Redis and using the Hash data structure to a new level. In the next section, we'll go a step further and discover how to develop applications or integrate Redis Stack with other systems using the standard JSON format.

Working with JSON

The JSON format does not need too much of an introduction. As a JavaScript native object, born for lightweight communication between web clients and servers, and adopted in general for electronic communications, it is supported by most client libraries and databases. Redis Stack does not make exceptions and extends the data modeling capabilities to JSON objects, together with the indexing features we've learned so far. Using the JSON data structure in Redis Stack, you can store, retrieve, and update **JSON documents** efficiently using the popular **JSONPath** syntax. The many commands to manipulate strings, counters, arrays, and object literals, and all the data stored in a JSON document, help address the requirements of several data modeling problems.

The JSONPath syntax

The JSONPath syntax helps with accessing a single element or multiple elements within a JSON document.

Using the `JSON.*` suite of commands together with **JSONPath**, you can work with the JSON data structure and perform operations on multiple elements. Examples of using JSONPath, whose complete documentation can be found online at `https://redis.io/docs/data-types/json/path/`, follow.

Let's store a JSON string, which includes properties (such as the name of an author), arrays (of text, tags, and numbers of geographical locations), and object literals. It can also store a combination of these elements, such as an array of objects as a list of books, as shown in the following example:

```
JSON.SET author:1 $ '{"name":"Stephen King", "genre":["horror",
"suspense", "crime"], "books":[{"isbn":"8845295303","title":"The
Shining", "year":1977},{"isbn":"8820062909","title":"It",
"year":1986},{"isbn":"8845294021", "title":"Carrie", "year":1974}]}'
```

The root of a document can be accessed using the `$` symbol in JSONPath. You can retrieve a value attached to the root path:

```
JSON.GET author:1 $.name
"[\"Stephen King\"]"
```

You can access an array by index, where the subscript operator, `[]`, accesses elements in an array:

```
JSON.GET author:1 $.books[0]
"[{\"isbn\":\"8845295303\",\"title\":\"The Shining\",\"year\":1977}]"
```

You can also search using a filter condition, using the `?()` syntax to specify a filter, and the `@` symbol to indicate to which attributes the filter must be applied, which is `isbn` in this case:

```
JSON.GET author:1 '$.books[?(@.isbn=="8845294021")]'
"[{\"isbn\":\"8845294021\",\"title\":\"Carrie\"}]"
```

You can only retrieve what you need from a JSONPath-based search by using the `.` (dot) syntax to select a child element:

```
JSON.GET author:1 '$.books[?(@.isbn=="8845294021")].title'
"[\"Carrie\"]"
```

Using the commands from the JSON suite, you can append an element (an object literal, in this example) to an array:

```
JSON.ARRAPPEND author:1 $.books '{"isbn":"886836204X","title":"Cujo"}'
4
```

In this example, we're iterating over all the object literals stored by an array and extracting the desired values:

```
JSON.GET author:1 '$.books.*.title'
["The Shining","It","Carrie","Cujo"]
```

You also have the option to interact with object literals directly:

```
JSON.OBJKEYS author:1 $.books[1]
1) 1) "isbn"
   2) "title"
   3) "year"
```

To conclude this introduction to the JSON data structure, you can format a JSON response in a human-readable format. Just connect with the command-line interface using the `redis-cli -raw` option:

```
JSON.GET author:1 INDENT "\t" NEWLINE "\n" SPACE " " $.books[1]
[
        {
                "isbn": "8820062909",
                "title": "It",
                "year": 1986
```

```
        }
]
```

The ability to model data as JSON and access it easily by using the concise JSONPath syntax allows you to store complex objects in a tree-like structure, with multiple nested levels. This capability, together with the well-known real-time features of Redis, contributes to simplifying electronic communications (in particular, between web frontends and backends) and breaking the data impedance mismatch down. In addition, by putting together JSON data structures with the indexing capabilities of Redis Stack, we have the full potential to model and search JSON documents.

Indexing a JSON document

JSON documents can be indexed in the same way as Hash documents, using a similar syntax, where we specify the desired type of index. This means that the equivalent index that we created for the KnowledgeBase dataset can be written using the following command:

```
FT.CREATE json_idx
ON JSON
PREFIX 1 json:
SCHEMA  $.title AS title TEXT
$.content AS content TEXT
$.creation AS creation NUMERIC SORTABLE
$.update AS update NUMERIC SORTABLE
$.tags AS tags TAG SEPARATOR "," SORTABLE
$.privacy AS privacy TAG
$.state AS state TAG
$.author AS author TAG
$.owner AS owner TAG
$.type AS type TAG
```

There are slight changes in the syntax if we compare indexing JSON documents to indexing Hash documents:

- The `ON JSON` clause defines the type of index to be created
- The attributes must be specified with their JSONPath

You can import the simple KnowledgeBase dataset with 20 documents in JSON format as follows:

```
cat jsonkb.txt | redis-cli
```

Besides the differences in the syntax to create the index, searching and aggregating the dataset does not depend on the format of the documents stored in the database. You would write queries like so for a full-text search:

```
FT.SEARCH json_idx "scalability" RETURN 1 title
1) (integer) 1
2) "json:vvnoino242"
3) 1) "title"
   2) "Scalability Configuration for Redis Cloud Databases"
```

You can also aggregate data using the `FT.AGGREGATE` command:

```
FT.AGGREGATE json_idx * GROUPBY 1 @type REDUCE COUNT 0 AS docs
1) (integer) 3
2) 1) "type"
   2) "troubleshooting"
   3) "docs"
   4) "2"
3) 1) "type"
   2) "how-to"
   3) "docs"
   4) "12"
4) 1) "type"
   2) "q&a"
   3) "docs"
   4) "6"
```

Alternatively, you can use the same arguments that we saw when we looked at using Hash, such as spellchecking, highlighting, summarizing, and others.

While a JSON document can replace a Hash document for the modeling and indexing capabilities we've explored so far, we can go beyond indexing a flat document and create multiple indexes, regardless of the position and cardinality of the attribute in the document. This means you can index the following:

- Arrays of text, tags, numbers, and geographical locations
- Individual elements in objects
- Multiple values in the document, known as multi-value indexing
- Arrays as embeddings, for vector similarity search

Let's consider a few examples to illustrate JSON's indexing capabilities.

Indexing arrays and objects

To explore how to index and search JSON documents, let's add some additional data to our database of authors so that the dataset includes three authors, where each author is associated with genres. Authors write books, and books are associated with `isbn`, `title`, and `year` details, as well as one or more `genre` attributes (stored in an array). Let's consider three authors. The first has three books listed:

```
JSON.SET author:1 $ '{"name":"Stephen King", "genre":["horror",
"suspense", "crime"], "books":[{"isbn":"8845295303", "title":"The
Shining", "year":1977, "genre":["suspense"]}, {"isbn":"8820062909",
"title":"It", "year":1986, "genre":["horror"]}, {"isbn":"8845294021",
"title":"Carrie", "year":1974, "genre":["horror"]}]}'
```

The second author has two books listed:

```
JSON.SET author:2 $ '{"name":"Javier Marías", "genre":["fiction",
"suspense", "essay"], "books":[{"isbn":"8483465698","title":"Tu rostro
mañana", "year":2007, "genre":["fiction"]}, {"isbn":"8499899714",
"title":"Los Enamoramientos", "year":2011, "genre":["fiction",
"suspense"]}]}'
```

The third author has just one book listed:

```
JSON.SET author:3 $ '{"name":"Haruki Murakami",
"genre":["sci-fi", "fantasy", "crime", "novel", "fiction"],
"books":[{"isbn":"8806216465", "title":"Norwegian wood", "year":1987,
"genre":["romance novel"]}]}'
```

Here are some examples of searches we may want to perform:

- Find an author by name
- Retrieve authors by genre
- Get all the books written in a range of time
- Discover what author has written a certain book

We can create the following index to satisfy these requirements:

```
FT.CREATE author_idx
ON JSON
PREFIX 1 author:
SCHEMA $.name AS name TEXT
$.genre AS genre TAG
$.books[*].year AS year NUMERIC SORTABLE
$.books[*].isbn AS isbn TAG
$.books[*].title AS title TEXT SORTABLE
```

This definition provides the name index for full-text search, so you can perform this query like so:

```
FT.SEARCH author_idx @name:stephen RETURN 1 name
1) (integer) 1
2) "author:1"
3) 1) "name"
   2) "Stephen King"
```

The genre index makes the $.genre array of tags searchable, so you can do the following:

```
FT.SEARCH author_idx '@genre:{horror}' RETURN 1 name
1) (integer) 1
2) "author:1"
3) 1) "name"
   2) "Stephen King"
```

The year, isbn, and title indexes have been created on the corresponding individual elements of the objects in the array of books. So, the following query would return the authors with books published in a certain range of years:

```
FT.SEARCH author_idx '@year:[1974, 1980]' RETURN 1 $.name
1) (integer) 1
2) "author:1"
3) 1) "$.name"
   2) "Stephen King"
```

The following query would perform a full-text search across all authors' books:

```
FT.SEARCH author_idx '@title:wood' RETURN 1 title
1) (integer) 1
2) "author:3"
3) 1) "title"
   2) "Norwegian wood"
```

Multi-value indexing

Another useful feature is the option to create multi-value indexes – that is, indexes of data stored at different paths, and matched by a JSONPath expression. Before the introduction of the multi-value indexing method, we could only index JSONPath expressions that resolved into a scalar. Now, we can do it on paths that return arrays. Let's introduce this useful feature with an example. Consider the JSON author:3 object, which defines the genre attributes at the author's level and the books' level. We can retrieve each genre qualifier for both the author and the related books as follows:

```
JSON.GET author:2 $.genre.*
"[\"fiction\",\"suspense\",\"essay\"]"
```

```
JSON.GET author:2 $.books[*].genre.*
"[\"fiction\",\"fiction\",\"suspense\"]"
```

We can also merge these with a single query by using `..` in the syntax:

```
JSON.GET author:2 $..genre.*
"[\"fiction\",\"suspense\",\"essay\",\"fiction\",\"fiction\",\"sus-
pense\"]"
```

With this result in mind – that is, a single JSONPath query returning an array of values (or multiple scalars using different JSONPath queries) – we can create an index that accounts for such values:

```
FT.CREATE author_idx
ON JSON
PREFIX 1 author:
SCHEMA $.name AS name TEXT
$..genre.* AS genre TAG
$.books[*].year AS year NUMERIC SORTABLE
$.books[*].isbn AS isbn TAG
$.books[*].title AS title TEXT SORTABLE
```

The `"$..genre.* AS genre TAG`" definition will index the values returned by the query with the `..` operator. Finally, we can search both the authors and the books that have a certain value indexed as TAG:

```
FT.SEARCH author_idx "@genre:{'romance novel'}" RETURN 1 name
1) (integer) 1
2) "author:3"
3) 1) "name"
   2) "Haruki Murakami"
```

The previous query returns the only author who has a book classified as `romance novel`. The following query returns authors who write fiction:

```
FT.SEARCH author_idx "@genre:{'fiction'}" RETURN 1 name
1) (integer) 2
2) "author:3"
3) 1) "name"
   2) "Haruki Murakami"
4) "author:2"
5) 1) "name"
   2) "Javier Mar\xc3\xadas"
```

Multi-value indexing is supported for the `TEXT`, `TAG`, `GEO`, `NUMERIC`, and `VECTOR` attributes, boosts the user search experience, and increases the chances of retrieving the data from multiple paths either in the document or across documents.

Extracting partial data from JSON documents

We have reviewed many indexing techniques and discovered the flexibility of using **JSONPath** to read, index, and search different portions of documents. An additional advantage of JSONPath is that it can be used in the `RETURN` clause to select what to return for the matched documents.

If we would like to search a document by tag and return its title, we would execute this command:

```
FT.SEARCH author_idx '@isbn:{8806216465}' RETURN 6 $.name AS Author
'$.books[?(@.isbn=="8806216465")].title' AS Title
1) (integer) 1
2) "author:3"
3) 1) "Author"
   2) "Haruki Murakami"
   3) "Title"
   4) "Norwegian wood"
```

Wrapping up, JSONPath helps retrieve the desired portion of a JSON document and is an essential asset to index, search, and retrieve data from a Redis Stack database.

The last type of index that both the Hash and the JSON documents support is the `VECTOR` type. We have postponed introducing the indexing of vectors until now because the topic demands a dedicated chapter, partly due to the innovation that this feature adds to database traditional searches and because modern use cases can be implemented with it, so it seems better to keep the discussion separate. In the following section, we will explore what options exist to build a recommendation engine, using the traditional approach based on scoring functions.

Redis Stack as a recommendation engine

Typically, we would retrieve documents based on their data, which means that we would resort to different indexing methods to perform a search, such as `TEXT`, `TAG`, or `NUMERIC`. However, to provide realistic recommendations, we can't just rely on the content or taxonomy of the information stored in a database – we must also rely on other methods that take into account the popularity and feedback from users who may have rated that content. This leads to the introduction of another variable: the relevance of the results. As an example, if a certain item is rated to be top-quality and affordable, our database should return this item rather than other items that are inferior or more expensive and sort the results by relevance.

In addition to searches based on the relevance of the documents, another type of recommendation can be based on the appearance of an item, or other properties that are also intrinsic, such as a textual description, an audio file, or other kinds of unstructured data.

Redis Stack provides methods to implement such recommendation engines via scores and similarity search.

Recommendation using scores

When creating an index, Redis Stack uses a scoring function to evaluate the relevance of the documents and present them sorted by score. Redis Stack uses a default **scoring function** (**TF-IDF**) but also allows for other functions (`TFIDF.DOCNORM`, `BM25`, `DISMAX`, `DOCSCORE`, and `HAMMING`), all based on the frequency of the terms that are being researched. It is also possible to extend Redis Stack with a custom scoring function. Let's review the default scoring mechanism using some book data samples:

```
JSON.SET book:8845295303 $ '{"author":1, "title":"The Shining",
"synopsis":"A family heads to an isolated hotel for the winter
where a sinister presence influences the father into violence",
"rating":0.83}'
JSON.SET book:8820062909 $ '{"author":1, "title":"It", "synopsis":"In
1960, seven pre-teen outcasts fight an evil demon who poses as a
child-killing clown. Thirty years later, they reunite to stop the
demon", "rating":0.83}'
JSON.SET book:8845294021 $ '{"author":1, "title":"Carrie",
"synopsis":"Carrie White unleashes her telekinetic powers after being
humiliated by her classmates at her senior prom.", "rating":0.8}'
JSON.SET book:8483465698 $ '{"author":2, "title":"Tu rostro mañana",
"synopsis":"Jaime Deza is a bit adrift in London until his old
friend Sir Peter Wheeler recruits him for a new career in British
Intelligence.", "rating":0.87}'
JSON.SET book:8499899714 $ '{"author":2, "title":"Los Enamoramientos",
"synopsis":"A novel of death and love, The Infatuations goes on to
explore the relationship of the narrator with the widow and with the
death of his best friend Miguel", "rating":0.70}'
JSON.SET book:8806216465 $ '{"author":3, "title":"Norwegian wood",
"synopsis":"The mutual passion of Toru and Naoko is marked by the
tragic death of their best friend years before.", "rating":0.92}'
```

Now, we can create a new index to search the synopsis:

```
FT.CREATE books_idx ON JSON PREFIX 1 book: SCHEMA $.synopsis AS
synopsis TEXT
```

If we want to research those authors that have the term "death" in the synopsis, we can execute the following search command:

```
FT.SEARCH books_idx death NOCONTENT
1) (integer) 2
2) "book:8499899714"
3) "book:8806216465"
```

Considering the context of the relevance of results, you may be wondering why `book:8499899714` comes before `book:8806216465`. For the explanation, you can review the algorithm that's used by Redis Stack to compute the scores using the `EXPLAINSCORE` option:

```
FT.SEARCH books_idx death NOCONTENT WITHSCORES EXPLAINSCORE
1) (integer) 2
```

```
2) "book:8499899714"
3) 1) "2"
   2) 1) Final TFIDF : words TFIDF 4.00 * document score 1.00 / norm 2
/ slop 1
     2) 1) (TFIDF 4.00 = Weight 1.00 * TF 2 * IDF 2.00)
4) "book:8806216465"
5) 1) "2"
   2) 1) Final TFIDF : words TFIDF 2.00 * document score 1.00 / norm 1
/ slop 1
     2) 1) (TFIDF 2.00 = Weight 1.00 * TF 1 * IDF 2.00)
```

As the term "death" appears twice for `book:8499899714` but only once for `book:8806216465`, `book:8499899714` has a higher score, so it is returned as the first result. Note how the score is `1.00` – this is a default value because no score was defined by the index. The `EXPLAINSCORE` command gives us some insight into the internals so that we can determine the relevance of results; however, we are not really in the realm of recommendations because this search was only based on the content of the document. To introduce the "human factor," the `rating` index of the books comes into play. To this purpose, let's drop and recreate the index as follows:

```
FT.CREATE books_idx
SCORE_FIELD $.rating
ON JSON
PREFIX 1 book:
SCHEMA $.synopsis AS synopsis TEXT
```

This new index instructs the scoring function to consider the user ranking indicated by `SCORE_FIELD`, which is expressed as an attribute between 0 and 1:

```
FT.SEARCH books_idx death NOCONTENT
1) (integer) 2
2) "book:8806216465"
3) "book:8499899714"
```

Having a look at the explanation, we have the following:

```
FT.SEARCH books_idx death NOCONTENT WITHSCORES EXPLAINSCORE
1) (integer) 2
2) "book:8806216465"
3) 1) "1.840000333786011"
   2) 1) Final TFIDF : words TFIDF 2.00 * document score 0.92 / norm 1
/ slop 1
     2) 1) (TFIDF 2.00 = Weight 1.00 * TF 1 * IDF 2.00)
4) "book:8499899714"
5) 1) "1.3999999761581421"
   2) 1) Final TFIDF : words TFIDF 4.00 * document score 0.70 / norm 2
```

```
/ slop 1
    2) 1) (TFIDF 4.00 = Weight 1.00 * TF 2 * IDF 2.00)
```

This time, the book's `rating` is used as the score to estimate the relevance of the documents, and not just the default value equal to `1.00`. If you decide to sort the results by the desired field using the `SORTBY` clause, the scoring mechanism won't be used.

If you would like to rely entirely on the ratings, it is possible to configure the desired scorer, as in this example, and the frequency of terms will not be considered:

```
FT.SEARCH books_idx death NOCONTENT WITHSCORES SCORER DOCSCORE
EXPLAINSCORE
1) (integer) 2
2) "book:8806216465"
3) 1) "0.92000001668930054"
   2) Document's score is 0.92
4) "book:8499899714"
5) 1) "0.69999998807907104"
   2) Document's score is 0.70
```

Finally, when the search includes more than one attribute to estimate the relevance (the title and the content of a document, for example), it is possible to boost one or more attributes using the desired weight when the index is defined. This functionality is delivered by the `WEIGHT` field option.

The next section concludes this chapter with an overview of Redis Stack as a session store, with a walk-through of the different options to model session data and the pros and cons of the available options.

Redis Stack as a session store

Now that we have seen the principal features of the two main data structures that can be created, indexed, and searched in Redis Stack, let's consider a conclusive example to understand what the Hash and JSON data structures offer to one of the most classical use cases: the **session store**. In *Chapter 2, Developing Modern Use Cases with Redis Stack*, we highlighted the importance of making session data available outside of the application server for different reasons, such as the scalability of the session store, high availability, load balancing, and, in the case of a session store that uses Redis as a backend, achieving real-time performance.

Redis offers many options to store and retrieve data efficiently. However, sessions store different types of data: metadata, lists, geographical locations, and entire objects. Finding the right data structure, using low-complexity data access patterns, and managing session expiration in a highly concurrent environment may be challenging. In this section, we will introduce some ideas for a solid session data management strategy:

- Redis Data structures for session data
- Modeling key-value pairs
- Modeling objects

- Modeling collections
- Session management for real-time applications

Redis data structures for session data

Let's approach session data modeling by introducing the typical data structures that help implement a physical data model with Redis.

String

Session data can be serialized in a String, a compact format that is also easy to manage. This data structure is often managed using serializable programming language interfaces, which help map software objects to strings and deserialize strings back to objects. While strings are a compact format, it is expensive to serialize and deserialize data. In addition, Redis Strings cannot be indexed by Redis Stack:

```
GET session:f2423g52
"creationTime:1673122876161;lastAccessedTime:1673122876162"
```

Hash

The Hash data structure is an intuitive and natural choice for session data as it can be indexed and allows direct access to properties. However, it does not allow you to nest data, and managing objects requires expensive serialization and deserialization operations:

```
HGETALL session:f2423g52
1) "creationTime"
2) "1673122876161"
3) "lastAccessedTime"
4) "1673122876162"
```

JSON

The JSON data structure offers a compact representation of session data – it allows nested data and satisfies a vast variety of queries:

```
JSON.GET session:f2423g52
"{\"lastAccessedTime\":1672475765650, \"creationTime\":1672475765649}"
```

Additional Redis data structures

Session data can also be saved in other data structures:

- Lists, Sets, Sorted Sets, Bitmaps, and more to offer unique features for modeling user information
- Data types can be operated with low-complexity commands

However, the variety of commands to operate with data structures may generate anti-patterns (recurrent `HGETALL` on huge Hashes, time-consuming scans (`HSCAN`), range searches with many results. and more). Because of this, data must be indexed to achieve real-time performance, and the indexable data structures are the Hash and the JSON ones.

Modeling key-value pairs

When it comes to adding key-value pairs to the session, both the Hash and the JSON data structures are a good fit.

Hash

Key-value pairs are stored in the Hash and the entire session can be retrieved using the `HGETALL` command:

```
HGETALL session:aaed7f84-555f-4083-b755-6d424e0c15f9
1) "lastAccessedTime"
2) "1673123039784"
3) "creationTime"
4) "1673123039783"
```

JSON

The `JSON.GET` command can be used to retrieve the entire session (as in the following example) or part of it:

```
JSON.GET session:ee93af76-796f-4649-9a92-66983aa4def5
"{\"lastAccessedTime\":1673300622,\"creationTime\":1673300622}"
```

The Hash and the JSON data structures both allow the following:

- Direct access to in-session key-value pairs
- Indexing for cross-session searches
- Queries to retrieve the sessions that were created at a point in time or within a certain period
- Sessions tagged by a certain label
- Full-text searches on text fields

Modeling objects

The Hash and JSON data structures can store objects when they've been transformed, but JSON is a natural choice for storing multiple nested objects. JSON is more flexible when it comes to indexing and searching:

```
JSON.GET session:ee93af76-796f-4649-9a92-66983aa4def5
"{\"lastAccessedTime\":1673300622,
```

```
\"creationTime\":1673300622,
\"cart\":[  {\"itemId\":\"hp-2341\",
             \"itemCost\":1990.99,
             \"quantity\":3},
             {\"itemId\":\"MacBook\",
             \"itemCost\":2990.99,
             \"quantity\":15}
          ],

\"Marvel\":\"Avengers\",
\"Disney\":\"Frozen\"}"
```

Redis Stack can index any nested field of an object (also located at multiple paths, using multi-value indexing) and perform powerful cross-session searches, so we can provide a solution to the following search problems:

- Search for a specific item in all the shopping carts
- Find the biggest orders across carts
- Retrieve older or newer carts
- Find the idle shopping carts
- Retrieve the open sessions close to a location

Modeling collections

Collections can be modeled using Lists, Sets, or Sorted Sets but cannot be indexed. The JSON data structure is a versatile option as it can store collections that can be indexed for cross-session searches. An example could be the ability to retrieve the user sessions that have visited a certain web page:

```
JSON.SET session:28og4f8-2643gf862g4
    $ '{"lastAccessedTime":1672475765650,
        "creationTime":1672475765649,
        "visited":[ "www.redis.com", "www.google.com"]
        }'
JSON.SET session:np9p09n-9f2743fbavs
    $ '{"lastAccessedTime":1672475765645,
        "creationTime":1672475765549,
        "visited":[ "www.redis.io", "www.microsoft.com"]
        }'
```

Using JSON, a full-text search can be done on arrays of strings or a JSONPath leading to multiple strings. Indexing and searching are also possible for arrays of numbers or geographic locations:

```
FT.CREATE session_idx
ON JSON
PREFIX 1 session:
SCHEMA
$.lastAccessedTime AS lastAccessedTime NUMERIC SORTABLE
$.creationTime AS creationTime NUMERIC SORTABLE
$.visited AS visited TEXT
FT.SEARCH session_idx '@visited:("www.redis.com")' RETURN 1 $.visited
1) (integer) 1
2) "session:28og4f8-2643gf862g4"
3) 1) "$.visited"
   2) "[\"www.redis.com\",\"www.google.com\"]"
```

Session management for real-time applications

When designing the data model of the session stored in a database, a variety of options are available. The requirements of a session stored in a database are as follows:

- Session TTL can be refreshed and session data expires at will
- Lazy loading of partial information from a session
- Extensibility to new session objects
- Searchable (in-session and cross-session)

In addition, data stored in Redis can be modeled as follows:

- Key-value pairs (metadata, attributes, and so on)
- Objects (including geographic locations)
- Collections (textual, numeric, objects, and so on)

High-performance session management must do the following:

- Allow indexing of properties, collections, and object properties
- Allow in-session and cross-session indexed searches

The natural choice to satisfy these requirements is to use the JSON data structure for properties, collections, objects, and geographical locations while making it possible to extend the session with additional data structures such as **HyperLogLog**, Lists, Streams, and more:

```
{
    "lastAccessedTime":1673354843,
    "creationTime":1673354843,
    "cart":[
        {
            "itemId":"hp-2341",
            "itemCost":1990.99,
            "quantity":3
        },
        {
            "itemId":"MacBook",
            "itemCost":2990.99,
            "quantity":15
        }
    ],
    "location":"34.638,31.79",
    ["www.redis.com","www.google.com"]
}
```

Session lazy loading

Session data can be partially loaded, thus avoiding the need to transfer bulky session data, which represents an overhead:

```
JSON.GET session:28og4f8-2643gf862g4  $.visited
"[[\"www.redis.com\",\"www.google.com\"]]"
JSON.GET session:28og4f8-2643gf862g4  $.lastAccessedTime
"[1672475765650]"
```

We can retrieve multiple values at once:

```
JSON.GET session:28og4f8-2643gf862g4 $.lastAccessedTime $.visited
"{\"$.lastAccessedTime\":[1672475765650],\"$.visited\":[[\"www.redis.
com\",\"www.google.com\"]]}"
```

Multi-object sessions

A session, including the principal JSON data structure plus additional data structures such as a List and HyperLogLog, can be stored in Redis by prefixing the session objects with the same session identifier:

```
KEYS *3354623a-78fb-45aa-80fb-fc8c7f6afeb5*
1) "session:3354623a-78fb-45aa-80fb-fc8c7f6afeb5:history"
```

```
2) "session:3354623a-78fb-45aa-80fb-fc8c7f6afeb5:trackvisits"
3) "session:3354623a-78fb-45aa-80fb-fc8c7f6afeb5"
```

Session expiration

It is important to highlight that every time the user interacts with the session, the session's **Time to Live** (**TTL**) needs to be refreshed, so the TTL of all the session keys must be updated at once. This causes processing overhead. As an example, if the user logs out, the session must expire immediately; if there is user activity, then the session must be extended. Client pipelines can be used to limit this overhead and transactions can be used to make this operation atomic.

Example of sessions using the JSON data structure

As an example of the potential of a session modeled as JSON and indexed by Redis Stack, let's consider this example of two sessions with some user data:

```
JSON.SET session:a30d0c64-4cad-4088-a9ef-f1889d182df4
$ '{"lastAccessedTime":1672475765650,"creation-
Time":1672475765649,"user":{"name":"John","last":"Doe"},"visit-
ed":["www.redis.com","www.google.com"], "location": "34.638,31.79",
"cart":[{"itemId":"hp-2341","itemCost":1990.99,"quantity":3},{"item-
Id":"MacBook","itemCost":2990.99,"quantity":15}]}'
JSON.SET session:18920ac6-a2f0-4019-8250-e0036d17d015
$ '{"lastAccessedTime":1672475765645,"creation-
Time":1672475765549,"user":{"name":"Jane","last":"Appleseed"},"visit-
ed":["www.redis.io","www.microsoft.com"], "location": "35.178,31.768",
"cart":[{"itemId":"invicta-jolly","itemCost":68.99,"quanti-
ty":1},{"itemId":"MacBook","itemCost":2990.99,"quantity":15}]}'
```

The index will be created for the following data:

- `NUMERIC SORTABLE` for `lastAccessedTime` and `creationTime`
- `TEXT` for the collection of visited URLs
- `TAG` for `itemId`
- `GEO` for the location of the user

The statement that creates the index is as follows:

```
FT.CREATE session_idx
ON JSON PREFIX 1 session:
SCHEMA
$.lastAccessedTime AS lastAccessedTime NUMERIC SORTABLE
$.creationTime AS creationTime NUMERIC SORTABLE
```

```
$.visited AS visited TEXT
$.cart[*].itemId AS itemid TAG
$.location AS loc GEO
```

A search to return all the sessions containing a MacBook in the shopping cart can be written as follows:

```
FT.SEARCH session_idx '@itemid:{MacBook}' RETURN 0
1) (integer) 2
2) "session:a30d0c64-4cad-4088-a9ef-f1889d182df4"
3) "session:18920ac6-a2f0-4019-8250-e0036d17d015"
```

A search to get a **shopping cart** item with that product in a session (unique key per cart) can be written as follows:

```
JSON.GET session:a30d0c64-4cad-4088-a9ef-f1889d182df4 '$.cart[?(@.
itemId=="MacBook")]'
"[{\"itemId\":\"MacBook\",\"itemCost\":2990.99,\"quantity\":15}]"
```

A search to get the sessions close to a given location (within a radius of 40km) can be written as follows:

```
FT.SEARCH session_idx '@loc:[34.5 31.5 40 km]' return 0
1) (integer) 1
2) "session:a30d0c64-4cad-4088-a9ef-f1889d182df4"
```

A search to return the last created session can be written as follows:

```
FT.SEARCH session_idx "@creationTime:[-inf, +inf]" RETURN 1
creationTime LIMIT 0 1 SORTBY creationTime DESC
1) (integer) 2
2) "session:a30d0c64-4cad-4088-a9ef-f1889d182df4"
3) 1) "creationTime"
   2) "1672475765649"
```

These are just a few examples of the potential of a session managed with Redis while exploiting the capabilities of Redis Stack. Combining the index types or extending the session data model beyond the JSON object and using streams, bitmaps, and Hyperloglog, Redis Stack provides the flexibility to solve any query and search problems while opening the path to complex session data analysis, not to mention its flexible aggregation capabilities.

In conclusion, the choice concerning the data model to be used for a session stored in Redis is a function of the requirements to store, fetch, and analyze the data in the session itself, plus additional needs such as session refresh or expiration on demand, and partial session data loading.

Standard sessions are often modeled in Redis using the Hash data structure for the metadata, key-value pairs, and objects (where objects are serialized using the default or a custom serializer), and for this purpose, it is possible to configure the most popular framework for the desired language to transparently enable session management in Redis:

- **Spring** with the **Spring Session Data Redis** module
- **Express** with the **connect-redis** `npm` package
- **Flask**, using the **Flask-Session** extension

In use cases where a compact session representation for collections, objects, and geographical locations is required, together with the ability to perform efficient in-session and cross-session queries and searches, the JSON data type is a flexible alternative for new use cases.

Summary

In this chapter, we dived into the modeling and indexing capabilities of Redis Stack. In particular, we experimented with the query syntax on some sample databases and learned about the possibilities that are offered by the search and aggregation features. In addition, we discovered several chances to enrich our applications using spellcheck, auto-completion, highlighting, summarizing, stemming, and more.

Once you were familiar with modeling, indexing, and searching through a database of Hash or JSON documents, you discovered how to implement a recommendation system using a scoring approach. We finished this chapter by modeling a session using Redis Stack's capabilities, with examples and the trade-offs of using one data structure rather than another provided. While the many features considered in this chapter provide a rich application design and development experience, more features will be added to Redis Stack, such as the ability to index new geometries, or new commands to query JSON documents. Stick around and check out the new Redis Stack releases to discover all the news.

In *Chapter 6, Redis Stack as a Vector Database*, you will learn how to store, index, and search vectors using the vector similarity search feature. You will also understand how to design a textual and visual recommendation engine using advanced AI/ML data models and other emerging use cases.

6

Redis Stack as a Vector Database

Vector similarity search (**VSS**) is a core functionality of Redis Stack, the foundation of a vast variety of use cases. In this chapter, we will go through the concepts you need to understand to make the most out of this capability. The main idea behind VSS is that Redis Stack can store, index, and search vectors, and vectors are an optimal representation of unstructured data (data without a data model and a structure, which is harder to organize) because vectors can be easily processed by machines and take advantage of optimized hardware such as GPUs. New techniques have emerged in the areas of AI and ML to help with the task of modeling, classifying, and understanding unstructured data such as images, audio files, text, and more. By leveraging this capability, it is possible to build systems that, while making sense of such data, resolve problems otherwise impossible to solve with traditional databases. **Unstructured data** is a relevant portion of the data that enterprises manage nowadays (estimates suggest that 80% of global data will be unstructured by 2025) and extracting value from such data is imperative. We'll introduce VSS in Redis Stack in steps, then present examples to help you implement a recommendation engine.

We will discuss the following topics:

- Vector embeddings for unstructured data modeling
- Storing the embeddings
- Indexing the embeddings
- Performing similarity search
- Performing hybrid queries
- Performing VSS range queries
- Recommendations based on visual search
- Integrating Redis with generative AI

Technical requirements

To follow along with the examples in the chapter, you will need to install

Redis Stack Server 7.2 or later in your development environment. Alternatively, you can create a free Redis Cloud subscription to get a free plan and use a managed Redis Stack database.

Vector embeddings for unstructured data modeling

Vector embeddings are lists of floating-point numbers that are used to describe the semantics of unstructured data. The principal feature of vector embeddings is that they have fixed sizes and allow a compact and dense representation of data in fewer bytes, compared to other encoding models. Features can be, in certain cases, engineered manually or using standard methods. An example of embedding can be the description of a color, expressed by the three RGB color components. So, using the RGB representation, we can express any color as an array of numbers:

```
[34, 93, 232]
```

While this approach will work perfectly with this and many other data modeling problems, nowadays, generating vector embeddings from unstructured data involves **deep learning** techniques. These aim to produce models that do the following:

1. Take the raw unstructured data as input (a bitmap file or a voice recording).
2. Capture the relevant and distinguishing features of the data (such as frequency peaks in a voice recording or sharp edges in a picture).
3. Dump the features into a vector embedding.

We won't dive into the models that perform this transformation from data to embeddings in this chapter. If you are curious about this topic, you will find a lot of bibliographies about models and their training methods online. There are many open pre-trained models that you can already use for free, such as those from **PyTorch**, **Hugging Face**, and **OpenAI**.

Let's consider an example. We will encode a short sentence into an embedding using the popular **Sentence Transformers** Python framework, a collection of models that produces embeddings of different sizes and specialized for different purposes, such as data clustering or semantic search. Let's pick a model from those available at `https://huggingface.co/sentence-transformers`. The library can be installed as follows:

```
pip install -U sentence-transformers
```

A snippet of code that calculates the embedding can be coded as follows:

```
from sentence_transformers import SentenceTransformer

model = SentenceTransformer('sentence-transformers/multi-qa-MiniLM-L6-
cos-v1')
embedding = model.encode("This is a technical document, it describes
the SID sound chip of the Commodore 64")
```

This specific model produces a vector of 384 floating-point numbers. Let's print the first 10 elements:

```
print(embedding[:10])
[ 0.00631137 -0.005189 -0.03774299 -0.09026785 -0.05783698  0.01209931
-0.02595172  0.01094836 -0.06051398  0.0521009 ]
```

Note that models are produced and tested with content of limited size. In this example, `multi-qa-MiniLM-L6-cos-v1` supports texts up to 512 words; longer texts are truncated, and the truncated portion is not considered. Make sure your text length suits the model you are using. If the number of words exceeds the supported length, an option is to split the content into chunks and generate multiple vector embeddings for a single document.

Storing the embeddings

Vectors are numerical representations of unstructured data and the transformation is performed using AI and ML models. Redis Stack can perform VSS on vectors that are locally stored. In this section, you will learn how to store vectors, a capability that turns Redis Stack into a *de facto* **vector database**.

Hashes

Vectors can be stored in Hash data structures or JSON documents as attributes contained in such document formats. Storing vectors in Hashes is a one-command operation that involves leveraging the NumPy library for scientific computing and its conversion utility, `astype`, which casts the vector to the desired format – in this case, a binary blob. Back to the former embedding generation example, we can now convert the vector and print a portion as follows:

```
import numpy as np
blob = embedding.astype(np.float32).tobytes()
print(blob[0 : 50])
```

This script outputs the following:

```
b'\x99\xcf\xce;\x87\x08\xaa\xbbe\x98\x1a\xbdZ\xde\xb8\xbdx\xe61\
xbd2<F<\xb3\x98\xd4\xbc\xbc`3<\x82\xddw\xbd\xc2gU=\xa8^\xbf\xbbM\x14Z\
xbd\x84%'
```

You are now ready to store this binary blob in the Redis Stack database. Check out the full example:

```
from sentence_transformers import SentenceTransformer
import numpy as np
import redis

r = redis.Redis(host='127.0.0.1', port=6379)
text = "This is a technical document, it describes the SID sound chip
of the Commodore 64"
model = SentenceTransformer('sentence-transformers/multi-qa-MiniLM-L6-
cos-v1')
embedding = model.encode(text)
blob = embedding.astype(np.float32).tobytes()
r.hset('doc:1', mapping = {'embedding': blob,
                            'genre': 'technical',
                            'content': text})
```

In this example, we have stored the embedding in a Hash, the original content, and a tag, `genre`. But you can think of including additional data or metadata in the same Hash so that you can add additional filters and perform hybrid searches.

JSON

JSON documents can store vectors as well. However, compared to Hashes, vectors are stored as arrays rather than blobs. We will use the NumPy library to convert the embedding into a Python list and store it with the content in the related properties in the document:

```
vector = embedding.tolist()
doc = {
    'embedding': vector,
    'genre': 'technical',
    'content': text
}
r.json().set("doc:1", '$', doc)
```

Indexing the embeddings

Now that we can generate a vector for the desired type of data using the corresponding ML model, we would like to index vectors for VSS. Here, we'll introduce the `VECTOR` field type which, together with `TEXT`, `TAG`, `NUMERIC`, and `GEO`, complete the types of data that can be indexed by Redis Stack. Using `redis-cli` to create an index as usual, we can index the embedding as follows:

```
FT.CREATE doc_idx
ON HASH
```

```
PREFIX 1 doc:
SCHEMA content AS content TEXT
genre AS genre TAG
embedding VECTOR HNSW 6 TYPE FLOAT32 DIM 384 DISTANCE_METRIC COSINE
```

We can index the JSON document in a similar fashion:

```
FT.CREATE doc_idx
ON JSON
PREFIX 1 doc:
SCHEMA $.content as content TEXT
$.genre AS genre TAG
$.embedding VECTOR HNSW 6 TYPE FLOAT32 DIM 384 DISTANCE_METRIC COSINE
```

This index includes the content of the document and the embedding and uses the related types: `TEXT` and `VECTOR`. In the next subsections, we will explain the meaning of the arguments for the vector similarity index.

The algorithms – FLAT and HNSW

When searching for the most similar vectors, we may choose between the FLAT and **Hierarchical Navigable Small World** (**HNSW**) algorithms. FLAT is also referred to as brute-force indexing because, to compute the most similar vector to the vector under analysis, the distance between the provided vector and all the vectors in the index must be computed, which can be expensive when this iterative approach is performed over many embeddings. The HNSW algorithm, on the other hand, is a graph-based probabilistic approach that scales better over many embeddings and provides fast results, but at the expense of precision. Some accuracy is sacrificed for the benefit of performance.

In summary, the HNSW algorithm is more complex than the FLAT algorithm in that it's faster but less accurate. The FLAT algorithm scales well with more shards (we will discuss multi-shard databases when we address the open source version of Redis Cluster and Redis Enterprise Cluster). Both the FLAT and HNSW algorithms are defined by three mandatory parameters: the type, the dimension, and the distance metric.

Type

The type that defines the embedding is either `FLOAT32` or `FLOAT64` for higher accuracy. Choose the type accordingly, depending on the embedding generated by the model. In the former example, the model produced embeddings of 32-bit floating point numbers.

Index dimension

This is just the dimension of the vector embedding: in our example, the chosen model generated embeddings of 384 numbers. Check what format is produced by the model of choice and configure this parameter accordingly.

Distance metrics

To look for the most similar vectors (this approach is also referred to as **K-nearest neighbors** or **KNN**), we need to define the distance between vectors. VSS in Redis Stack supports three distances:

- **L2, the Euclidean distance between vectors**: This distance, when applied to two points in the Cartesian plane, is calculated as the distance of the segment interconnecting the two points (calculated using the Pythagorean theorem on the horizontal and vertical coordinates of the points). When dealing with higher vector dimensions, the formula to calculate the distance does not change. Since `u` and `v` are two *n*-dimensional vectors, the **Euclidean distance** is calculated as follows:

$$d\left(u, v\right) = \sqrt{\sum_{i=1}^{n}(u_i - v_i)^2}$$

  This distance is effective when the vectors describe continuous features, and when the magnitude of the distance matters (the vector is describing a physical property, such as geographical coordinates or other multi-dimensional coordinates, where the distance between points in the related space matter).

- **COSINE, the cosine distance between vectors**: The **cosine similarity** considers the cosine of the angle between the vectors (when the angle is 0, the cosine is 1, which represents the maximum similarity). The cosine similarity does not account for the magnitude of the vectors being compared. The cosine distance is complementary to cosine similarity (obtained by subtracting the value of the cosine similarity from 1). This distance is appropriate when the magnitude of the vectors is not important when describing the unstructured data (for example, when dealing with a model that generates an embedding for a text, or when the element of the vectors is scaled by a weight, but the weight itself is irrelevant, as in the case of vector normalization). This distance is often a good choice when you're dealing with the similarity of documents or image comparison. It is also a good option for high-dimensional vector spaces:

$$dist\left(u, v\right) = 1 - \frac{\sum_{i=1}^{n} u_i \times v_i}{\sqrt{\sum_{i=1}^{n} u_i^2} \times \sqrt{\sum_{i=1}^{n} v_i^2}}$$

- **IP, the inner product of vectors**: This distance looks at both the angle between the vectors and their magnitude. Note that this distance is equivalent to cosine similarity if vectors are normalized (vectors are scaled to have a length equal to 1):

$$dist\left(u, v\right) = 1 - \sum_{i=1}^{n} u_i \times v_i$$

  Rather than using the Euclidean or cosine distances, the inner product can be chosen to emphasize the importance of considering both the magnitude and the alignment of the vectors when describing the data. As an example, recommender systems may consider detecting similarities between arrays of user ratings, where both the preferences (a user favors determined movie genres) and the magnitude (the rating itself) matter in the comparison.

Performing similarity search

Now that we have created an index that's suitable to the vector length and type (`FLOAT32` or `FLOAT64`), and we have chosen the right distance concerning the data represented by the vector embeddings (we care about the orientation of the vectors, or we are also interested in their magnitude), we can perform a comparison. Let's consider a simple scenario based on the former example. We have three sentences in our database stored as Hashes, along with their vector embeddings:

- **doc:1** stores *This is a technical document, it describes the SID sound chip of the Commodore 64*
- **doc:2** stores *The Little Prince is a short story by Antoine de Saint-Exupéry, the best known of his literary productions, published on April 6, 1943 in New York*
- **doc:3** stores *Pasta alla carbonara is a characteristic dish of Lazio and more particularly of Rome, prepared with popular ingredients and with an intense flavour.*

We will calculate the corresponding embeddings and store them in the database. Then, we will test this minimalistic database to suggest a recommendation when the user is reading this content:

This post is about 8 bits computers, such as Commodore 64, ZX Spectrum, and other home computers.

The relevant search is performed by this short Python code:

```
q = Query("*=>[KNN 2 @embedding $vec AS score]")
                    .return_field("score")
                    .dialect(2)
res = r.ft("doc_idx").search(q, query_params={"vec": model.
encode(text).astype(np.float32).tobytes()})
print(res)
```

In this command, we specify the following:

- There's no filter in the query. This is expressed by the `*` `symbol.`
- `KNN`, which is set to `2`. This sets the number of closest vectors to the `$vec` vector, which is passed in the query we want to retrieve.
- The `@embedding` attribute, which points to the vector embedding in the Hash data structure.
- The `$vec` placeholder. This will be assigned the vector later, at query execution time.
- The `score` alias. While it is not mandatory to retrieve the score, we want to demonstrate what scores look like and use the alias to sort the results by score (the score is equivalent to the distance). It is also possible to sort the results by the score. This can be specified by using the predetermined `__<vector_field>_score` value. In this example, it would be `__embedded_score`.
- `dialect`, which is set to 2 (alternatively, we can set `DEFAULT_DIALECT` using `FT.CONFIG SET`). The requirement to use VSS is to configure this dialect.

Once executed, this command will return a coherent recommendation – that is, the expected document, `doc:1`. Here, we are interested in vintage computers:

```
Result{2 total, docs: [Document {'id': 'doc:1', 'payload': None,
'score': '0.482430696487'}, Document {'id': 'doc:2', 'payload': None,
'score': '0.99235022068'}]}
```

Let's try another piece of input text:

The Adventures of Pinocchio is a fantasy novel for children written by Carlo Collodi, pseudonym of the journalist and writer Carlo Lorenzini, published for the first time in Florence in February 1883.

The recommendation will correctly return a result in the context of literature for kids:

```
Result{2 total, docs: [Document {'id': 'doc:2', 'payload': None,
'score': '0.76663184166'}, Document {'id': 'doc:3', 'payload': None,
'score': '0.949324011803'}]}
```

You have learned how to execute vector search operations, and now you will explore how to refine your search with additional filters. For example, you may restrict the results only to a particular category of documents. Such operations are possible using hybrid queries.

Performing hybrid queries

Hybrid queries are VSS queries mixed with ordinary search algorithms (numeric, text, tag, and geo). When running hybrid queries with VSS, it is possible to include business logic in the query to enrich the search criteria and simplify the client application code. These conventional filters are pre-filters to the vector search operation and are meant to simplify the similarity search by reducing the computational effort to retrieve the KNN results. An example based on the previous proof of concept can be written by replacing * with the desired query. In this case, this is a filter with the `genre` tag that retrieves the closest documents in the "technical" category:

```
q = Query("@genre:{technical}=>[KNN 2 @embedding $vec AS score]")
                  .return_field("score")
                  .sort_by("score")
                  .dialect(2)
```

Additional options are available to customize the vector search when hybrid queries are adopted, such as the pre-filter query attributes, to deal with a large set of vectors, and additional algorithm-specific attributes, to fine-tune the search algorithm for the best trade-off between accuracy and speed. Refer to the documentation at `https://redis.io/docs/interact/search-and-query/advanced-concepts/vectors/` for more details.

Performing VSS range queries

To understand what range queries are in the context of VSS, an edge case would be searching for two element vectors that model the coordinates of points in a bi-dimensional Cartesian plane. Another example would be geographical locations expressed with longitude and latitude. In these cases, a range query that uses VSS would find closer points in this bi-dimensional space, so within the desired distance from the query vector. Thinking of multi-dimensional spaces, we can imagine the most different use cases. Using VSS range queries, we want to discover relevant content within a predefined similarity range, instead of looking up the KNN similar vectors.

We can customize the example we've considered so far and rewrite the search operation as follows:

```
q = Query("@embedding:[VECTOR_RANGE $radius $vec]=>{$YIELD_DISTANCE_
AS: score}") \
    .sort_by("score") \
    .return_field("score") \
    .dialect(2)

query_params = {
    "radius": 0.8,
    "vec": model.encode(text).astype(np.float32).tobytes()
}
res = r.ft("doc_idx").search(q, query_params)
```

This syntax retrieves all the vectors with a distance less than 0.8 from the embedding representing the description of "Pinocchio." So, once again, we get the expected result, "The Little Prince:"

```
Result{1 total, docs: [Document {'id': 'doc:2', 'payload': None,
'score': '0.76663184166'}]}
```

Recommendations based on visual search

We have seen a basic example of semantic similarity search, but there are other ways of generating recommendations from the item under consideration. One is by looking at its appearance. Using the pre-trained models in the **PyTorch** library, we can extract embeddings from images and associate them with their Hash or JSON representation in the database. The sample Python excerpt we'll be looking at makes use of the **Img2Vec** wrapper library, which can be installed as follows:

```
pip install img2vec_pytorch
```

This script opens a file and produces an embedding of 1,024 numbers using the **densenet** model. Let's prototype a simple application with three items in the database – a glass, a spoon, and a cup:

Figure 6.1 – Training images for VSS

This Python snippet of code will create the index:

```
index_def = IndexDefinition(prefix=["item:"])
schema = (VectorField("embedding", "HNSW", {"TYPE": "FLOAT32", "DIM":
1024, "DISTANCE_METRIC": "COSINE"}))
r.ft("item_idx").create_index(schema, definition=index_def)
```

This code will load the Img2Vec library and the image, and then store the image object together with the embedding. We will repeat this action for all three items:

```
img2vec = Img2Vec(cuda=False, model='densenet')
img = Image.open('spoon.jpg').convert('RGB')
spoon = img2vec.get_vec(img)
r.hset('item:spoon', mapping = {'embedding': spoon.astype(np.float32).
tobytes()})
img = Image.open('glass.jpg').convert('RGB')
glass = img2vec.get_vec(img)
r.hset('item:glass', mapping = {'embedding': glass.astype(np.float32).
tobytes()})
img = Image.open('cup.jpg').convert('RGB')
cup = img2vec.get_vec(img)
r.hset('item:cup', mapping = {'embedding': cup.astype(np.float32).
tobytes()})
```

Now, we can test this prototype with an image sample of a glass:

Figure 6.2 – Test image for VSS

This code sample generates a vector embedding for the test image of a glass and performs VSS. This compares the test embedding with the stored embeddings and returns the closest vector that's associated with the most similar image:

```
img = Image.open('test.jpg').convert('RGB')
test = img2vec.get_vec(img)
q = Query("*=>[KNN 1 @embedding $vec AS score]").return_
field("score").dialect(2)
res = r.ft("item_idx").search(q, query_params={"vec": test.astype(np.
float32).tobytes()})
print(res)
```

The expected result will be a glass:

```
Result{1 total, docs: [Document {'id': 'item:glass', 'payload': None,
'score': '0.235672473907'}]}
```

In these examples, we stored the embeddings in Hashes. However, note that by opting for a JSON document, it is possible to store multiple embeddings in the same document using the multi-value indexing capability, when multiple vectors are returned by a JSONPath expression. You would use this option when an object is described by several embeddings, and you want them all to be searchable by the VSS feature.

Integrating Redis with generative AI

The rise of conversational AI took the world by storm in the early months of 2023 thanks to the advent of powerful **large language models** (**LLMs**) such as ChatGPT. ChatGPT versions 3.5 and 4, which were presented around March 2023, have surprised users with unprecedented quality answers and the ability to solve complex and structured problems, produce ideas, organize and edit texts, and generate source code, all by using natural and conversational questions in the desired language. This has impressed the world in a wide variety of scenarios and use cases. While such a paradigm shift has been driven by the ChatGPT assistant, which is available for free to the public, the possibility of turning the usual applications and services into smart assistants has been accelerated by pay-as-you-go service models by OpenAI and other providers, democratizing the access to such advanced capabilities.

However, training such systems is extremely time-consuming and resource-intensive. For example, training ChatGPT 4 took over a month and dozens of GPUs, which led to freezing the training set in time and cutting off forthcoming knowledge. This intrinsic feature of LLMs poses a constraint on several kinds of applications: working with fresh data is not possible when integrating an LLM technology into a service. Given this background, new techniques are becoming popular to circumvent such limitations. LLMs are being enabled to assist users even in the case of recent updates to the corpus of knowledge and provide answers when the model hasn't been trained on specific content.

Redis, as a high-performance, in-memory data platform, can play a pivotal role in addressing the challenges of LLM-based use cases:

- **Context retrieval for retrieval augmented generation** (**RAG**): Pairing Redis with LLMs enables these models to access external contextual knowledge. This contextual knowledge is crucial for providing accurate and context-aware responses, preventing the model from generating incorrect or "hallucinated" answers. By storing and indexing vectors that model unstructured data, Redis ensures that the LLM can retrieve relevant information quickly and effectively, enhancing its response quality.
- **LLM conversation memory**: Redis allows all conversation history (memories) to be persisted as embeddings in a vector database to improve model quality and personalization. When a conversational agent interacts with the LLM, it can check for relevant memories to aid or personalize the LLM's behavior. This feature enables seamless topic transitions during conversations and reduces misunderstandings.
- **Semantic caching**: LLM completions can be computationally expensive. Redis helps reduce the overall costs of ML-powered applications by caching input prompts and evaluating cache hits based on semantic similarity using VSS. This caching mechanism ensures that frequently requested information is readily available, optimizing response times and resource utilization.

Introducing such architectures and concepts is outside the scope of this basic introduction to vector search, but you will find that Redis and its Redis Stack capabilities are backing many frameworks and services that operate with LLMs. You can refer to the current frameworks and services:

- LangChain
- LlamaIndex
- Azure OpenAI and Microsoft Semantic Kernel
- Amazon Bedrock

Now, let's summarize what we've learned.

Summary

In this chapter, we learned how Redis Stack can store and index vectors to perform similarity searches and recommend similar documents. The power of VSS is that it can be used to find similar matches from incomplete or uncorrelated data. It can also leverage innovative AI/ML models, different search algorithms such as FLAT or HNSW, which focus on the precision or speed of the search, and different distances so that the most suitable option can be configured concerning the entity described by the vector embedding. VSS has been used for **recommendation engines**, but there are additional and relevant use cases that are trending right now, such as **question answering**, where we take advantage of generative models and their ability to take a set of prompts and perform text completion from the results of VSS so that we can provide complete answers out of them.

Data classification is another use case: by pre-training the database with a set of vectors modeling known objects (labeled by an identifier), it is straightforward to guess what object is under analysis using VSS. Redis Stack plays a central role in these innovative scenarios when used as a vector database together with the VSS feature, and shines for online, real-time search operations. Note that there are many open datasets to experiment with VSS in the area of recommendation engines, so you can test several models, distances, and algorithms and achieve the best trade-off between precision and speed.

In *Chapter 7, Redis Stack as a Time Series Database*, you will learn how to store data points in a time series. Through practical examples, you will learn how to complement data points with metadata labels and use multiple labels for filtering, searching, querying, and aggregating the samples using the built-in reducer functions.

7

Redis Stack as a Time Series Database

Redis Stack, as we learned in *Chapter 1, Introducing Redis Stack*, is also capable of handling a particular data type called time-series data points.

Time series are a sequence of data points collected and recorded over time at regular intervals. In a **time series**, the data points are typically measured by intervals ranging from hourly to daily, weekly, monthly, or yearly. Time-series data can represent various types of observations, such as stock prices, weather data, sales figures, or economic indicators, among others.

Time-series analysis is the process of using statistical techniques to study and forecast trends, patterns, and correlations within the data. This can help in understanding the underlying structure and behavior of the data, as well as making predictions about future values.

In this chapter, you will explore various aspects of Redis Stack for time series, including storing and managing data, understanding the use cases it addresses, enriching data points with labels, utilizing built-in functions for filtering, querying, and aggregating data, and visualizing aggregations as charts using **RedisInsight**. In particular, we will cover the following topics:

- Working with time series
- Adding labels to data points
- Aggregation framework
- Compaction rule

To begin, let's discuss the prerequisites for following this chapter.

Technical requirements

To follow along with this chapter, you need the following:

- Redis Stack server version 7.2 or later up and running. As introduced in *Chapter 3, Getting Started with Redis Stack*, the easiest way to set up a fully functional Redis Stack is by using Redis Cloud.
- Additionally, you will need to download and install **RedisInsight** software on your workstation. Please refer to *Chapter 10, RedisInsight – the Data Management GUI*, for instructions on how to download and install **RedisInsight**. By following the guidance provided in this chapter, you will be able to use the software effectively.

Why Redis Stack for Time Series?

Redis Stack, with its high-performance capabilities, can ingest and process large volumes of data efficiently. As you delve deeper into this chapter, you will learn about various built-in features that Redis Stack provides for working with time-series data:

- **High-performance**: Redis Stack for Time Series is designed to provide high-speed data ingestion, querying, and processing, leveraging the in-memory nature of Redis.
- **Data retention policies**: Redis Stack for Time Series allows you to set data retention policies to automatically expire older data points based on time. This helps to manage storage efficiently, especially when dealing with large volumes of time-series data.
- **Downsampling and aggregation**: Redis Stack for Time Series provides built-in support for data aggregation and downsampling, allowing you to reduce the granularity of data and store aggregated values over time. The available aggregation functions include average, minimum, maximum, sum, and count.
- **Time-based querying**: Redis Stack for Time Series offers advanced functionality for efficient data retrieval and querying. It specifically allows users to query and retrieve data points effectively within specified time ranges, utilizing its sophisticated time-based querying feature for enhanced performance.
- **Label-based indexing**: Time-series data benefits from the addition of indexed labels, which significantly enhance data organization and retrieval efficiency. By indexing these labels, querying based on metadata becomes more precise and streamlined, greatly improving the management and access of data according to distinct, user-defined attributes and characteristics.
- **Compression**: Redis Stack for Time Series uses a lossless compression algorithm called Gorilla to store time-series data efficiently, reducing memory usage without compromising data integrity.

Let's begin working with time series.

Working with time series

As mentioned at the beginning of the chapter, a time series is a sequence of data points collected and recorded over time at regular intervals. Redis Stack provides a rich API to manage data points collected into a time series.

To start with an example, you will need to create a time series. The simplest method to accomplish this is by utilizing the `TS.CREATE` command followed by a key, representing the time series name, as shown here:

```
TS.CREATE key
```

However, there are additional parameters that can be employed when creating the time series, as outlined here:

```
TS.CREATE key [RETENTION retentionTime] [ENCODING
[UNCOMPRESSED|COMPRESSED]] [CHUNK_SIZE size] [DUPLICATE_POLICY policy]
[LABELS label value..]
```

Each parameter can be adjusted for performance optimization, reducing memory footprint, or enhancing querying and aggregation capabilities, as detailed here:

- `key`: This is the key that identifies the time series.
- `RETENTION`: This is the retention period, expressed in milliseconds, after which the sample expires. The expiration of samples is solely dependent on the time difference between their timestamp and the timestamps supplied in the subsequent `TS.ADD`, `TS.MADD`, `TS.INCRBY`, and `TS.DECRBY` calls linked to the same key. If it's set to `0`, the default value, the sample never expires.
- `ENCODING`: This option sets the encoding format for series samples and offers two options:
  - `COMPRESSED`, which compresses the samples
  - `UNCOMPRESSED`, which stores the raw samples in memory

  Generally, `COMPRESSED` is recommended as it reduces memory usage and typically results in better performance by reducing memory accesses, resulting in up to a 90% reduction in memory. However, if the timestamps or values are highly irregular and infrequent, `UNCOMPRESSED` may be a better choice.
- `CHUNK_SIZE`: This refers to the initial allocation size in bytes for the data segment of each new chunk in Redis, although be aware that the actual memory consumption may be higher. Modifying the "chunk size" with `TS.ALTER` will not impact existing chunks. However, depending on your use case, consider the following tradeoffs when creating smaller or larger chunks:
  - **Insert performance**: Smaller chunks result in slower inserts (more chunks need to be created)
  - **Query performance**: Queries for a small subset when the chunks are very large are slower, as we need to iterate over the chunk to find the data

    - Larger chunks may take more memory when you have a very large number of keys and very few samples per key, or less memory when you have many samples per key

  The value must be a multiple of 8 and fall within the range of 48 to 1,048,576. If not specified, the default value is determined by the global `CHUNK_SIZE_BYTES` configuration of the database, which is set to 4,096 (equivalent to one memory page) by default.

- `DUPLICATE_POLICY`: There are several options available for handling the insertion (using `TS.ADD` and `TS.MADD`) of multiple samples with identical timestamps, and the policy can be chosen from among the following:

    - `BLOCK`: Disregard the new value and return an error.
    - `FIRST`: Ignore the new value.
    - `LAST`: Replace the existing value with the new one.
    - `MIN`: Update the value only if the new one is lower than the current value.
    - `MAX`: Update the value only if the new one is higher than the current value.
    - `SUM`: If a previous sample exists, add the new sample to it, resulting in an updated value equal to the sum of the previous and new values. If no previous sample exists, set the updated value to the new value.

  If not specified, the policy defaults to the global `DUPLICATE_POLICY` configuration of the database, which is set to `BLOCK` by default.

- `LABELS`: This refers to a collection of label-value pairs that signify the metadata labels associated with a key, and function as a secondary index.

  Commands such as `TS.MGET`, `TS.MRANGE`, and `TS.MREVRANGE` work with multiple time series based on their respective labels. The `TS.QUERYINDEX` command retrieves all time-series keys that match a specific filter, which is determined by their labels.

With a fundamental understanding of how time series operate, let's create one to monitor the visitor count for the `https://www.mortensi.com/` website, using **RedisInsight** or `redis-cli`, as demonstrated here:

```
TS.CREATE mortensi.com
```

The previous command generates a time series identified by `mortensi.com`. To view its details, use the `TS.INFO` command followed by the key, as shown here:

```
TS.INFO mortensi.com
1) "totalSamples"
2) "0"
3) "memoryUsage"
4) "4184"
```

```
5) "firstTimestamp"
6) "0"
7) "lastTimestamp"
8) "0"
9) "retentionTime"
10) "0"
```

The information mentioned in the previous code snippet relates to the cardinality of samples within the time series, including such details as the timestamps of the first and last inserted sample and the retention time upon which the sample is based:

```
11) "chunkCount"
12) "1"
13) "chunkSize"
14) "4096"
15) "chunkType"
16) "compressed"
17) "duplicatePolicy"
18) "null"
19) "labels"
20) (empty list or set)
21) "sourceKey"
22) "null"
23) "rules"
24) (empty list or set)
```

The final set of information relates to the number of checks available, the utilized size, and the specific type, which, in this context, is denoted as `"compressed"`. Furthermore, the data reveals details concerning the duplication policy, attached labels, source key, and a forthcoming exploration into the compaction rule, which will be delved into later in this chapter.

Currently, our time series is empty, but we can observe its default settings.

To track users visiting the `mortensi.com` website, we need to add a data point that includes the visit's date and time and keeps a count of the visits. In this scenario, our data point will function as a counter.

Let's proceed by adding our initial data point to the `mortensi.com` time series, as demonstrated here:

```
TS.ADD mortensi.com * 1
```

The asterisk symbol (`*`) means that the timestamp is provided by the server clock at the time of insertion.

For this specific use case (tracking the number of visitors to a site), the approach mentioned above may not be optimal, as it would require maintaining a counter on the client side, incrementing it, and updating the time series with the new value.

Thankfully, Redis Stack for Time Series offers a built-in `TS.INCRBY` command that was designed precisely for such scenarios, by enabling atomic increments.

Let's experiment by executing the `TS.INCRBY` command a few times using **redis-cli** or directly within RedisInsight:

```
> TS.INCRBY mortensi.com 1
(integer) 1682433895397
> TS.INCRBY mortensi.com 1
(integer) 1682433896518
> TS.INCRBY mortensi.com 1
(integer) 1682433897428
> TS.INCRBY mortensi.com 1
(integer) 1682433898284
```

As observed, each time a data point is entered, the server clock insertion timestamp is returned. Redis Stack for Time Series also includes `TS.DECRBY`, which is an atomic command for decrementing a value. The value specified as a parameter in both commands represents the increment or decrement to be applied to the current value.

To obtain the total number of visitors, you need to execute the `TS.GET` command followed by the time-series key:

```
> TS.GET mortensi.com
1) "1682433898284"
2) "5"
```

The command will provide the total number of visitors along with the timestamp of the most recent insertion.

Statistics become more fascinating as the time intervals and data volumes increase, particularly when visualized as charts. RedisInsight makes it possible to display such time series data in graphical format.

First, we need to generate a larger set of data points. To do this, remove the existing time series and create a new one using a Python script that populates daily visitor data for the `mortensi.com` website from January 1st, 2023, to April 30th, 2023.

The `timeseries-mortensi.py` file can be retrieved in the following repository: `https://github.com/PacktPublishing/Redis-Stack-for-Application-Modernization`. Download the file, modify the settings to connect to your Redis Stack server, and execute the script using the following command:

```
python timeseries-mortensi.py
```

Upon executing the script, a time series with the key `mortensi.com` is generated, containing data points from January 1st, 2023, to April 30th, 2023, with values ranging between 1 and 1000. RedisInsight offers the ability to visualize query results as charts, which is particularly useful for time series data.

Next, launch the RedisInsight application, navigate to the **Workbench** section, and enter the following command:

```
TS.RANGE mortensi.com - +
```

Proceed to run the command by clicking on the green play button.

After execution, the query results will be displayed as a chart, as shown here:

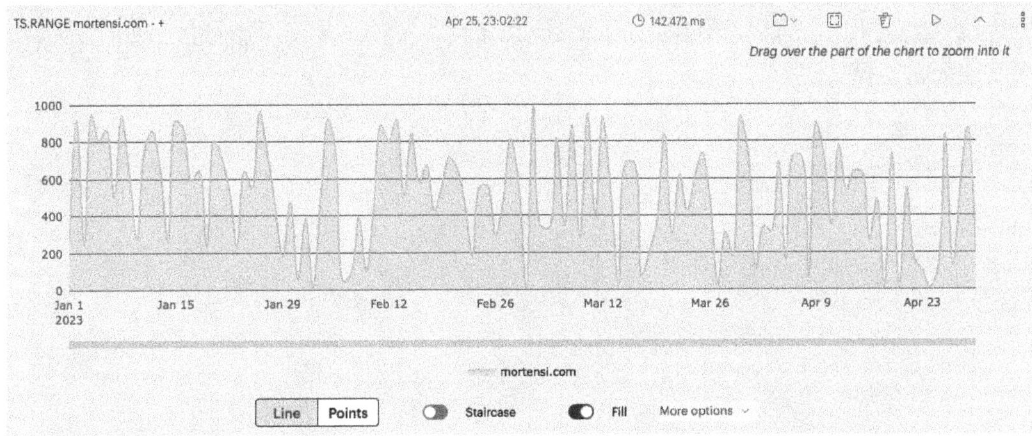

Figure 7.1 – RedisInsight representing time-series data points as chart

`TS.RANGE` retrieves a range of data points from a specific time-series key based on the provided timestamp range. The command returns an array of data points, where each data point consists of a timestamp and its corresponding value.

Similar charts can be generated for various aggregation intervals, such as weekly, bi-weekly, or monthly, depending on the data point timestamp precision and specific use case. It would be intriguing to compare the statistics of the `mortensi.com` site with another outstanding site, `foogaro.com`.

Up to now, we have covered the process of creating a time series and adding data points to it. While the primary objective of a time series is to collect data points, metadata plays a fundamental role in facilitating the searching, querying, and aggregation of these data points for analytical purposes. In the following section, you will delve into the understanding and application of metadata to achieve these tasks effectively.

Adding labels to data points

Labels are metadata attached to time series data points to provide additional context or information about the data. They are key-value pairs that help group, query, filter, or aggregate data. This makes it easier to manage and analyze large volumes of time-series data. For example, you might use labels to indicate the data source, measurement units, or the device or location from which the data was collected. By using labels, you can perform more granular and focused queries on your time-series data, making it easier to understand trends, relationships, and patterns.

Let's apply a few labels to the `mortensi.com` site. Since its time series already exists, we can add labels by modifying the current time series as follows:

```
TS.ALTER mortensi.com LABELS dev python database redis
```

After applying the labels, the `TS.INFO` command for the `mortensi.com` time series will display them as shown here:

```
TS.INFO mortensi.com
1) "totalSamples"
2) "120"
3) "memoryUsage"
4) "4242"
5) "firstTimestamp"
6) "1672527600000"
7) "lastTimestamp"
8) "1682805600000"
9) "retentionTime"
10) "0"
```

As discussed earlier, the initial set of information is concerned with the quantity of data points and their corresponding timestamps. In the following code section, we will explore further details specifically related to the labels. Labels are metadata in the form of key-value pairs, assigned to data points for the purposes of categorization and filtering. They may consist of either string or numeric values and are typically incorporated into a timeseries during its creation, as shown in the following code:

```
11) "chunkCount"
12) "1"
13) "chunkSize"
14) "4096"
15) "chunkType"
16) "compressed"
17) "duplicatePolicy"
18) "null"
19) "labels"
20) 1) 1) "dev"
       2) "python"
    2) 1) "database"
       2) "redis"
21) "sourceKey"
22) "null"
```

```
23) "rules"
24) (empty list or set)
```

Let's now download another Python script named `timeseries-foogaro.py`, which can be retrieved from the usual repository.

Download the file, modify the settings to connect to your Redis Stack server, and execute it using the following command:

```
python timeseries-foogaro.py
```

Upon executing the script, a time series with a key of `foogaro.com` is generated, containing data points from January 1st, 2023, to April 30th, 2023, with values ranging between 1 and 1,000.

It's now time to compare those two sites and see who has more visitors. Instead of using the `TS.RANGE` command, the `TS.MRANGE` command will be used as it retrieves a range of data points from multiple time series keys, based on the provided timestamp range and filters. This command is useful when you want to query data across multiple time series with similar characteristics or labels, which is exactly our next use case.

Again, launch the RedisInsight application, navigate to the **Workbench** section, and enter the following command:

```
TS.MRANGE - + FILTER database='redis'
```

After execution, the query results will be displayed as a chart, as depicted here:

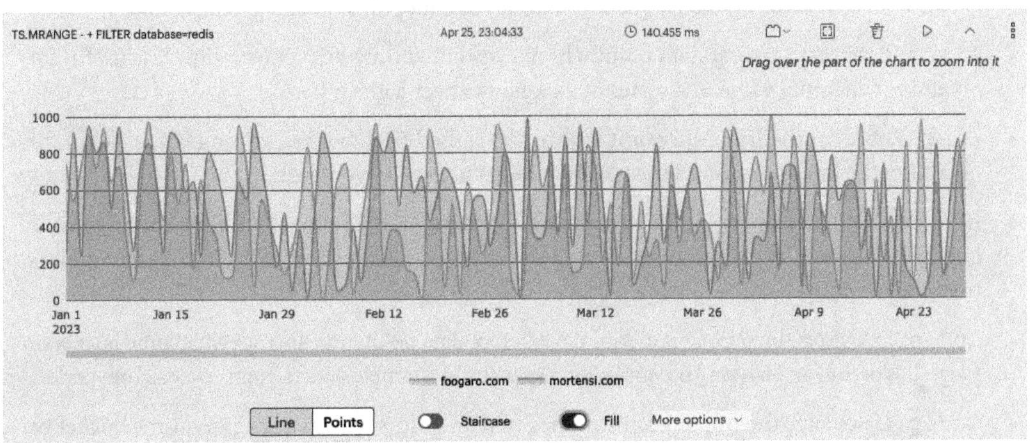

Figure 6.2 – RedisInsight example showing two time series

As observed, labels can serve as markers, enabling the comparison of multiple time series simultaneously to discern variations. However, this is not the sole purpose of labels. In the following section, we will explore how labels can be employed in conjunction with built-in aggregation functions to enhance the analytical capabilities further.

Aggregation framework

The Redis Stack for Time Series aggregation framework provides functions that enable users to perform operations such as calculating the average, sum, minimum, maximum, count, or standard deviation of data points, within a specific time bucket or range. By using these functions, you can derive insights, detect trends, and analyze patterns in your time-series data more effectively.

The following is a list of aggregation functions:

- `avg`: Calculates the average (mean) value of data points within a specified time bucket or range. It is useful for analyzing and summarizing time-series data to understand trends and patterns over time.
- `sum`: Calculates the total (sum) of data points within a specified time bucket or range. It is useful for aggregating time-series data to understand the cumulative effect or total value of the data points over time.
- `min`: Calculates the minimum value of data points within a specified time bucket or range. It is useful for determining the lowest value in a series of data points over a given period.
- `max`: Calculates the maximum value of data points within a specified time bucket or range. It is useful for determining the highest value in a series of data points over a given period.
- `range`: Calculates the difference between the maximum value and minimum value of data points within a specified time bucket or range.
- `count`: Calculates the total number of data points within a specified time bucket or range. It is useful for determining the frequency or count of data points over a given period.
- `first`: Retrieves the first data point within a specified time bucket or range. It is useful for obtaining the initial value of a series of data points over a given period.
- `last`: Retrieves the last data point within a specified time bucket or range. It is useful for obtaining the final value of a series of data points over a given period.
- `std.p`: Calculates the population standard deviation of data points within a specified time bucket or range. It is useful for analyzing the spread or dispersion of a series of data points over a given period.
- `std.s`: Calculates the sample standard deviation of data points within a specified time bucket or range. It is useful for analyzing the spread or dispersion of a sample of data points over a given period.
- `var.p`: Calculates the population variance of data points within a specified time bucket or range. It is useful for analyzing the level of variability or dispersion in a series of data points over a given period.
- `var.s`: Calculates the sample variance of data points within a specified time bucket or range. It is useful for analyzing the level of variability or dispersion in a sample of data points over a given period.

- `twa`: Calculates the time-weighted average of data points within a specified time bucket or range. It is useful for analyzing the average value of a time-series data set, considering the duration and distribution of the data points over time.

Getting back to our two websites, `mortensi.com` and `foogaro.com`, you may want to aggregate the data points to make meaningful comparisons. In this case, you can use the built-in function to add up the values of the data points for each website over a given time period.

To use the `sum` function in RedisInsight, you can execute a query using the `TS.MRANGE` command, specifying the time range and the interval of aggregation. The result will be the sum of the data points for each time bucket within the specified time range.

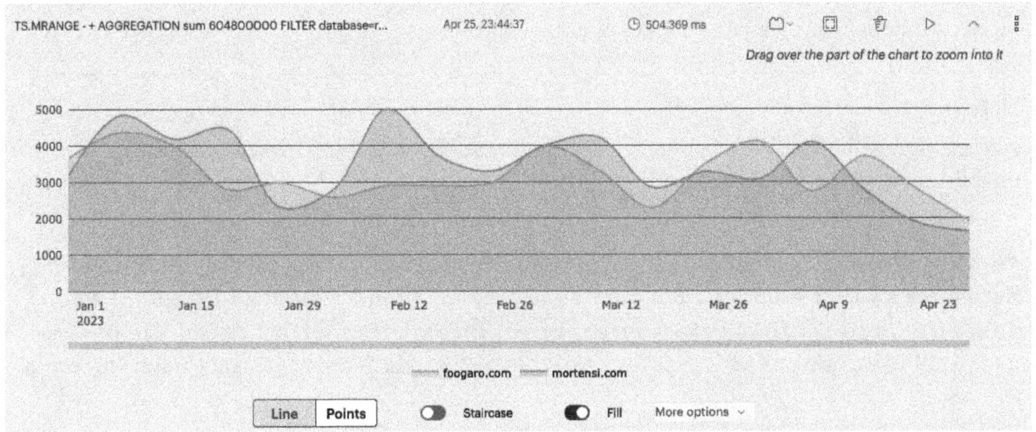

Figure 6.3 – RedisInsight using the aggregation framework

Up to this point, we have explored the process of creating time series, adding data points, and utilizing labels to enhance time series analysis, leveraging aggregation functions for relevant insights. However, it is important to be mindful of the footprint generated by this data, considering both memory consumption and performance implications during aggregation operations. To address this, Redis Stack for Time Series offers a set of rules known as the "compaction rule," which enables dataset reduction. In the upcoming section, we will delve into the details of the compaction rule and its application.

Compaction rules for Time Series

In Redis Stack for Time Series, a compaction rule is a mechanism used to downsample data points and reduce data storage requirements over time. As time-series data grows and accumulates, it often becomes less important to store high-resolution data for older timestamps. Compaction rules help to maintain a balance between data storage and resolution requirements.

A compaction rule is a user-defined policy that dictates how the data points should be aggregated over a given time period (e.g., every minute, hour, or day) and retained in a downsampled series. The rule can specify the aggregation method, such as average, minimum, maximum, sum, or count, among the others described in the *Aggregation framework* section of this chapter.

For example, you can set up a compaction rule to downsample data every 5 minutes using the average aggregation function. This rule would create a new time series key where each data point represents the average value of the original data points within a 5-minute interval. By applying compaction rules, you can store long-term historical data efficiently while retaining the desired level of granularity.

To create a compaction rule in Redis Stack for Time Series, use the `TS.CREATERULE` command to define the compaction rule, specifying the source time-series key, the destination time-series key, the aggregation function, and the time bucket interval.

> **Note**
>
> Aggregation will only be applied to the data points added to the source series following the establishment of the compaction rule.

Let's extend our example of tracking the visitors for the `mortensi.com` website, by relying on our GitHub repository at the following URL: `https://github.com/PacktPublishing/Redis-Stack-for-Application-Modernization`. The Python script that extends our previous example is called `timeseries-mortensi-weekly.py`, which implements the following steps:

1. Deletes the `mortensi.com` time series key.
2. Creates a new `mortensi.com` time series key.
3. Creates a `new mortensi.com:weekly` time series key.
4. Creates a new compaction rule that retains only the sum of the weekly visitors.
5. Loads the new `mortensi.com` time series with randomly generated new data points.

While the `mortensi.com` time series is being populated with data points, the compaction rule comes into play by automatically processing these data points. As the rule is applied, it aggregates the data according to the specified method and time bucket. In this case, the data is compacted on a weekly basis. Once the data is processed, it is then added to the `mortensi.com:weekly` time series. This process ensures that the weekly time series remains up to date with the compacted data, providing a more manageable and efficient view of the original dataset.

Upon completion, both time series will have 120 data points and 17 data points, respectively. Let's have a look at the browsing section of RedisInsight, as depicted here:

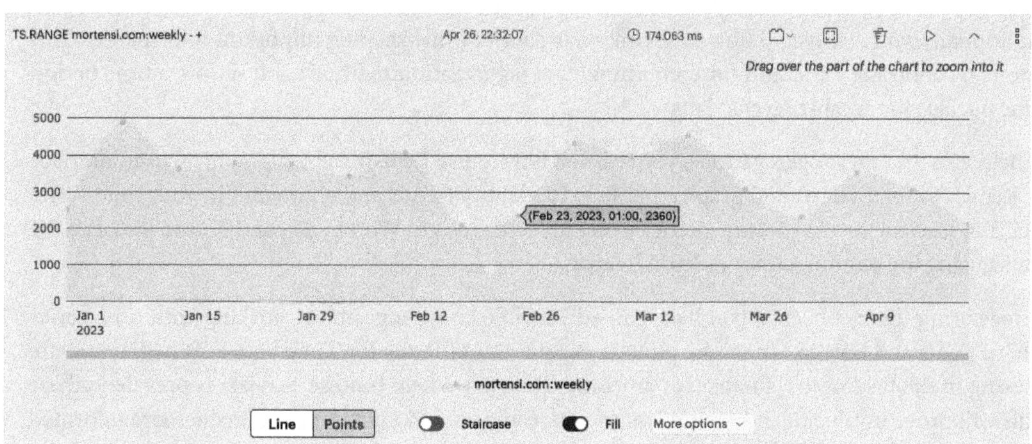

Figure 6.4 – RedisInsight showing a time series provided by the compaction rule

Redis Stack for Time Series provides a wide range of capabilities that can be leveraged to build expressive frontends for real-time insights into time-series data. Plotting utilities available in various programming languages such as Python, R, and JavaScript can be utilized to create visually appealing charts and graphs that help to identify trends, patterns, and anomalies in time-series data.

In addition to these plotting utilities, various statistical functions such as mean, sum, min, max, and standard deviation can be employed to analyze and aggregate time-series data points within a given time range or time bucket. By visualizing these aggregated data points using the plotting utilities, it becomes easier to identify key insights and optimize metrics for better performance.

These expressive frontends can be used in a variety of industries and use cases, including monitoring system performance, analyzing user behavior, and tracking business metrics. By identifying trends, anomalies, and patterns in the data, businesses can quickly identify issues or opportunities for optimization, make data-driven decisions, and evaluate the success of various strategies or campaigns.

Overall, the ability to build expressive frontends for time-series data is a powerful tool that can be used to gain valuable insights into any time-series dataset, and Redis Stack for Time Series can transform time-series data into actionable insights that drive business success.

Summary

In this chapter, you learned about the basics of working with time-series data in Redis. You learned how to insert data points into Redis Stack for Time Series and how to add labels to those data points to make them more easily identifiable and searchable.

You also learned about the aggregation framework in Redis for Time Series, which allows you to analyze and aggregate data points within a specified time range or time bucket using various statistical functions such as mean, sum, min, max, and standard deviation. By utilizing the aggregation framework, you can gain deeper insights into your time-series data and identify trends, patterns, and anomalies more easily.

Additionally, you discovered how to shrink your dataset while keeping important information. This is done by choosing a method for combining data (aggregation method) and setting a time period (time bucket) for organizing the data.

To help visualize these aggregations, you learned how to use RedisInsight, a graphical user interface for Redis, to create charts and graphs that help to identify trends and anomalies in your time-series data. You learned how to execute queries using the RedisInsight Workbench and how to visualize the results using the plotting utility in RedisInsight.

By mastering these concepts, you have gained valuable knowledge about working with time-series data in Redis and how to utilize the built-in capabilities of Redis for Time Series. Whether you are working in the field of IoT, finance, or any other industry where time-series data is prevalent, these skills will prove invaluable in helping you to better understand your data and make more informed decisions based on that data.

In *Chapter 8, Understanding Probabilistic Data Structures*, you will learn the fundamentals of the counting algorithms implemented in the form of probabilistic data structures. These constitute a category of data structures that offer highly accurate approximations of answers, achieved within a significantly reduced time frame and minimal memory consumption.

8
Understanding Probabilistic Data Structures

The probabilistic data structures of Redis Stack are packed into a set of capabilities also known as Bloom filters. Such structures owe their name to Burton Howard Bloom, a computer scientist who introduced the concept of a probabilistic data structure in 1970 to resolve the problem of verifying whether an item belongs to a set. By using hash data representations, it is possible to achieve a sufficient approximation to the problem under analysis, allowing false positives (the item may belong to the set), but without false negatives (the item definitely does not belong to the set).

The Bloom filter has since become a widely used data structure in computer science. It is used in various applications, such as spell-checking, network routing, content filtering, and DNA sequence analysis.

Probabilistic data structures process large volumes of data in real time with minimal memory requirements. This chapter covers several types of probabilistic data structures and their applications, such as detecting fraud in credit card transactions, analyzing network traffic patterns, and monitoring user behavior on a website. Throughout this chapter, you will find that we sometimes refer to these structures as **sketches**. Probabilistic data structures are called sketches as they provide an approximate view of data from the desired perspective, much like a sketch is a simplified representation of a real object. Probabilistic data structures can enable fast, scalable, and low-memory data processing for real-time analytics. We will cover the following data structures:

- HyperLogLog
- Bloom filter
- Cuckoo filter
- Count-Min sketch
- Top-K
- t-digest

Technical requirements

To follow along with the examples in this chapter, you will need to install Redis Stack Server 7.2 or later in your development environment. Alternatively, you can create a free Redis Cloud subscription to get a free plan and use a managed Redis Stack database.

HyperLogLog

HyperLogLog was the first probabilistic data structure available in Redis, theorized and published in 2003 by Marianne Durand and Philippe Flajolet. HyperLogLog is an efficient solution to count the number of unique occurrences in a set, which, in practice, is the cardinality of the set. This is especially useful when accuracy is not required: the count is probabilistic but presents a very low error. HyperLogLog does not store any information as the items that are added pass through a hashing function, so it is not possible to remove elements once they are counted.

HyperLogLog is the simplest probabilistic data structure and using it is as easy as adding elements to it using the `PFADD` command:

```
PFADD mortensi.com:1hnsn9n6kb:012023 IGaJ9c5KqYHFUEogCQWc
PFADD mortensi.com:1hnsn9n6kb:012023 XUq9br38-SYFOVpfN-vq
PFADD mortensi.com:1sneb4qq3t:012023 bmGteHMoGpAKbtk4X-9Y
PFADD mortensi.com:1sneb4qq3t:022023 IGaJ9c5KqYHFUEogCQWc
```

Using the former commands, we can track the monthly unique visitors of individual web pages of the `https://www.mortensi.com` website, so we have chosen a key name that is descriptive of the website, the page identifier, and the month of the year. The unique visitor is anonymously identified by, for example, the session identifier (`IGaJ9c5KqYHFUEogCQWc`, for example).

We can count the visited pages with the `PFCOUNT` command:

```
PFCOUNT mortensi.com:1hnsn9n6kb:012023
(integer) 2
PFCOUNT mortensi.com:1sneb4qq3t:012023
(integer) 1
PFCOUNT mortensi.com:1sneb4qq3t:022023
(integer) 1
```

Calculating the number of unique visitors of a certain page across the year is as easy as using the `PFMERGE` command, which combines two or more HyperLogLogs into one:

```
PFMERGE mortensi.com:1sneb4qq3t:2023 mortensi.com:1sneb4qq3t:012023
mortensi.com:1sneb4qq3t:022023
OK
PFCOUNT mortensi.com:1sneb4qq3t:2023
(integer) 2
```

Now that we know how to count unique items in a set using up to 12 KB of memory and with good approximation (with a standard error of 0.81%), let's discover how to verify whether an item belongs to a set. For that, we will use the Bloom filter.

Bloom filter

A **Bloom filter** is one of the probabilistic data structures supported by Redis Stack and is used to test whether an item is a member of a set. It is crucial as a data deduplication solution – that is, for removing duplicated data from a set. It is a memory-efficient and fast data structure that uses a bit array and a set of hash functions to determine whether an item is in the set or not. Testing for membership to the filter can return "possibly in the set" or "definitely not in the set," which means that false positives are possible, but false negatives are not. Imprecisions (or approximations) are around the corner in every aspect of life, and digital computing does not make any difference. Think of the lossy compression algorithms for images (JPEG) or audio files (MP3): we can still enjoy media files and not even realize there is a loss of quality. A Bloom filter simplifies the management and speed of solutions that require the existence or membership verification.

The verification is accurate when it discards an item has not been added to the filter yet, so false negatives are not possible. When accuracy is mandatory in positive cases, the user can double-check the source of data to discard false positives. The adoption of the filter helps because in this case, it limits access to the data source and reduces the time to produce an accurate answer. In addition, the filter suits those datasets that contain sensitive information because the original data is not saved.

Using the Bloom filter is straightforward. Imagine a scenario where a new user will subscribe to your portal by creating an account. The user will provide an email and a username, and you would like to verify whether the username is already being used by some other account. You have created and provisioned the filter for previous accounts using the `BF.ADD` command (or `BF.MADD` to add more items to the filter at once):

```
BF.ADD service:username mortensi
BF.ADD service:username lfoogaro
BF.ADD service:username bmay
BF.ADD service:username jdeacon
```

The existence of an item in the filter can be verified using the `BF.EXISTS` command:

```
BF.EXISTS service:username mortensi
(integer) 1
BF.EXISTS service:username fmercury
(integer) 0
```

If the username is available, the user can proceed and create the account, and the application server can add the username to the filter so that subsequent checks will find that this username has been taken. You can also check multiple elements at once:

```
BF.MEXISTS service:username mortensi fmercury
1) (integer) 1
2) (integer) 0
```

You can check the cardinality of a filter (that is, the number of users) with `BF.CARD`:

```
BF.CARD service:username
(integer) 4
```

Note that the probability of collisions can be reduced by specifying the desired error ratio (refer to the `BF.RESERVE` command). However, reducing the error increases the memory requirements and computation time as larger hashes are required.

Some other scenarios where Bloom filters represent an efficient solution are as follows:

- **Spam filtering**: Maintaining a list of malicious URLs or IPs to prevent spam or fraud.
- **Fraud detection**: Checking whether a credit card number belongs to a list of blocked or suspicious credit cards (stolen or cloned). This is particularly useful because such a filter could also be shared between financial institutions without the risk of storing the number in clear text.
- **Suspicious activity**: Verifying user activity (geographical location, date and time of activity, category of a product being purchased, and so on) and preventing authentication or allowing certain operations until authentication or verification is completed using a stronger method.
- **Ad placement and recommendations**: Using the Bloom filter, you can answer questions such as "Has the user seen this ad?" and then act accordingly.
- **Spell-checking**: If a word does not belong to a filter, it is misspelled.

Regarding the fraud detection use case, Bloom filters offer a streamlined and effective solution. For instance, we can employ Bloom filters to add verified user locations and subsequently verify whether a login attempt originates from a known location. This approach ensures that the user has not authenticated from a new or suspicious location. Additionally, Bloom filters simplify the process of monitoring user behavior, allowing us to track their activities during specific time intervals.

Modern fraud detection systems employ algorithms that calculate **real-time transaction risk scoring**. These systems analyze various factors such as transaction information, user profiles, behavioral biometrics, geolocation, IP/device data, and account details using predictive ML models. Redis is suitable for serving such models when used as an online feature store. However, for smaller solutions, you can swiftly and effectively utilize Bloom filters to check whether a specific transaction is part of a collection of recognized fraudulent patterns.

The Bloom filter offers a practical solution to numerous scenarios where complex problems can be simplified with a reliable approximation. Similarly, Cuckoo filters exhibit high efficiency in these particular use cases, albeit with some subtle distinctions. Let's delve into their details.

Cuckoo filters

Cuckoo filters are an evolution of Bloom filters that were published in 2014 and address the limitations of Bloom filters, especially around collision handling. This filter inherits its name from the cuckoo bird, famous for laying its eggs in the nests of other bird species and leaving them to be raised by the host bird. In doing so, the cuckoo pushes the other eggs or chicks out of the nest. This behavior describes the implementation of Cuckoo filters. Differently from Bloom filters, Cuckoo filters use a fingerprint-based technique that allows for the fast and efficient handling of collisions and reduces the rate of false positives while maintaining the same space requirements as Bloom filters.

Instead of storing the hashed version of an item as Bloom filters do, Cuckoo filters use multiple locations, or buckets, to store the fingerprint representation of the item. When a new item is added to the filter and a collision occurs at a candidate bucket, the existing item is moved to another candidate bucket. If that bucket is also occupied, the filter keeps searching until a bucket without the fingerprint is found or the filter reaches the maximum number of attempts to kick out existing items. This approach reduces the rate of false positives while maintaining the same space requirements as Bloom filters.

The items are stored through their fingerprint, after which it is possible to locate them. It's also possible to delete them. Let's review the usage of this filter.

We can use the `CF.ADD` command to add elements to the filter:

```
CF.ADD service:username mortensi
CF.ADD service:username lfoogaro
CF.ADD service:username bmay
CF.ADD service:username jdeacon
```

Note that thanks to the multi-bucket fingerprint-based implementation, we can also insert the same item multiple times and count them. If the items are repeated and you want to account for repetitions, `CF.COUNT` returns the number of times the item *may* be in the filter:

```
CF.ADD service:username mortensi
(integer) 1
CF.COUNT service:username mortensi
(integer) 2
```

`CF.DEL` removes items from the filter:

```
CF.DEL service:username mortensi
(integer) 1
CF.COUNT service:username mortensi
(integer) 1
```

Overall, Cuckoo filters provide an alternative to Bloom filters with similar error rates. Use cases where the Cuckoo filter is a valid solution are the same as those listed for the Bloom filter, with the difference that Cuckoo filters also allow elements to be deleted. Now, let's continue our journey into probabilistic data structures by introducing the Count-Min sketch structure, which supercharges HyperLogLog with the frequencies of the different items being counted.

Count-Min sketch

The **Count-Min sketch** probabilistic data structure, like HyperLogLog, counts the items that have been added, with the difference that the Count-Min sketch counts the number of times specific items have been added – that is, their frequency.

When using a Count-Min sketch data structure, any frequency counts below a predetermined threshold (established by the error rate) should be disregarded. The Count-Min sketch serves as a valuable tool for counting element frequencies in a data stream, especially when dealing with higher counts. Nevertheless, very low counts are often perceived as noise and are typically discarded in this context. To start using the data structure, we have the option to initialize it either based on the probabilities to be maintained or on the desired dimensions. It is important to note that the dimensions of the Count-Min sketch play a significant role because to merge two Count-Min sketches, they must have identical dimensions.

We can initialize it using the `CMS.INITBYDIM` command while passing the name, the width, and the depth and indicating the number of counters in the structure and the depth:

```
CMS.INITBYDIM key width depth
```

To understand the definition, consider that the Count-Min sketch is implemented as several arrays of counters – that is, a two-dimensional array with `width` as the number of counters and `depth` as the number of hash functions used. The larger the depth, the smaller the probability of an element that has a count below the threshold colliding with elements that have a count above the threshold, resulting in more accuracy but also more overhead to maintain and update the data structure.

We won't dig into the theory of the Count-Min sketch probabilistic data structure as the algorithm is in the public domain and detailed information can be found on multiple websites. Instead, let's look at an example of counting the items sold in a day in a grocery store. Assuming we would like to count 50 items and we have chosen a depth of 5, we would create the structure as follows:

```
CMS.INITBYDIM grocery:25042023 50 5
```

Now, we can use the Count-Min sketch to introduce the items sold in a day:

```
CMS.INCRBY grocery:25042023 orange 1
CMS.INCRBY grocery:25042023 orange 5
CMS.INCRBY grocery:25042023 lemon 1
CMS.INCRBY grocery:25042023 apple 3
```

To test the frequencies, we can query the data structure using the `CMS.QUERY` command:

```
CMS.QUERY grocery:25042023 orange
1) (integer) 6
CMS.QUERY grocery:25042023 apple
1) (integer) 3
```

This probabilistic data structure, invented by Cormode and Muthukrishnan in 2003, answers the question "How many times did this value appear in the data stream?" so the use cases where it is helpful to employ such a data structure are those where we must count, out of a high volume of data, occurrences of an item. The following data structure is not only relevant for counting events but also optimized to sort them by frequency: let's introduce the Top-K structure.

Top-K

The **Top-K** data structure is used to keep track of items with the highest rank, such as the top players in a leaderboard. The ranking, or score, is often based on the count of how many times an item appears in the data source (such as a stream), making the data structure ideal for identifying elements with the highest frequency. Among the most common use cases of this data structure are leaderboards, trending entities in a system, detecting network anomalies, and DDoS attacks. Here, the Top-K data structure can help answer questions such as "Which top addresses or IPs have the highest surge in the flow of requests?"

Let's dive into an example of using the Top-K data structure and insert a few items into it. First, we must initialize it using the following command:

```
TOPK.RESERVE key topk [width depth decay]
```

In addition to `key`, which specifies the Top-K name, `topk` indicates the number of top items we want to keep track of, and `width` indicates the number of counters. As seen with other data structures, it is possible to configure how sensitive the data structure is to collisions by choosing `depth` and `decay`.

Similar to Cuckoo filters, Top-K uses buckets to store fingerprints and counters. This method employs a two-dimensional array characterized by its width and depth:

- `width` represents the number of buckets within each array
- `depth` signifies the number of arrays or hash functions employed

Collisions can be avoided using the HeavyKeeper algorithm, which relies on exponential decay. When a hash collision occurs (two elements compete for the same bucket), the algorithm initiates a reduction in the counter of the current occupant of the bucket. However, this reduction doesn't occur with every collision. Instead, the probability of a decrease is determined by an exponential function of the counter's current value.

This means that the more substantial the counter value (indicative of significant flows, often referred to as "elephant flows"), the greater the likelihood that the element remains in the bucket despite collisions. Conversely, for smaller counter values (representative of less significant flows, often termed "mouse flows"), there is a higher probability of the element being displaced from the bucket during collisions. This approach allows the algorithm to dynamically adapt, prioritizing the retention of elements with higher counts while efficiently managing collisions and maintaining the integrity of the Top-K approximation.

Typically, a good initial configuration involves setting the following:

- `width` to `topk*log(topk)`
- `depth` to `log(topk)` or a minimum of `5`
- The `decay` rate to `0.9`

It's advisable to conduct tests to refine these parameters based on the characteristics of your data.

Let's proceed with creating and using Top-K to store some players' scores:

```
TOPK.RESERVE players 10
TOPK.INCRBY players "john" 5
TOPK.INCRBY players "tod" 10
TOPK.INCRBY players "john" 3
TOPK.INCRBY players "bill" 5
```

In this example, we initialized the Top-K data structure named `players` with a capacity of 10 elements. Then, we inserted some players and a score. Now, we can retrieve the top-k players from the data structure using the following command:

```
TOPK.LIST players WITHCOUNT
1) tod
2) (integer) 10
3) john
4) (integer) 8
5) bill
6) (integer) 5
```

This command will return a list of the *k most* frequent elements stored in the Top-K data structure, along with their counts.

Before we look at the next probabilistic data structure, let's conclude this introduction with a summary of the principal use cases for Top-K:

- **Network analysis/DDoS prevention**: Locating the Top-K highest rates in network analysis is crucial. Sudden fluctuations in certain packets may indicate increased traffic going into or coming out of specific nodes, which can provide insights for mitigating DDoS threats, managing bandwidth usage, improving system efficiency, and so on.
- **Leaderboards**: Rankings are usually stored as sorted sets. However, when there are vast amounts of users, memory consumption can be reduced by utilizing Top-K. It helps save space without compromising functionality.
- **Trending hashtags (or other resources, such as pages, videos, and so on)**: Top-K manages trending hashtags on social media platforms (or any kind of content in the related hosting platform).

Now, let's conclude our walk-through of probabilistic data structures with the last and most recent data structure: t-digest.

t-digest

t-digest is a data structure for estimating quantiles from a data stream or a large dataset using a compact sketch.

The t-digest data structure enables the resolution of various inquiries, such as "What proportion of values in the data stream is less than a specific value?" and "How many values in the data stream are below a given threshold?" To better understand t-digest, we need to define quantiles and percentiles.

A **quantile** is a value or cut point that divides a dataset into *intervals* with equal proportions or frequencies of observations. As an example, the median is an example of a quantile as it divides the dataset in half (that is, 50% of observations below and 50% above).

A **percentile** represents a specific position within a dataset, where a certain percentage of the data falls below that position. For example, if a value is at the 75th percentile of a dataset, it means that 75% of the data falls below that value. Percentiles are used to understand the distribution of data and to compare observations to others within the same dataset.

In short, quantiles are like percentiles, but instead of dividing a dataset into 100 equal parts, they divide it into a specified number of intervals, each with an approximately equal number of observations.

Having defined these concepts, let's dig into t-digest using the following commands, where we will add some data to t-digest using the `TDIGEST.CREATE` command:

```
TDIGEST.CREATE temperatures
TDIGEST.ADD temperatures 20
TDIGEST.ADD temperatures 43
TDIGEST.ADD temperatures 38
```

```
TDIGEST.ADD temperatures 24
TDIGEST.ADD temperatures 41
```

In this example, we have created a digest named `temperatures` and added some data points representing temperatures to the digest using the `TDIGEST.ADD` command.

Using the `TDIGEST.QUANTILE` command, we can calculate an estimate for a specific quantile of the data:

```
TDIGEST.QUANTILE temperatures 0.5
1) "38"
TDIGEST.QUANTILE temperatures 0.9
1) "43"
```

In this example, 38 degrees is the threshold item that divides the set of temperatures into two groups, also called the **median**. The 0.9 quantile, on the other hand, has 90% of the points to its left.

The output of this command is an estimate of the value at the required quantiles.

t-digest offers the useful `TDIGEST.CDF` command, which stands for cumulative distribution function, which helps determine the rank or fraction of observations that are smaller or equal to a given value. This feature can be highly beneficial in addressing queries such as "What is the percentage of observations with a value less than or equal to *X*?" Using the minimal dataset we introduced previously, we can test the command as follows:

```
TDIGEST.CDF temperatures 38
1) "0.5"
```

Similarly, the `TDIGEST.RANK` command calculates the number of observations rather than the percentage:

```
TDIGEST.RANK temperatures 38
1) (integer) 2
```

In this section, we have just scratched the surface of the t-digest sketch: there are additional commands you will find useful in many use cases. Overall, t-digest is a valuable data structure in scenarios such as the following:

- **Network monitoring**: As an example, you can measure the distribution of latencies in a network (what fraction of the connections has latency above/below a certain value?). This information can help you troubleshoot eventual slowness and pinpoint root causes.
- **Online gaming**: You might be wondering what threshold or minimum score should be included in the *X*% of best players of the game. In this case, you would use t-digest with the desired percentile.

- **Prevention of denial of service**: Using the t-digest sketch, it is possible to detect whether the latest received packets (as an example, in the last second) exceed a percentage of already observed packets in a certain time window.

With that, let's summarize what we've learned.

Summary

In this chapter, we introduced probabilistic data structures, also known as "sketches." We explained their strengths in different areas, such as fraud detection, online gaming, network, device analysis, and social media trends analysis. We also learned how to use the right data structures for the right use cases and understood that using such solutions is often an acceptable compromise between accuracy, performance, and the usage of resources, especially when dealing with datasets of exceptional size or that contain big data. In addition, we discussed how accuracy can be fine-tuned and the guarantees of outcomes when a certain item is tested against a specific sketch. To learn more about probabilistic data structures and understand how to achieve acceptable accuracy, refer to the *Sizing* section in the documentation at `https://redis.io/docs/data-types/probabilistic/`.

In *Chapter 9*, *The Programmability of Redis Stack*, we will dive into the strengths of Redis Stack as a data platform and show use cases for subscribing to and managing database events. We will also introduce the stream processing features and learn how to design powerful data flows.

Part 3: From Development to Production

In addition to the traditional Lua server-side scripts and functions, Redis Stack introduces a JavaScript serverless engine that enables users to write and execute custom functions directly on data stored in Redis. This feature supports various use cases, such as write-behind caching to sync Redis changes with backend databases, and streaming and event processing to respond to events in Redis using its diverse data structures and capabilities.

Additionally, Redis Stack includes RedisInsight, a graphical desktop manager that connects to Redis Stack databases. This tool provides visualization tools for various data models stored in Redis. Traditionally used as an in-memory cache alongside a primary database, Redis Stack extends Redis's capabilities, making it suitable as a standalone, multi-model primary database for diverse applications.

The content in this part also covers the transition from a development environment to deploying Redis at scale, highlighting the effort and maintenance required in monitoring and managing databases. Redis Enterprise and Redis Cloud offer solutions to these challenges, providing an intuitive UI that eases the workload for system and database administrators. This simplifies the management of Redis databases, particularly in larger, scaled environments.

This part contains the following chapters:

- *Chapter 9, The Programmability of Redis Stack*
- *Chapter 10, RedisInsight – the Data Management GUI*
- *Chapter 11, Using Redis Stack as a Primary Database*
- *Chapter 12, Managing Development and Production Environments*

9
The Programmability of Redis Stack

In this chapter, we'll explore Redis Stack's programmability features and show you how they can be used in different situations. For quite a while, software engineers and database administrators have been making the most of stored procedures in relational databases. There are several good reasons for that: managing SQL procedures all in one place, easily troubleshooting procedure flows, staying separate from the chosen client library, and, most importantly, getting things done quickly.

Redis started off by allowing users to write Lua scripts and run them locally, giving them a taste of this capability. But with Redis Stack, server-side programming has been taken to a whole new level. You can now write intricate business logic in either Lua or JavaScript and execute it as close to your data as possible. There is no need for back-and-forth trips to a distant server.

In this chapter, we'll show you how to implement complex behaviors using Lua and JavaScript. We'll also dive into the world of asynchronous and distributed programming in a clustered environment. Additionally, we'll unveil the power of triggers, which let your application respond to keyspace events and execute your logic when data is added, updated, or deleted.

Plus, we'll teach you how to minimize interactions with clients, reducing round-trip times and enabling you to run fast and efficient operations directly within the database.

In this chapter, we are going to cover the following:

- The single-threaded architecture
- Programming complex business logic with Redis Stack
- Lua scripting
- Redis Functions
- Triggers and functions
- Comparing Lua scripts, Lua functions, and JavaScript functions

Technical requirements

To follow along with the examples in the chapter, you will need to do the following:

- Install Redis Stack Server 7.2 or later on your development environment. Alternatively, you can create a free Redis Cloud subscription to get access to a free plan and use a managed Redis Stack database.
- Create a clustered version to test the triggered remote functions using Redis Stack. You can refer to *Chapter 12, Managing Development and Production Environments*, to learn how to do it.
- You can download and import the *World* dataset from this book's repository if you'd like to test the examples that we propose in this chapter: `https://github.com/PacktPublishing/Redis-Stack-for-Application-Modernization`.

The single-threaded architecture

Redis incorporates a single-threaded architecture, which is a distinctive design in the realm of databases and caches. While "single-threaded" may suggest that only one thread runs within the Redis process, this assumption is not entirely accurate. A Redis server comprises multiple threads dedicated to specific tasks, such as key expiration, statistics, and threaded I/O to handle concurrent connections. However, the primary focus is on the main thread responsible for executing commands and managing data storage and retrieval. This single-threaded design ensures that commands are processed sequentially, avoiding complex synchronization issues such as deadlocks and long-running locks. By eliminating interaction between different clients, this implementation reduces the number of stages data and instructions must pass through and enables immediate access to data, a crucial aspect for real-time execution.

With the main thread executing commands, a single Redis Stack Server instance does not scale beyond a single CPU core. To address scalability beyond the single core, the Redis OSS Cluster API and Redis Enterprise offer solutions that will be discussed in detail in *Chapter 12, Managing Development and Production Environments*. Regarding command execution, the serialized approach ensures exclusive access to the keyspace and allows for the efficient atomic execution of multiple commands using the `WATCH/MULTI/EXEC` transactions. However, it also implies that prioritizing low-complexity commands over lengthy, blocking scans is necessary. While Redis Stack's secondary indexing features enhance data retrieval by eliminating the need for time-consuming scans such as `HSCAN`, `ZSCAN`, and others, it's important to handle scripts or functions carefully to prevent extended blocking of concurrent clients. Exclusive access to the keyspace requires consideration of the complexity of commands, especially when implementing complex actions with Redis Stack's programmability features, which we'll discuss next.

Programming complex business logic with Redis Stack

To illustrate the programmability features of Redis Stack, let's explore scenarios where we can solve problems through a sequence of actions. As an example, to identify click spam, we can employ various methods, such as counting events in a time span using the `ZCOUNT` method of the sorted set data structure. Using `ZCOUNT`, we can find the number of clicks from a user during a defined time window. If the count received surpasses a certain threshold, we identify it as anomalous and execute a series of actions, such as throttling user interactions or logging out the user, and maybe sending a warning notification. Another example where we can leverage Redis Stack's programmability features is in an e-commerce application. When an order is placed, we may need to respond to the updated data and adjust the inventory count accordingly. By incorporating Redis Stack, we can efficiently handle such updates and ensure accurate inventory management.

These are just a few instances where we can utilize Redis Stack to solve common problems. The possibilities extend to various use cases, including data manipulation or normalization during insertion, as well as identifying and handling fraudulent attempts by blocking specific IP addresses or users. Redis Stack empowers developers to address these challenges seamlessly and efficiently.

In the realm of databases, **triggers** and **stored procedures** play a vital role in automating actions performed on the stored data in response to specific events. Stored procedures offer the advantage of moving the logic for these actions from the client application to the database itself. This transfer simplifies code management, including versioning and troubleshooting, while also enhancing performance. By executing procedures locally within the database, the need for round-trip communication is eliminated, resulting in faster processing, and the proximity of data reduces additional overhead.

Redis has long supported **Lua scripting**, which enables the atomic execution of multiple actions on local data. While Lua scripting is straightforward and intuitive, the advent of **Redis functions** represents an evolution of this feature. Redis functions provide several advantages, such as script persistence (unlike Lua scripts, which are not persisted and must be reloaded upon database restart) and structured management (enabling the organization of functions into libraries). To further expand on the programmability features of Redis Stack, **triggers and functions** come into play, offering complete control over data events and the ability to react to them using custom functions written in JavaScript.

In summary, Redis Stack offers a powerful set of programmability features. With Lua scripting, Redis functions, triggers, and JavaScript functions, developers have a range of tools at their disposal to automate actions, enhance performance, and ensure efficient data event management in Redis. Let's start our journey with the first and most well-known Lua programmability features.

Lua scripting

With Redis, developers can write Lua scripts and execute them within Redis. Lua is a lightweight scripting language known for its simplicity and efficiency, and Redis has leveraged its power to perform complex operations on stored data since Redis 2.6.0. Lua scripting offers several benefits, such as allowing the execution of multiple commands atomically, meaning all the commands within a Lua script will be executed as a single unit of work, ensuring consistency. This is particularly useful to ensure they are executed without interruption or interference from other clients.

By executing Lua scripts, the network round trips between the application and the server are removed, improving performance. Lua scripts are sent to Redis as an atomic block of instructions and executed directly on the server, eliminating the need to send multiple commands and receive responses individually.

Redis provides a Lua interpreter with a set of Redis-specific Lua functions that allow you to interact with Redis data structures, such as strings, lists, sets, and hashes. These functions enable various operations, including data manipulation, conditional clauses, iterations, and transaction-like behavior.

To use Lua scripting in Redis, you can write Lua code within the `EVAL` command. Let's test a few commands in a Redis Stack instance where the *World* dataset has been preloaded. A single command is executed using the following signature:

```
EVAL <script> <number_of_keys> [<key1> ... <keyn>] [<arg1> ... <argn>]
```

The `EVAL` command is fed with the script, the number of keys that'll be passed to the script, a list of keys, and a list of arguments, all separated by spaces. In the script, access to the database and the arguments is possible, considering the following:

- Interacting with Redis is possible using the `redis` object singleton
- Scripts are parametrized with keys (accessed with `KEYS[id]`), arguments (accessed with `ARGV[id]`), or both

In the following example, the script receives a key (so the related hash data structure is read) and a message, used to format the output:

```
EVAL "local name = redis.call('HGET', KEYS[1], 'Name') return
ARGV[1]..name" 1 'city:123' 'The city you requested is '
"The city you requested is Ezeiza"
```

It is possible to cache Lua scripts identified by a unique script hash with the `SCRIPT LOAD` command. Once the script has been cached, it can be invoked using the hash:

```
SCRIPT LOAD "local name = redis.call('HGET', KEYS[1], 'Name') return
ARGV[1]..name"
"42740b7c393c61b71ba7a0cd58b707bc3f7a04ca"
```

The `EVALSHA` commands take the Lua script hash as an argument along with any required parameters, and Redis executes the script and returns the result.

For complex business logic, the Lua scripts can be written to a file as follows:

```
#!lua
local name = redis.call('HGET', KEYS[1], 'Name')
return ARGV[1]..name
```

Then the script can be executed from the `redis-cli` command-line client as follows:

```
redis-cli --eval script.lua 'city:123' , 'The city you requested is '
"The city you requested is Ezeiza"
```

Alternatively, it can be cached as usual, again, from the file:

```
redis-cli -x script load < script.lua
"60304f8d51782b9f601032be84a0b3011b644295"
```

You can clean up the cache with `SCRIPT FLUSH`, kill a long-running script using `SCRIPT KILL`, and more. Note that Lua scripts are volatile, so any cached script won't survive a server restart: Lua scripts are not part of the server and are always managed by clients. An additional feature of Lua scripting is support for read-only Lua scripts, enforced by the `EVAL_RO` command (and the equivalent `EVALSHA_RO` for cached scripts):

```
EVAL_RO "local name = redis.call('HGET', KEYS[1], 'Name') return
ARGV[1]..name" 1 'city:123' 'The city you requested is '
"The city you requested is Ezeiza"
```

Changing the script used as an example and adding an `INCR` command, instead, will fail if executed with `EVAL_RO`:

```
EVAL_RO "local name = redis.call('HGET', KEYS[1], 'Name') redis.
call('INCR', 'cnt') return ARGV[1]..name" 1 'city:123' 'The city you
requested is '
(error) ERR Write commands are not allowed from read-only scripts.
script: 08c94c021a86b797dfb361f29cc3f9c9bb3d8d5a, on @user_script:1.
```

Lua scripting in Redis is a powerful feature that provides flexibility and performance optimizations when working with Redis data. It allows you to perform complex operations efficiently, reducing network overhead and ensuring the atomicity of multiple Redis commands. However, maintaining and organizing scripts across multiple clients is complicated and error-prone and scripts cannot call other scripts, which makes reusing code impossible. Redis functions, introduced in Redis 7, supersede Lua scripts and overcome such limitations and many more.

Redis functions

Redis functions are an evolution of ephemeral scripting in Redis. They provide similar functionality as scripts but are considered first-class software artifacts within the database. Functions are managed and persisted by Redis, ensuring their availability through data persistence and replication. Unlike scripts, functions are declared before use and do not need to be loaded during runtime.

Here are some advantages of Redis functions over Lua scripts:

- **Persistence and replication**: Redis manages functions as part of the database and stores them alongside the data itself ensuring their persistence (RDB snapshots and/or append-only files) and replication along with the data. Functions are considered integral components of the database, making them readily available without the need for external management.
- **Simplified development and code sharing**: Functions belong to libraries, and libraries can contain multiple functions. Functions within the same library can call each other, enabling code sharing and modular development. Libraries are updated as a whole, providing a consistent and atomic update mechanism.
- **Atomic execution**: Like transactions and Lua scripts, the execution of a function in Redis is atomic. This means that the effects of a function either have not happened yet or have already happened. Function execution blocks all server activities during its execution, ensuring atomicity and consistent behavior across connected clients.

Let's see an example to load and execute a function. Functions can be loaded as strings:

```
FUNCTION LOAD "#!lua name=mylib\n redis.register_function('city_fetch_
name', function(keys, args) local name = redis.call('HGET', keys[1],
'Name') return args[1]..name end)"
"mylib"
```

Functions can also be listed:

```
FUNCTION LIST
1) 1) "library_name"
   2) "mylib"
   3) "engine"
   4) "LUA"
   5) "functions"
   6) 1) 1) "name"
         2) "city_fetch_name"
         3) "description"
         4) (nil)
         5) "flags"
         6) (empty array)
```

Differently from the basic Lua scripting feature, Redis functions can be invoked by their name using the `FCALL` command:

```
FCALL city_fetch_name 1 'city:123' 'The city you requested is '
"The city you requested is Ezeiza"
```

The entire library can be deleted using the following command:

```
FUNCTION DELETE mylib
OK
```

It is possible to develop a library with multiple functions in a single Lua source code file:

```
#!lua name=mylib

local function city_fetch_name(keys, args)
    local name = redis.call('HGET', keys[1], 'Name')
    return 'The city is '..name
end

local function city_fetch_district(keys, args)
    local district = redis.call('HGET', keys[1], 'District')
    return 'The district is '..district
end

redis.register_function('city_fetch_name', city_fetch_name)
redis.register_function('city_fetch_district', city_fetch_district)
```

You can import the library as follows (in this example, see how the library is replaced using the `REPLACE` option):

```
cat mylib.lua | redis-cli -x FUNCTION LOAD REPLACE
"mylib"
```

Redis functions promote **code reuse**, so the invocation of functions from other functions *within the same library* is supported. This facilitates the sharing of code between functions by utilizing a shared code base in library-internal methods:

```
#!lua name=mylib

local function myincr()
    redis.call('INCR', 'cnt')
    return 'OK'
end
local function city_fetch_name(keys, args)
    local name = redis.call('HGET', keys[1], 'Name')
    myincr()
    return 'The city is '..name
end
redis.register_function('city_fetch_name', city_fetch_name)
```

Another useful feature of Redis functions is the ability to set functions as read-only. This can be achieved by specifying the `no-writes` flag at function registration time and executing the function with the `FCALL_RO` command. By default, functions allow write operations, so attempting to execute a function with `FCALL_RO` will fail:

```
FCALL_RO city_fetch_name 1 city:123
(error) ERR Can not execute a script with write flag using *_ro
command.
```

The correct function definition is as follows:

```
#!lua name=mylib

local function city_fetch_name(keys, args)
    local name = redis.call('HGET', keys[1], 'Name')
    return 'The city is '..name
end

redis.register_function{
    function_name='city_fetch_name',
    callback=city_fetch_name,
    flags={ 'no-writes' }
}
```

Now the execution with the `FCALL_RO` command is successful:

```
FCALL_RO city_fetch_name 1 city:123
"The city is Ezeiza"
```

Flags are supported by Redis functions and Lua scripts. The additional flags supported are as follows:

- `allow-oom`: Allows a script to execute even when the server is **out of memory** (**OOM**). By default, Redis denies the execution of flagged scripts in an OOM state. This flag enables the script to call any Redis command, including those not allowed in this state.
- `allow-stale`: Enables running flagged scripts against a stale replica when the `replica-serve-stale-data` config is set to `no`. It allows scripts that do not access data to run on stale Redis replicas but commands accessing stale data will still be restricted.
- `no-cluster`: Causes the script to return an error in Redis Cluster mode, preventing its execution on cluster nodes.
- `allow-cross-slot-keys`: Allows a script to access keys from multiple slots, breaking the usual rule of single-command access. However, it is generally discouraged as applications should access keys from a single slot at a time, especially when using Redis Cluster.

Overall, Redis functions offer improved management, persistence, atomicity, and flexibility compared to traditional Lua scripting. They provide a more integrated and reliable approach for extending Redis functionality with user-provided logic, promoting code reuse.

Triggers and functions

The latest addition to Redis Stack is the capacity to respond to specific events happening in your Redis database and define business logic that executes the desired actions. These events can be triggered by changes to the data, such as adding a new key-value pair. When an event occurs, the specified **JavaScript function** is automatically executed. However, this is not the only way to execute the desired functions: Redis Stack supports two types of triggers for execution while supporting manual user execution. For a summary, see the following:

- **User functions**: Functions can be executed manually, using the `TFCALL` or `TFCALLASYNC` command
- **Keyspace triggers**: These triggers are activated when there are changes to the data stored in Redis, and they execute the desired function
- **Stream triggers**: Whenever new items are added to a Stream, these triggers are activated and execute the desired function

The advantage of using triggers is that you can keep your business logic within the database itself, eliminating the need for duplicating the logic across multiple services or applications. These functions are executed synchronously and without any delay.

For example, in an e-commerce application, when an order is placed, the trigger executes the related function, which can update the inventory by reacting to the changed data. Similarly, if a database receives data from different applications, you can use a function to apply the transformation logic and ensure consistency across different domains. To deploy functions, you need to provide a JavaScript file. While this is easy for small projects, it becomes more challenging to maintain as projects become larger and more complex. However, the JavaScript community offers deployment tools such as **Webpack**, which can help manage and bundle the code effectively. It's important to note that when using JavaScript in a function, you should ensure that the JavaScript libraries you use are compatible with the popular **V8 engine**, which is the engine powering this functionality.

Let's now dive into writing functions. We will start with simple examples that can be executed manually, and then dive into the core functionality that enables automatic function execution in response to data events.

Anatomy of a function

Users can register functions using the `TFUNCTION LOAD` command, which can be invoked using the `TFCALL` and `TFCALLASYNC` commands:

```
TFUNCTION LOAD "#!js api_version=1.0 name=greetings\n redis.
registerFunction('hello_world', ()=>{return 'Hello world!';})"
```

Let's examine the syntax of building and loading a function into Redis:

- The functions are written in the JavaScript language.
- The functions are organized in libraries: a library can contain multiple functions.
- A library is introduced by the `#!js` shebang.
- The minimum version of the supported JavaScript API is specified with `api_version` (refer to the documentation for the list of supported versions). This is required in order to follow the life cycle of the JavaScript API and plan maintenance through API deprecation cycles.
- The name of the library is specified by `name=greetings`.

Any function in a library can be executed by specifying the library and the function names separated by a dot, followed by the number of keys, the list of keys, and the list of arguments:

```
TFCALL <library_name>.<function_name> <number_of_keys> [<key1> ...
<keyn>] [<arg1> ... <argn>]
```

Then, the execution of the former function is carried out as follows:

```
TFCALL greetings.hello_world 0
"Hello world!"
```

A function can be edited in a file, rather than loading it as a string. We can write the following code in the `greetings.js` file:

```
#!js api_version=1.0 name=greetings

redis.registerFunction('hello_world', function(){
    return 'Hello world!';
});
redis.registerFunction('ciao_mondo', function(){
    return 'Ciao mondo!';
});
```

Note that attempting to import the library again does not overwrite the former library:

```
redis-cli -x TFUNCTION LOAD < ./greetings.js
(error) Library greetings already exists.
```

When the library needs to be updated, we indicate it using the REPLACE option:

```
redis-cli -x TFUNCTION LOAD REPLACE < ./greetings.js
OK
```

This way, we have access to the newly added function:

```
TFCALL greetings.ciao_mondo 0
"Ciao mondo!
```

So far, we have explored how to define a function with the proper header and name. Let's now dive into accessing the database to implement complex behaviors using the data in the keyspace.

Working with data

Calling Redis commands inside of a JavaScript function is possible with a `client` object. The function gets the `client` object as the first argument, which allows interaction with the database using the `call` method. Subsequent parameters are keys and/or arguments. Create and import the following function:

```
redis.registerFunction('create_user', function(client, id, name){
    client.call('SET', 'user:' + id, name)
    client.call('INCR', 'users')
    return 'User created'
});
```

Execute it using the following command:

```
TFCALL greetings.create_user 0 123 "Dan Brown"
"User created"
GET user:123
"Dan Brown"
GET users
"1"
```

Here are a couple of other useful commands:

- `TFUNCTION DELETE <NAME>`, which deletes a library
- `TFUNCTION LIST`, which lists the functions loaded in the server and helps you to check their version at a glance

We have all the pieces to write complex JavaScript functions and work with the data stored in Redis. In the following sections, we will introduce typical implementations that leverage the power of local function execution.

Batch processing

Now that we have learned how to write, load, and execute functions in a library manually, let's do something useful with our functions. Edit the `counter.js` file and load it into Redis:

```
#!js api_version=1.0 name=counter

redis.registerFunction('count', function(client){
    var count = 0;
    var cursor = '0';
    do {
        var res = client.call('scan', cursor, 'MATCH', 'city:*');
        cursor = res[0];
        var keys = res[1];
        keys.forEach((key) => {
            count += 1;
        });
    } while(cursor != '0');
    return count;
});
```

The `count` example function is designed to perform a scan, using the `SCAN` command, of the keyspace and count the keys whose name is prefixed with 'city:'. This is a problem we could easily solve by creating an index with `FT.CREATE` and retrieving its cardinality; however, the example is a demonstration of the flexibility of the Redis Stack JavaScript programmability feature. Upon execution, the result is returned correctly:

```
TFCALL counter.count 0
(integer) 4079
```

Normally, the `SCAN` command executed from the `redis-cli` command-line client, or from any client library for the desired programming language, is blocked only for the duration of the batch. This means that to perform a full scan of the keyspace, we would invoke `SCAN` in multiple batches, providing the next cursor in each subsequent batch scan. This is the preferred behavior to avoid blocking the server with the execution of a long-running scan of the entire keyspace. However, executing scans in the previous `do-while` loop would block the server's main thread until the keyspace is entirely scanned. This is the same behavior as Lua scripts and functions and is the default behavior of JavaScript functions, but Redis Stack JavaScript functions rely on the native asynchronous nature of the V8 engine, and support asynchronous execution. Let's see how this works.

Asynchronous functions

The default behavior of JavaScript functions is synchronous; the execution of a function is atomic and all the changes that are made to data while a function is running will be seen by other clients when the function concludes the execution. This behavior ensures that no changes are made by other clients to data while the function is running, which may be a desirable behavior, but it causes the main thread to be locked until the function completes, so other clients can't be served until it completes.

When the atomicity of a function is not a requirement, it is possible to execute the function asynchronously in a coroutine. Asynchronous functions will be launched in a separate thread, freeing the main thread, which, therefore, remains available to other clients. Let's see this with an example. Add the following two functions to an existing library:

```
redis.registerFunction('sync_loop', function(){
    var count = 0;
    do{
        count += 1;
    } while(count != '300000000');
    return 'Very long loop';
});

redis.registerAsyncFunction('async_loop', async function(){
    var count = 0;
    do{
        count += 1;
    } while(count != '300000000');
    return 'Very long async loop';
});
```

The functions will both execute in a tight loop, but the `sync_loop` function will run in the main thread, while the `async_loop` function will run in a coroutine. You can test the execution of the first function as usual:

```
TFCALL counter.sync_loop 0
```

Note that functions blocking the main thread for too long will be timed out; this is the case for the `sync_loop` function:

```
TFCALL counter.sync_loop 0
(error) Err Execution was terminated due to OOM or timeout
```

This behavior is configurable using the `lock-redis-timeout` configuration value, to extend the maximum amount of time in milliseconds that a library can lock Redis. You can change the value as follows, just for demonstration purposes:

```
CONFIG SET redisgears_2.lock-redis-timeout 30000
```

Use the `TFCALLASYNC` command to execute an asynchronous function:

```
TFCALLASYNC counter.async_loop 0
```

When running the asynchronous version of the function, test from another Redis session that it is possible to execute some arbitrary commands (a `GET` command, for example). If you launch the same commands from another session when the synchronous function is executing, you will notice that the execution is put on hold.

You can pass an optional `client` argument to the asynchronous function that is distinct from the `client` argument accepted by synchronous functions, seen earlier. Unlike the regular `client` argument, this client (`async_client`, in the following example) does not permit the invocation of Redis commands. Instead, it blocks Redis and enters an atomic section where the atomicity property is activated once again: whatever is executed within the scope of the `block` call has exclusive access to Redis. Proof of this behavior is in the following example. If you execute the following function, you will notice, once more, that the command blocks other sessions:

```
redis.registerAsyncFunction('async_block_loop', async function(async_
client){
    return async_client.block(function(redis_client){
        var count = 0;
        do{
            count += 1;
        } while(count != '300000000');
        return 'Very long async and blocking loop';
    });
});
```

While running an asynchronous function and making it block may seem counter-intuitive, this design is used to guarantee single-threaded access to the keyspace, the distinctive feature of Redis, and, at the same time, permit non-blocking atomic batch executions within the server itself. To understand this concept with an example, let's rewrite the `count` function to make it asynchronous:

```
redis.registerAsyncFunction('async_count', async function(async_
client){
    var count = 0;
    var cursor = '0';
    do {
        async_client.block((client)=>{
            var res = client.call('scan', cursor, 'MATCH', 'city:*');
            cursor = res[0];
            var keys = res[1];
            keys.forEach((key) => {
                count += 1;
            });
        });
    } while(cursor != '0');
    return count;
});
```

This function returns the same result as the synchronous version, but it guarantees the following:

- The batch scan is executed atomically
- Access to the keyspace is exclusive
- Other clients can execute commands between batches

This implementation has the same consistency guarantees as the analogous client library version, but with all the benefits of local execution within the database.

Cluster awareness

Redis Stack JavaScript functions can be used in clustered environments, so it is possible to invoke remote JavaScript functions from a shard to remote shards in a Redis cluster. For more on this, see *Chapter 12, Managing Development and Production Environments,* where the open source Redis Cluster (sometimes referred to as Redis OSS Cluster to avoid confusion with Redis Enterprise clusters) is described in detail.

The shard on which the command is run (the originating shard) propagates the command to the other shards in a cluster using the `runOnShards` API and collects all their results before returning a merged response.

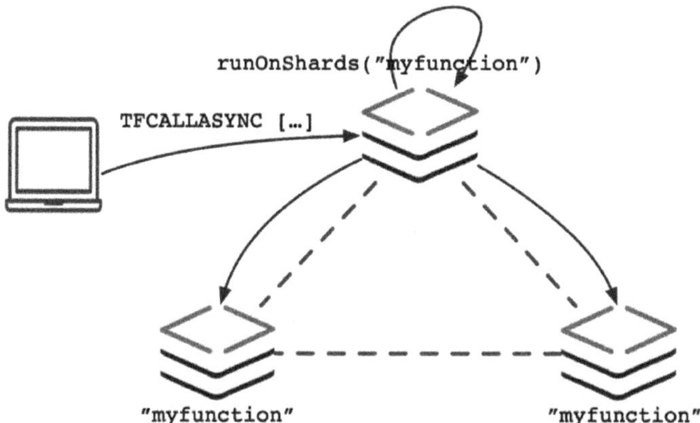

Figure 9.1: Remote JavaScript functions execution

The `registerClusterFunction` API enables remote functions in a library. This API allows you to declare a remote function that performs actions on all the shards of a cluster. When using `registerClusterFunction`, you provide the name of the remote function (which will be used to call it later) and its code. It's important to note that the remote function should be written as a coroutine (an async function) that will be executed in the background on the designated remote shard. Note also that remote functions can only perform read operations. An attempt to perform a write operation will result in an error.

In the following example, we define the remote `stringcounter` function to count the number of strings in the shard, and the originating `nstrings` function to invoke the remote functions and aggregate the results:

```
#!js api_version=1.0 name=clustercounter

redis.registerClusterFunction("stringcounter", async(async_client) =>
{
    var count = 0;
    var cursor = '0';
    do {
        async_client.block((client)=>{
            var res = client.call('SCAN', cursor, 'TYPE', 'string');
            cursor = res[0];
            var keys = res[1];
            keys.forEach((key) => {
                count += 1;
            });
        });
    } while(cursor != '0');
    return count;
});
redis.registerAsyncFunction("nstrings", async(async_client) => {
    let res = await async_client.runOnShards("stringcounter");
    let results = res[0];
    let errors = res[1];
    if (errors.length > 0) {
            return errors;
    }
    let sum = BigInt(0);
    results.forEach((element) => sum+=BigInt(element));
    return sum;
});
```

In addition to the `runOnShards` API, the `runOnKey` API is also available, which runs the remote function on the shard responsible for a given key.

Keyspace triggers

We have explored the essential characteristics of Redis Stack for developing JavaScript functions. So far, we have learned how to develop functions and execute them manually. Manual execution proves valuable for maintenance tasks and even for actions across all the shards of a Redis OSS cluster. Similarly, clients can utilize JavaScript functions to perform complex actions. While the synchronous and asynchronous execution capabilities of the V8 engine help in developing business logic that is closely tied to the data, the real differentiating factor between JavaScript functions and Lua functions is their ability to respond to events. This distinctive feature transforms JavaScript functions into triggered functions.

Besides the manual invocation of functions using the `TFCALL` command, it is possible to register event listeners that will trigger a function execution every time a watched key is changed. Simple examples where a trigger would be a good fit might be the following:

- Keeping track of changes and deletions, and storing the names of the affected keys in a list
- Listening for all `HINCRBY` operations on the elements of a hash that have a determined prefix and synchronously updating a user's level when the score reaches 1,000

Let's test the subscription to events with the following example:

- We are subscribing to events against the keys prefixed with the `user:` namespace
- We check the command that triggered the event, and if it is a deletion, we act and specify what's going to happen next
- The triggered actions will be the incrementing of a counter and logging a message into the server's log

The following code implements this behavior:

```
redis.registerKeySpaceTrigger("del_logger", "user:", function(client,
data){
    if (data.event == 'del'){
        client.call("INCR", "removed");
        redis.log(JSON.stringify(data));
        redis.log("A user has been removed");
    }
});
```

You can test this trigger as follows; creating and deleting a key will trigger the execution of the `del_logger` function:

```
GET removed
(nil)
HSET user:145345 name "Dan" last "Brown"
(integer) 2
DEL user:145345
(integer) 1
GET removed
"1"
```

A quick check of the server's log verifies that the condition has been met, and the information is logged. Note that it is not possible to see the data in the key that has been deleted; only the key name is visible:

```
1:M 05 Jun 2023 13:17:44.847 * <redisgears_2> 'redisgears::compiled_
library_api' {"event":"del","key":"user:145345","key_raw":{}}
1:M 05 Jun 2023 13:17:44.847 * <redisgears_2> 'redisgears::compiled_
library_api' A user has been removed
```

Using triggers, it is possible to keep track of key evictions and expiration. However, because of the probabilistic nature of these events, eviction and expiration do not guarantee the trigger will happen at the exact time the key was set to expire/be evicted.

Trigger guarantees

In `MULTI/EXEC` transactions or Lua scripts/functions, notifications are fired at the end of atomic execution. Consequently, all event notifications will see the last value that was written. To illustrate this, consider the following example, which captures changes on keys prefixed by `"captured:"`.

```
redis.registerKeySpaceTrigger("trigger_test", "captured:",
function(client, data){
    var value = client.call('GET', data.key);
    redis.log(value);
});
```

When testing the trigger with two sequential changes, the changes will be reflected normally in the log:

```
SET captured:123 maria
SET captured:123 john
... 'redisgears::compiled_library_api' maria
... 'redisgears::compiled_library_api' john
```

However, let's say we submit the same changes in the context of a Redis transaction:

```
MULTI
SET captured:123 maria
SET captured:123 john
EXEC
```

In that case, the trigger will be invoked at `EXEC` time, resulting in the same value being captured twice:

```
... 'redisgears::compiled_library_api' john
... 'redisgears::compiled_library_api' john
```

To resolve this issue of notifications within the context of transactions or the execution of atomic scripts/functions, an optional function argument called `onTriggerFired` is available. This function is fired immediately after the key change and allows us to read the content of the key. The content is then added to the `data` argument, which is passed to the actual trigger function that can process the data:

```
redis.registerKeySpaceTrigger("trigger_test", "captured:",
function(client, data){
    redis.log(data.value);
},{
    onTriggerFired: (client, data) => {
        data.value = client.call('GET', data.key);
    }
});
```

By executing the changes in a transaction, all individual events can be captured:

```
... 'redisgears::compiled_library_api' maria
... 'redisgears::compiled_library_api' john
```

This section concludes the introduction to the keyspace triggers. In the next section, we will discover another powerful feature of Redis Stack – stream triggers.

Stream triggers

Redis Stack provides an API that allows registering a stream consumer to a Redis Stream data structure and removes the need to invoke any additional command to read from the stream. Writing a stream trigger follows similar syntax rules to those already seen; in detail, you will specify the following:

- `consumer`: Specifies the name of the consumer.
- `stream`: Specifies the prefix of the stream names that will trigger the callback.
- `callback`: Specifies the function to be invoked for each element in the stream. The callback can be invoked synchronously or asynchronously, following the respective invocation rules on the shard storing the stream and originating the event.
- `window`: Determines how many elements can be processed simultaneously.
- `isStreamTrimmed`: Specifies whether we want to trim the stream after the data is processed by the consumer.

The following example shows how to subscribe to events added to a Redis stream:

```
redis.registerStreamTrigger(
    "consumer",
    "tickets",
    function(client, data) {
```

```
        redis.log(JSON.stringify(data, (key, value) =>
            typeof value === 'bigint'
                ? value.toString()
                : value
        ));
        client.call("INCR", "ntickets");
    },
    {
        isStreamTrimmed: false,
        window: 3
    }
);
```

The `consumer` function subscribes to events added to the stream prefixed by `"tickets"`, and upon insertion of events in the streams, it logs the received data and increments a counter. Load the function in the usual way:

```
redis-cli -x TFUNCTION LOAD REPLACE < ./counter.js
```

Test it by adding some data to a Redis stream:

```
XADD tickets * movie "The Godfather" paid "35"
"1685976466162-0"
XADD tickets * movie "Interstellar" paid "7"
"1685976485381-0"
```

A quick review of the log file will display the received data:

```
1:M 05 Jun 2023 14:47:46.195 * <redisgears_2> 'redisgears::compiled_
library_api' {"id":["1685976466162","0"],"stream_
name":"tickets","stream_name_raw":{},"record":[["movie","The
Godfather"],["paid","35"]],"record_raw":[[{},{}],[{},{}]]}
1:M 05 Jun 2023 14:48:05.387 * <redisgears_2>
'redisgears::compiled_library_api' {"id":["1685976
485381","0"],"stream_name":"tickets","stream_name_
raw":{},"record":[["movie","Interstellar"],["paid","7"]],"record_
raw":[[{},{}],[{},{}]]}
```

Trigger guarantees

While the shard storing the stream and originating the event is up and running, the callback is executed only once per event added to the stream. In case of failure (such as a shard crash), at least one execution of the callback is guaranteed.

The ability to process data added to Redis streams in real time enables countless applications. For example, data can be transformed and stored in indexed JSON documents for real-time search and aggregation, thus transforming Redis into an integrated data platform capable of loading, transforming, and processing events.

With this section, we have concluded the walk-through of the programmability features of Redis Stack. Let's review the differences between all the methods discussed so far.

Comparing Lua scripts, Lua functions, and JavaScript functions

To provide a better understanding of the programmability features in the Lua and JavaScript languages, we have prepared a concise summary in the following table, highlighting the key differences:

	Lua Scripts	**Lua Functions**	**JavaScript Functions**
Persistence	No. The application reloads the scripts on server restart.	Yes.	Yes.
Language	Lua.	Lua.	JavaScript.
Application awareness	The client controls the execution.	The client controls the execution.	Automated execution. Clients can execute functions.
Execution	Sync: blocks the main Redis thread.	Sync: blocks the main Redis thread.	Sync and async: can use a background thread.
Parameters	Keys, arguments.	Keys, arguments.	Keys, arguments, event data.
Atomicity	The script is an atomic action.	The function is an atomic action.	Atomic action. Not atomic when working with cross-shard data.
RDBMS analogy	Advanced queries/complex joins.	Stored procedure.	Triggers. Stored procedure.
Cluster	Only local shard execution.	Only local shard execution.	Cross-shard.

Table 9.1 – Key differences between Lua scripts, Lua functions, and JavaScript functions

Let's summarize the key takeaways from this chapter.

Summary

In this chapter, we have summarized the evolution of the programmability features of Redis, since the first Lua scripting feature was added in Redis 2.6.0, passing through the introduction of Redis functions in Redis 7, up to the most recent additions to Redis Stack – the introduction of the V8 engine and the ability to write JavaScript functions.

While Lua scripts and functions (which allow complex actions as close to the data as possible to be written) are of great value to developers, JavaScript functions and the asynchronous nature of the V8 engine provide an unprecedented capability to offload part of the processing load to coroutines, while preserving a single-threaded data access model, which is the distinguishing feature of the Redis Server architecture. In addition, the support for clustered environments with remote functions expands the manageability of data when working with sharded databases. Finally, the real-time stream processing capability of Redis Stack elevates Redis to a versatile data platform, capable of ingesting, transforming, storing, and indexing data for a wide array of purposes.

This chapter serves as a concise introduction to Redis Stack's programmability. We recommend consulting the related documentation to gain insights into developing, configuring, and debugging your code; this will enable you to harness the full potential of local code development on Redis databases. You can also find several examples to experiment with in your Redis Stack installation.

In *Chapter 10, RedisInsight – the Data Management GUI*, we present the main features of RedisInsight, a monitoring and performance analysis tool that offers a range of features for enhanced software development and troubleshooting. With RedisInsight, users gain access to metrics, including memory usage, throughput, and latency. These key metrics empower users to identify slow commands and bottlenecks. RedisInsight is invaluable for monitoring and optimizing software performance, making it an indispensable tool.

10

RedisInsight – the Data Management GUI

An essential aspect of the Redis Stack revolves around the developer experience. The developer journey extends beyond just the availability of libraries and frameworks; it also encompasses the suite of tools provided to augment the development process.

One of the key tools offered by Redis is **RedisInsight**, a comprehensive **graphical user interface** (**GUI**). This GUI serves as a gateway to interact with your Redis databases visually.

RedisInsight offers a broad spectrum of features, from visually exploring your data to crafting queries based on your specific requirements. It serves as an invaluable asset when debugging and troubleshooting, providing insights into your data like never before.

Chapter 7, Redis as a Time Series Database, thoroughly demonstrated the efficient usage of RedisInsight, showcasing how you could visualize time series data points graphically. Just as it allows you to visualize time-series data, RedisInsight also facilitates access to other data types, enabling you to query and visualize them effectively.

But to harness the power of RedisInsight, we first need to acquire the software. The journey starts with downloading and installing the software, setting the stage for you to dive into the extensive capabilities that RedisInsight offers.

In this chapter, you will acquire the knowledge to do the following:

- Establish a connection with Redis Stack databases
- Navigate through your keys
- Interact with your data efficiently
- Conduct automatic data analysis
- Test and diagnose issues in your PubSub channels

To begin, let's discuss the prerequisites for following this chapter.

Technical requirements

To follow along with this chapter, you need to have RedisInsight installed in your local environment.

To obtain RedisInsight, start by navigating to the official Redis website here: `https://redis.com/redis-enterprise/redis-insight/`

Once there, locate and click on the **Download RedisInsight Now** button, which will direct you to a form. Fill in all the required details on the form. After you've completed the form, click **DOWNLOAD**. This action will trigger the download of the RedisInsight software.

As the download progresses, the installation wizard will guide you through the rest of the setup process. Follow its instructions carefully to ensure smooth installation. Upon the completion of the installation process, you are free to launch and explore your freshly installed RedisInsight.

As of the time at which this guide was written, the latest available version of RedisInsight is 2.36.0 Be sure to stay updated and take advantage of the enhancements and fixes that come with each new version.

Connecting to the Redis Stack database

When you first launch RedisInsight, you'll be greeted by the initial application screen, represented as follows:

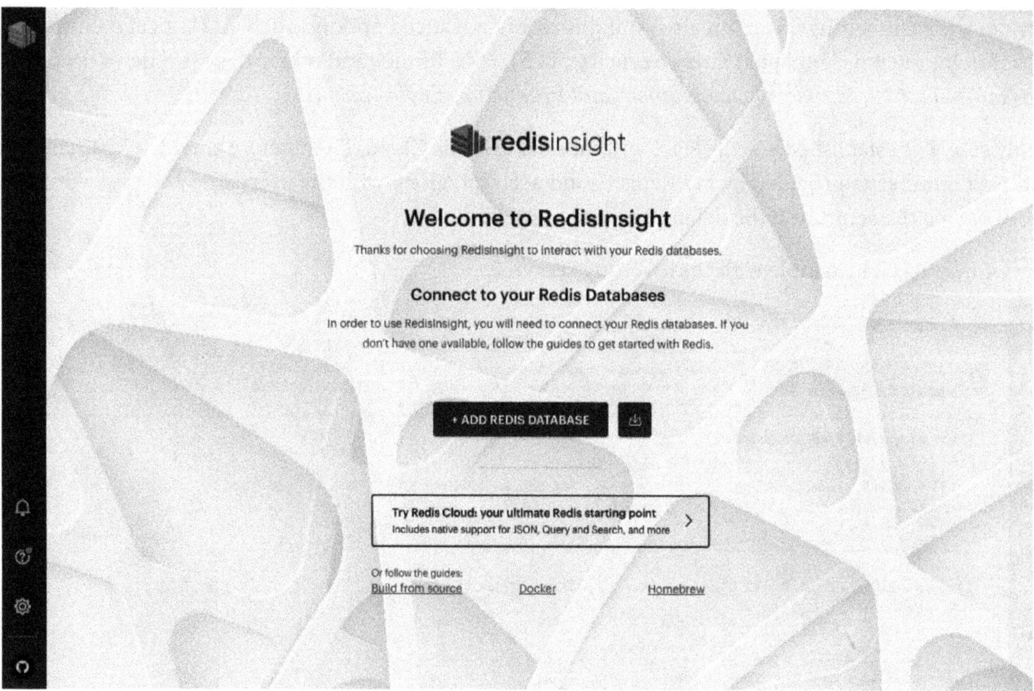

Figure 10.1 – RedisInsight welcome screen

The application first prompts you to establish a connection with a Redis database. Start this process by clicking on the **ADD REDIS DATABASE** button.

Connecting to a Redis database can be achieved in multiple ways. You can manually input the connection parameters, such as the IP address, port number, username, and password. Alternatively, you can utilize the auto-discovery feature offered by the **Sentinel** protocol or use the features provided by **Redis Cloud** and **Redis Enterprise** that you will learn about later in this chapter.

Let's begin with the manual connection approach. You'll need to enter the following:

- **Host**: The **fully qualified domain name** (**FQDN**) of the IP address of your database endpoint
- **Port**: The port to which your database is exposed
- **Database Alias**: The name of your database, a mnemonic identifier that will appear in your RedisInsight database list
- **Username** and **Password**: The credentials required for authentication to your Redis Stack database
- **Timeout** (in seconds): The time after which RedisInsight will stop trying to connect to your Redis Stack database

Besides the basic settings, you can also configure more advanced options, such as a logical database, data decompression, **Transport Layer Security** (**TLS**), SSH Tunnel, and others that we'll delve deeper into in *Chapter 12, Managing Development and Production Environments.*

In my case, I've established a Redis Stack instance using Redis Cloud. I'll therefore enter the hostname and port number as provided by my Redis Cloud account, along with the username and password I chose during the setup, and the default timeout value.

The following is an example with these settings entered:

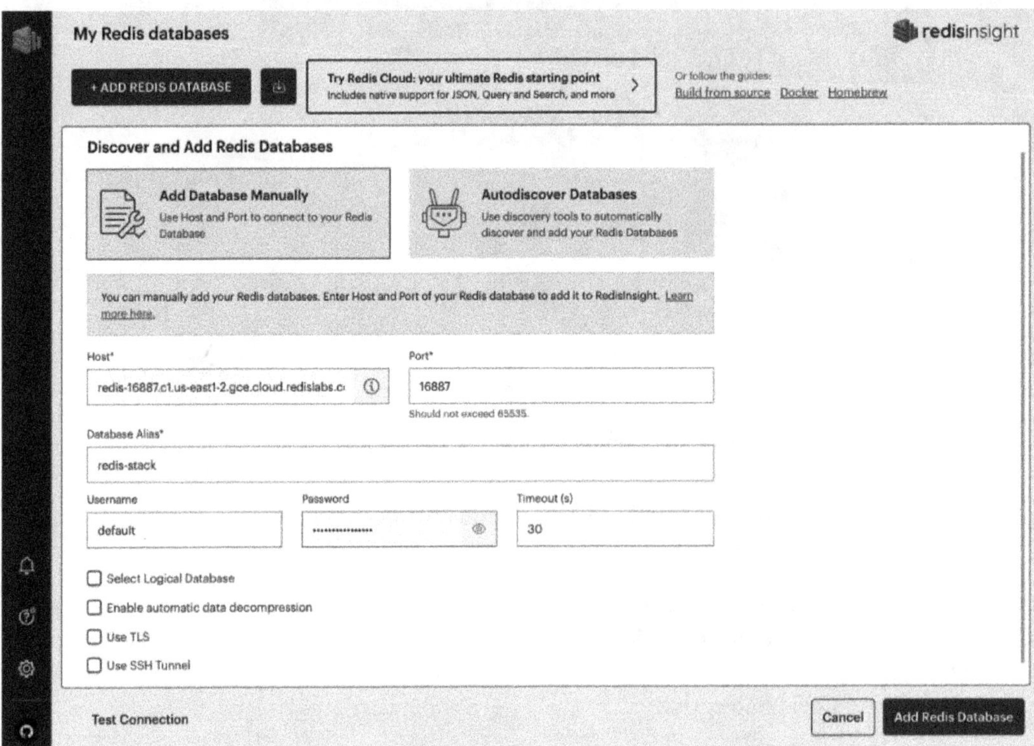

Figure 10.2 – Configuring database access in RedisInsight

After inputting your connection parameters, you can verify the setup by clicking on the **Test Connection** button located at the bottom left of the user interface. A pop-up banner reading **Connection successful** will appear if the test is successful. Alternatively, you can directly add the Redis database by clicking the **Add Redis Database** button at the bottom-right corner of the interface.

Once a successful connection is established, RedisInsight will display a banner stating **Database has been added** and the newly connected database will appear in the database list, as depicted in the following screenshot:

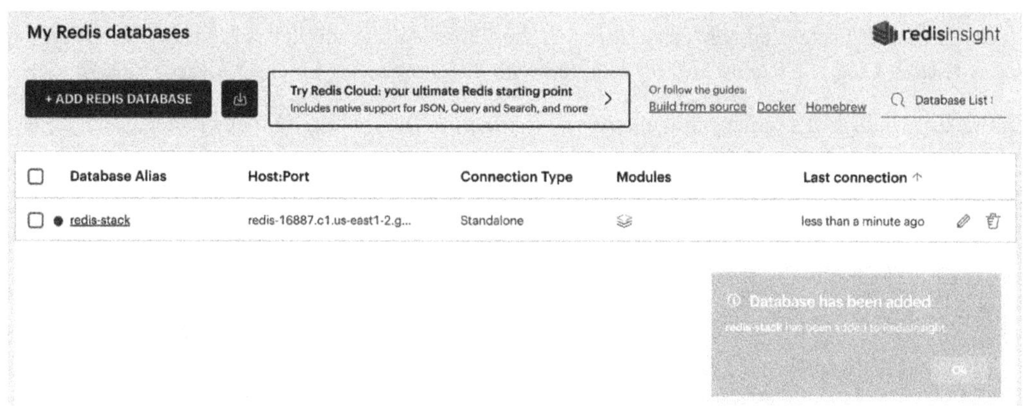

Figure 10.3 – RedisInsight database list

By clicking on the database alias, RedisInsight will connect to the selected database using the credentials you provided.

It's now the moment to delve into the contents of your Redis Stack database.

Browsing keys

The moment you select the database, RedisInsight establishes a connection and presents you with the following view:

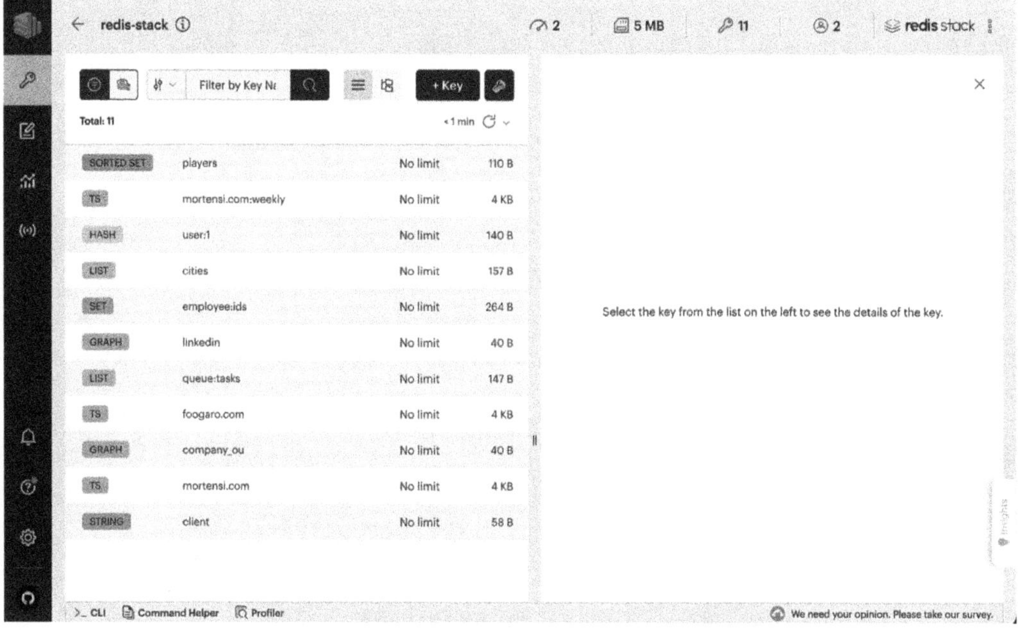

Figure 10.4 – RedisInsight browsing keys

The user interface displays a list of keys stored in the Redis Stack. Each key is identified by its type (such as **HASH**, **LIST**, **SET**, etc.) and represented with different colors for easier differentiation.

Atop this list, you'll find a toolbar that allows you to organize the list based on key patterns, which is the default setting. You can do this by entering a prefix and clicking on the magnifying glass icon or simply pressing *Enter*. The following screenshot provides a visual reference for this feature:

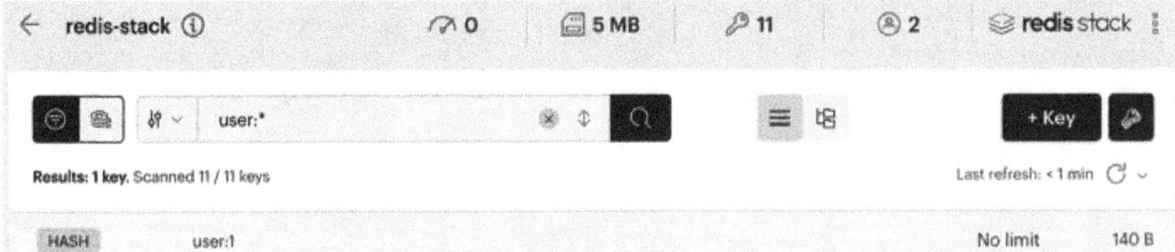

Figure 10.5 – RedisInsight key prefix

Additionally, the toolbar features a button that allows you to exclusively filter and display keys of a specific type, as shown here:

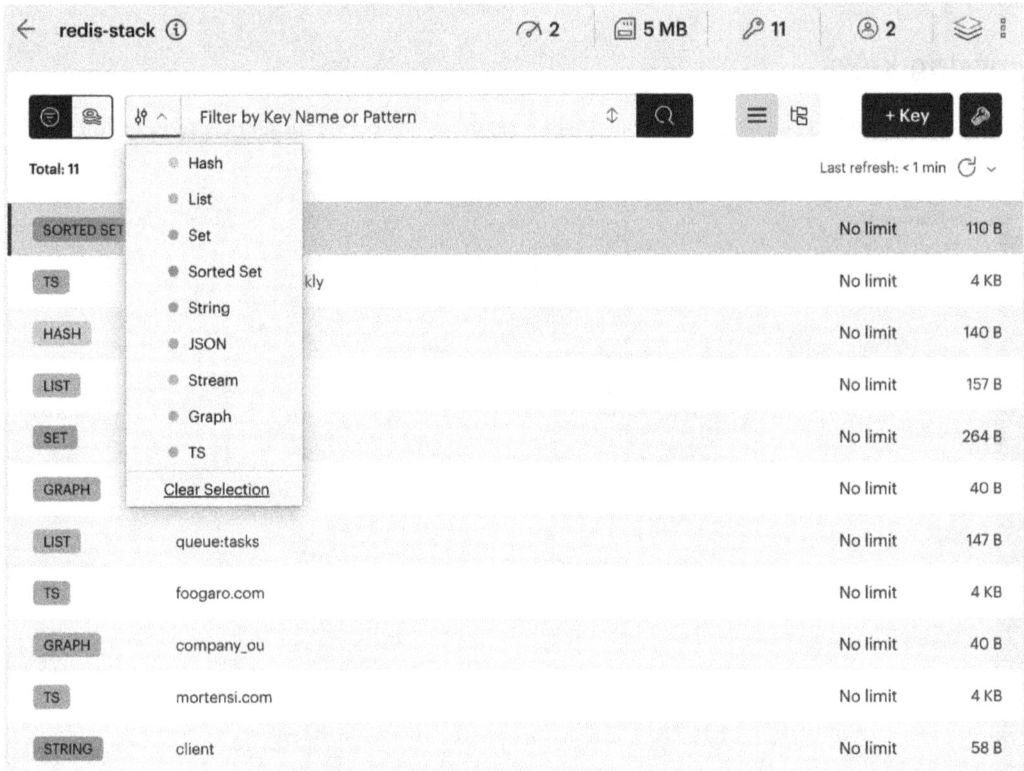

Figure 10.6 – RedisInsight key types

Alternatively, you can choose to view the list by values. This option, indicated by a search-lens icon, requires the selection of an index if one is available.

An alternative view to the standard list is the tree representation. In this mode, the key hierarchy is designated by the key separator. For instance, in the case of the `user:1` key, the colon `:` acts as the separator:

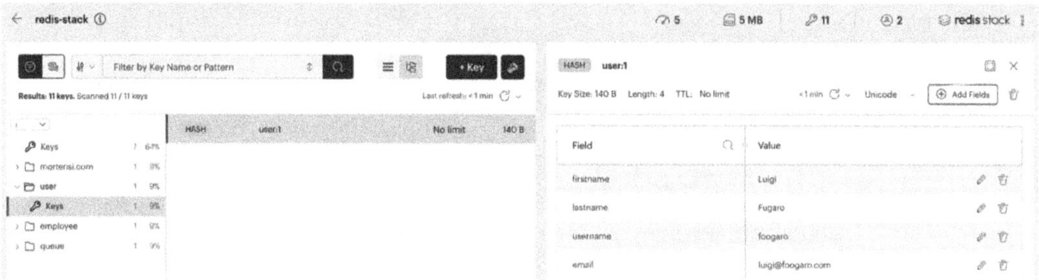

Figure 10.7 – RedisInsight key tree view

By selecting any key from the list, you can view its corresponding value in relation to its encoding or type. For instance, the **Time Series** (**TS**) data type doesn't display automatically, but it can be viewed in the workbench panel. This aspect was covered in detail in *Chapter 7, Redis Stack as a Time Series Database*.

Until now, we have viewed data already present within a Redis database, such as that generated in previous chapters. However, sometimes, for demonstrative or learning purposes, there is a need to generate and interact with data. RedisInsight provides a section specifically dedicated to this aspect. So, let's move on to the next section, regarding data interaction.

Interacting with data

Interacting with your data efficiently is enabled by the workbench feature in RedisInsight. The workbench section, represented by the second icon on the vertical panel on the left side, refers to a section of the tool where you can interact with its Redis databases. It allows you to write and execute Redis commands, query data, view results, and generally interact with your data.

For example, you could run aggregation queries, visualize time-series data as charts, or even zoom in to specific parts of a chart (to revert to the original view after zooming, simply double-click anywhere on the chart).

A useful interactive feature of this chart allows you to zoom in to any specific section of the data. This can be achieved by dragging your cursor over the desired section of the chart, demonstrated as follows:

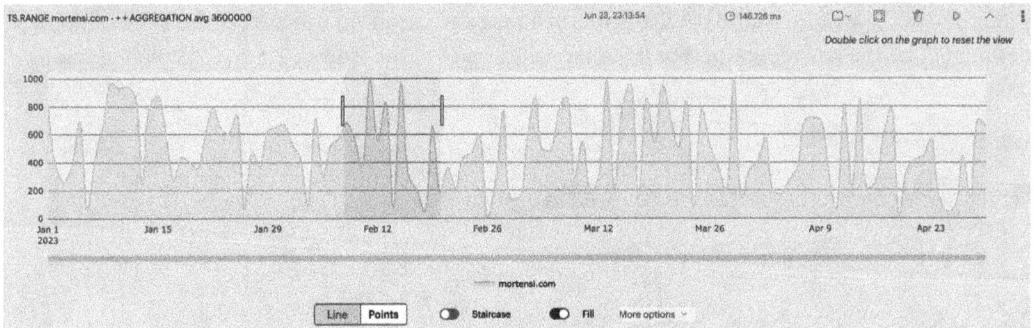

Figure 10.8 – RedisInsight Time Series chart zoom interaction

The chart representation isn't limited to a single style. You can customize it in various ways. You can choose to represent the data points with lines or points and decide whether to fill the space between the lines with color. You can also adjust the scale of the chart between linear and logarithmic and define labels for the *X* and *Y* axes for better data comprehension.

The workbench allows for a high degree of interaction with your data, providing a practical and visual means of working with the various features and data structures offered by Redis.

The workbench section also includes tutorials and learning materials to assist you in getting more value from your Redis databases. This could involve guides on handling JSON documents, creating indexes, or using Redis as a vector database for similarity searches. You can also learn more about probabilistic data structures, which you will have explored in *Chapter 8*, *Understanding Probabilistic Data Structures*.

Essentially, the workbench is like a playground or laboratory for developers working with Redis databases. It provides a space where you can experiment, learn, and manage your data in a user-friendly way, and serves as a fantastic resource to deepen your understanding of these concepts and operations.

Now, let's shift our attention to the next section of the left-side panel named **Analysis Tools**, designed to help you assess your database and offer recommendations.

Analyzing data

The analysis tools provide insights into the kinds of data types in your database and their distribution. They also monitor performance and flag any slow queries.

First, let's delve into data distribution. The **Database Analysis** section offers **Data Summary** where you can view the breakdown of your data. To generate this summary, you'll need to collect all your data by clicking on the **New Report** button located in the top-right corner. Following this, your **Data Summary** should be visible and may resemble the following:

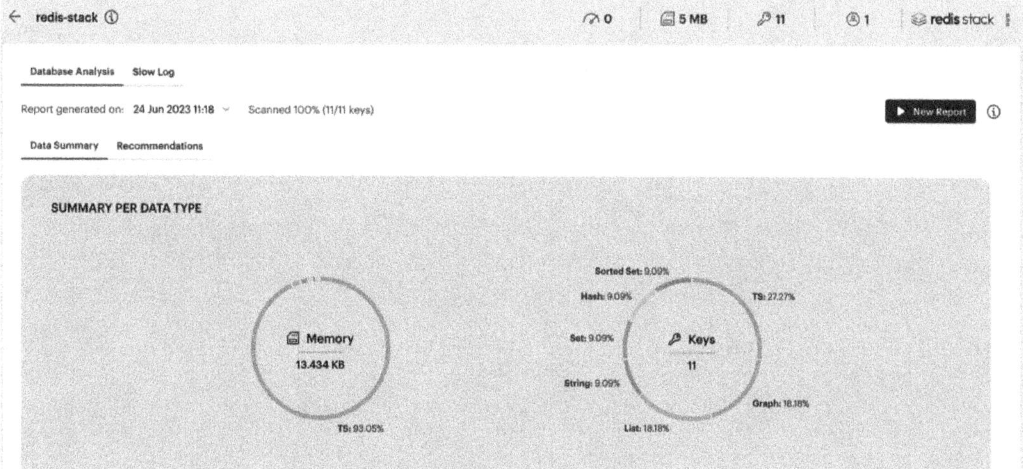

Figure 10.9 – RedisInsight Data Summary report

Another useful feature is a dedicated section for monitoring memory consumption. This provides insights into whether your data will be freed due to expiration or eviction policies:

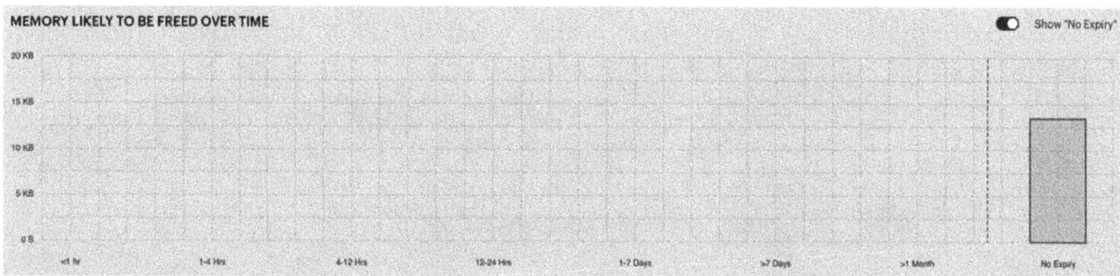

Figure 10.10 – RedisInsight memory consumption forecast

Two additional sections, **TOP NAMESPACES** and **TOP KEYS**, provide further granularity. **TOP NAMESPACES** gives an overview of your key patterns based on memory usage and the number of keys:

Key Pattern	Data Type	↓ Total Memory	Total Keys
mortensi.com:*	TS	4.133 KB	1
employee:*	SET	264 B	1
queue:*	LIST	147 B	1
user:*	HASH	140 B	1

Figure 10.11 – RedisInsight TOP NAMESPACES

Meanwhile, **TOP KEYS** displays the most memory-intensive keys and those that contain the most elements:

Key Type	Key Name	TTL	↓ Key Size	Length
TS	mortensi.com	No limit	4.188 KB	120
TS	foogaro.com	No limit	4.18 KB	120
TS	mortensi.com:weekly	No limit	4.133 KB	17
SET	employee:ids	No limit	264 B	2
LIST	cities	No limit	157 B	3
LIST	queue:tasks	No limit	147 B	1
HASH	user:1	No limit	140 B	4
SORTED SET	players	No limit	110 B	3
STRING	client	No limit	58 B	8
GRAPH	linkedin	No limit	40 B	4 265
GRAPH	company_ou	No limit	40 B	11

Figure 10.12 – RedisInsight TOP KEYS

Equally important is the **Slow Log** section, which relates to performance. Any requests sent to Redis Stack taking longer than 10 milliseconds will appear in this log. For illustrative purposes, I've adjusted the slowness threshold to 1 microsecond to capture some entries:

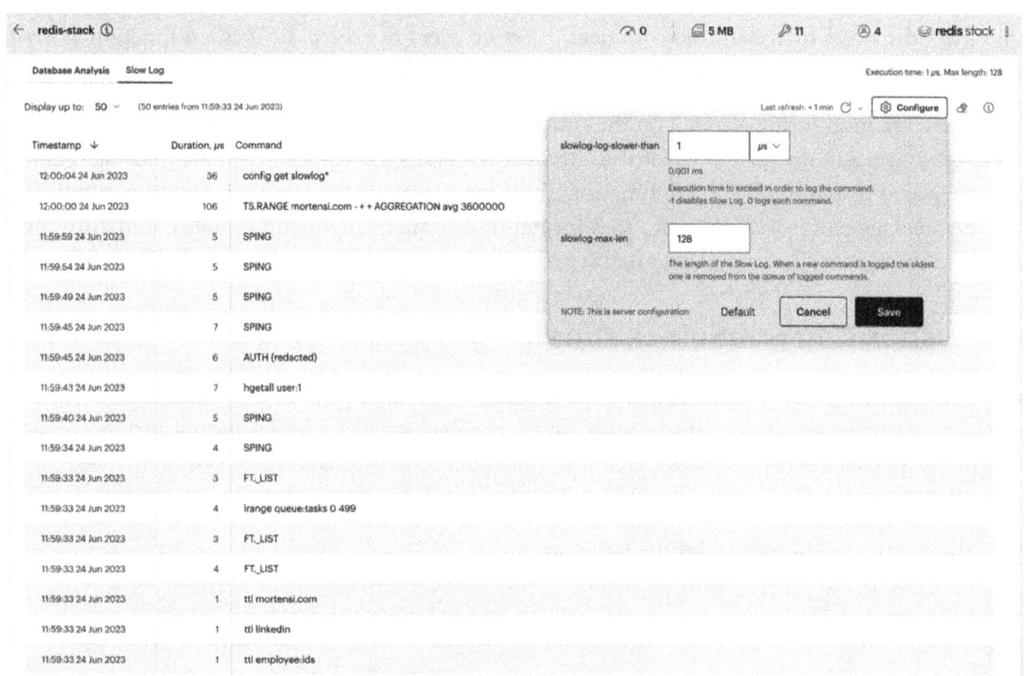

Figure 10.13 – RedisInsight Slow Log

This feature is particularly useful for debugging and troubleshooting, as it provides the exact timestamp of the query, its execution time, and the query itself.

Another critical feature in RedisInsight for monitoring is the Profiler. Be aware that the Profiler may impact the performance of your Redis Stack server, so its use is not recommended in a production environment.

To start the Profiler, click on the **Start Profiler** button, then try issuing a few commands in the **CLI**. These commands should appear in the **Profiler** section as follows:

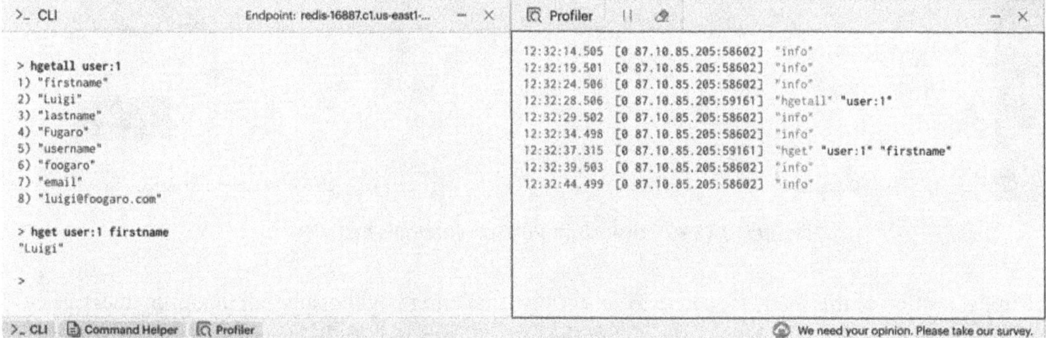

Figure 10.14 – RedisInsight Profiler with CLI

In my case, I can observe that an **info** command is issued every five seconds. This is a function of my Redis Cloud usage, which continuously monitors the system's health.

As we have seen, monitoring is based on the concept of an event, which can be represented by a log line or a message. Among its many features, Redis Stack offers the ability to publish messages and receive messages through the PubSub functionality. This allows for the implementation of publish/subscribe message patterns, a powerful tool for handling data changes and updates. RedisInsight allows us to test this feature as well, and that is precisely what we will learn about in the next section.

Troubleshooting PubSub channels

Access the PubSub feature by clicking on the fourth icon (signal symbol) in the left-side panel. This interface allows you to experiment with your PubSub channel for both sending and receiving messages. As we have covered in earlier chapters, PubSub is Redis's broadcasting system that enables your applications to instantly transmit and receive messages.

At first glance, the interface provides the following view:

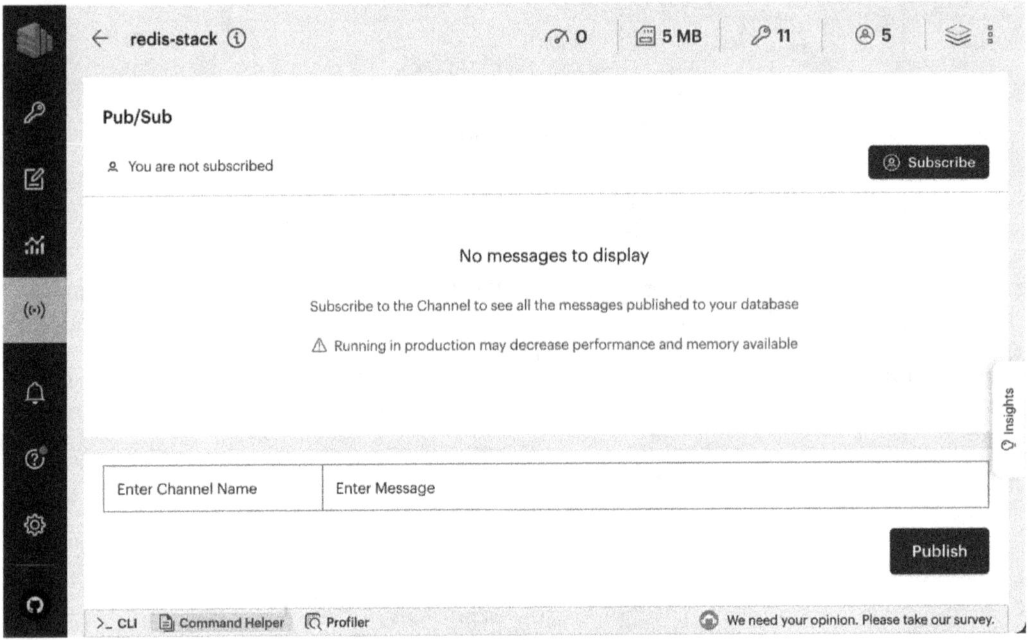

Figure 10.15 – RedisInsight PubSub channels first view

The upper section of this interface caters to subscribers, meaning it will display all incoming messages. By clicking on the **Subscribe** button located in the top-right corner, RedisInsight will subscribe to all channels, executing the **PSUBSCRIBE** * command.

The lower section of this interface enables you to publish messages. Here, you can input the name of the channel through which the message will be published and the content of the message itself. By clicking the **Publish** button located in the bottom-right corner, your message will be broadcast, as depicted in the following screenshot:

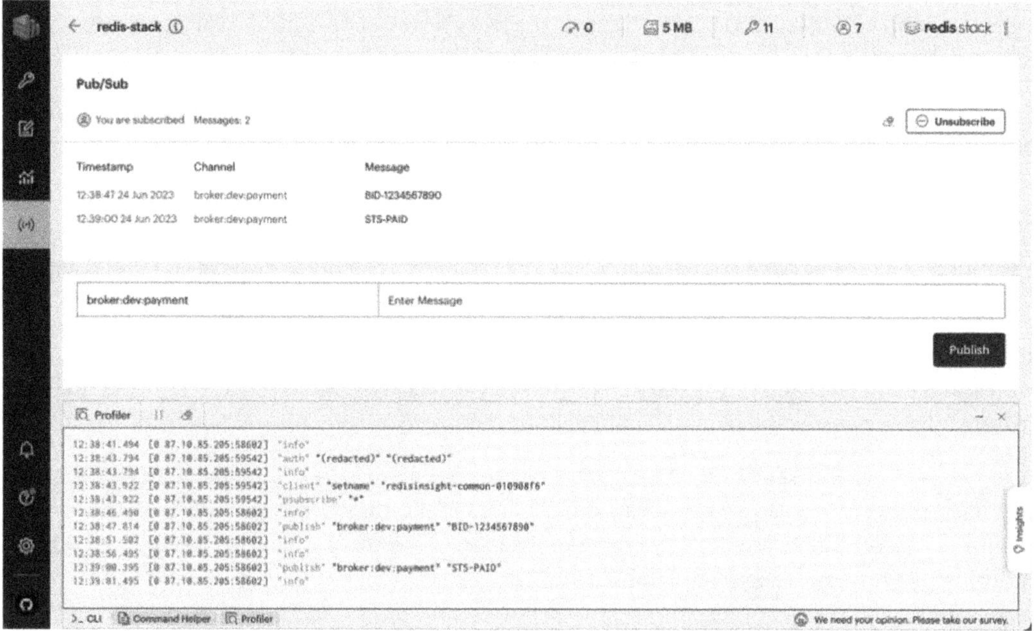

Figure 10.16 – RedisInsight PubSub example flow with Profiler enabled

The PubSub interface in RedisInsight provides a practical way to test and explore Redis's real-time messaging system, helping you to understand its capabilities and behavior.

The hands-on experience that RedisInsight's PubSub interface provides is not just beneficial – it's invaluable to anyone looking to master the intricacies of real-time messaging in Redis Stack. By actively using this interface, you have gained practical knowledge on how to publish messages to specific channels and how to subscribe to those channels to receive updates. This isn't merely theoretical understanding; it's applied learning that equips you with the skills needed to implement effective messaging workflows in a live Redis environment.

Summary

RedisInsight is a robust GUI designed to make working with Redis databases much simpler and more intuitive. It allows you to interact with your databases visually, enabling you to more easily access your data, run queries, and troubleshoot any issues. This is extremely beneficial, as it streamlines many of the tasks associated with managing a Redis database, ultimately saving you time and effort.

Furthermore, RedisInsight isn't just about ease of use – it also provides powerful features and functionality that can assist you in optimizing the performance and utilization of your Redis databases.

In this chapter, you have acquired valuable skills with the use of RedisInsight, starting with the process of downloading and installing the application. Furthermore, you've also learned how to establish a connection with a Redis database, which forms the basis for most operations you'll perform with Redis. This is a critical step in managing and manipulating your data effectively using RedisInsight.

Additionally, you've also learned how the analysis tools provide essential insights into data type distribution and database performance, empowering you to make informed decisions to optimize your Redis setup.

Furthermore, you've also been introduced to the Profiler, a crucial tool in RedisInsight that allows for real-time monitoring of your Redis databases, enhancing your ability to observe and understand their operational behavior.

Finally, you've been acquainted with the PubSub feature in RedisInsight, an invaluable tool that allows for the testing of publish-subscribe patterns in your Redis databases, thereby bolstering your ability to ensure reliable message exchange in your applications.

In *Chapter 11*, *Using Redis Stack as a Primary Database*, you will delve into the essentials of employing Redis Stack as the main database for serving multi-model applications. Here, you will explore how to capitalize on the robust persistence capabilities of Redis Stack, reinforcing your knowledge and skills in utilizing this versatile database technology.

11
Using Redis Stack as a Primary Database

In the previous chapters, we have covered most of the topics that concern software architects and engineers at the time of mapping the business logic of an application to the concrete physical data model using Redis. As a professional used to working with relational databases or document stores, you have learned to make the most of Redis using the core data structures and discovered the features delivered in Redis Stack, such as enhanced searches and queries, and working with JSON documents. Modeling entities and relationships with the traditional Hashes or the standard JSON format together with the ability to create indexes on different fields of documents stored in such formats shifts Redis from the realm of caches to that of **database management systems** (**DBMSs**).

Redis has long been used as a cache, and the original design encouraged such use, offering real-time performance and a predictable footprint, with efficient expiration and eviction algorithms. This means that Redis has historically been paired with other authoritative data stores. However, we will see that with the proper understanding of the features and configurations a primary store should have, Redis guarantees the highest level of reliability among databases without compromising data consistency and availability.

In this chapter, we will introduce the properties of a primary database and discuss the guarantees that architects demand from the data layer when designing an architecture. In this chapter, we will cover the following topics:

- What is a primary database?
- Redis as a primary database
- The BASE and ACID properties
- Configuring Redis for durability, consistency, and availability

Provided the consistency and availability properties of Redis Stack are equivalent to those of Redis, the references to Redis and Redis Stack you will find in this chapter are interchangeable.

Technical requirements

To follow along with the examples in the chapter, you will need to install Redis Stack Server 7.2 or a later version on your development environment. Alternatively, you can create a free Redis Cloud subscription to achieve a free plan and use a managed Redis Stack database.

What is a primary database?

There is no formal definition of what a **primary database** is and what requirements it should have; the interpretation of what features a primary database should support largely depends on the use case the data store fulfills. However, by looking at how traditional DBMSs are used as primary and often unique solutions in the data layer, we can sketch a few traits:

- A database can be considered primary when it is the authoritative source of data and stores the most recent copy of data. Secondary databases instead serve read-only workloads, either using the same technology as the primary database (using proprietary master-replica protocols) or as in-memory caches (using methods such as change data capture).
- A primary database serves mixed **online transactional processing** (**OLTP**) workloads, such as searches or scans and lookups, and may have analytical processing capabilities.
- A primary database is reliable and can stand single software or hardware failures, supporting failovers to redundant copies and recovery from backups in case of massive disasters.
- A primary database must scale as the amount of data and/or operations increase.

Redis and Redis Stack both support highly available and scalable deployments by configuring a Sentinel cluster or configuring Redis as a multi-shard cluster. Redis Enterprise as a multi-tenancy data platform with Redis Stack capabilities improves the availability and scalability of Redis to a production-grade DBMS. We will cover the difference between Redis open source and Redis Enterprise in *Chapter 12, Managing Development and Production Environments*. In this chapter, we will focus on data consistency when using Redis as a primary database.

Redis as a primary database

When Redis is deployed in a replicated topology with Sentinel agents or as a Redis cluster, it fulfills the typical requirements of a DBMS in terms of availability and scalability. Redis supports backups and recovery to a consistent state in case of major issues. In terms of hardening, Redis provides user permission management via **access-control lists** (**ACLs**), traffic encryption, and additional security features. Tools for benchmarking, monitoring, and auditing a Redis or Redis Stack database are available as well, and together with a rich set of client libraries, the Redis ecosystem integrates with all kinds of software architectures. We'll discuss the manageability of Redis in scalable and available scenarios in the next chapter and compare the different flavors: open source, Enterprise, and Cloud. In this section, we'll focus on the discussion around using Redis as an authoritative source of data.

Redis is commonly adopted as a cache to speed up data lookups and alleviate the pressure on primary data stores. Redis is also used for secondary index searches when replicating data from an authoritative data source, such as a **relational DBMS** (**RDBMS**), and speeding up searches and queries on documents modeled as Hash or JSON formats. In these contexts, Redis is a secondary data store that replicates changes from a primary store and offers sub-millisecond latency to lookups, searches, and queries. However, Redis shines as a primary database if used for many use cases: as a session store, as an authentication token store, as an online feature store, as a geo-positioning server, or as a vector database, to give a few examples. In such scenarios, there is no dependency on primary stores and Redis is the only mission-specific database. And, as such, while it is unfeasible to adapt the same database technology for several heterogeneous uses, we can certainly state that Redis is a suitable primary database in multiple scenarios. When using Redis in such use cases, we cannot help but stop for a moment and ponder the trade-off between data consistency and availability. Architects and database administrators, aware of the fact that NoSQL databases tend to privilege availability and partition tolerance (the BASE properties: Basically Available, Soft State, and Eventual Consistency) over consistency for the benefit of scalability and performance, may wonder how safe it is to use Redis as an authoritative data store, especially when considering it in the context of the ACID properties.

The BASE and ACID properties

Grouping the properties of Redis is immediate and serves the purpose of understanding where it fits between the ACID and BASE models. While relational databases usually follow the **ACID consistency model**, Redis, as a NoSQL real-time in-memory data store with support for replication and scalability, and used as a key-value, data structure, document, and vector store, fulfills the BASE properties. The BASE model does not stand necessarily as a replacement for the ACID model, but suggests the idea that databases may privilege some properties rather than others or blend them in order to excel in specific use cases. Let's introduce the BASE and ACID properties and discover how Redis fulfills them.

The BASE properties

Let's examine what the BASE properties are and see why Redis complies with them, as most of the **NoSQL** databases do. The idea of the BASE properties for distributed systems was presented in 1999 by the computer scientist Eric Brewer in the context of the formulation of the CAP theorem. The properties are as follows:

- **Basically Available**: Redis is still available in case of failure. Given the support of one or multiple replicas per master instance, either in a Sentinel deployment, in a Redis Cluster, or deploying the Enterprise or Cloud flavors, Redis guarantees high availability and resilience in case of the master instance crash and other failures.
- **Soft State**: Stored data may change even without user interaction. This is the case of delayed replicas that need to catch up with the replication lag, so their state is updated as replication progresses. In addition, when Redis is configured as a cache, data eviction and expiration are

additional examples of data changes that determine the soft state. In a strongly consistent distributed system, instead, consistent data is available on all the replicas at any time, so regardless of user interactions, the guarantee is that the data will not change over time (hard state).

- **Eventual Consistency**: An eventually consistent system may present a temporary lapse of time during which copies of the data (master and replica) are not consistent. However, the system guarantees that after user input, the data will be replicated and available in all the replicas, hence consistent with the master copy of the data. Redis-replicated databases are eventually consistent. Replication is asynchronous for the benefit of high performance.

NoSQL databases surged as a compromise to the strict ACID model, which enforces data consistency but poses constraints on the availability of data and limits performance by enforcing a series of strategies to maximize reliability. That said, we can still consider the degree of compliance of Redis to the ACID properties; that'll help set the right expectations when Redis is used as a primary database, especially in case of errors or failures.

The ACID properties

We have stated that Redis does not privilege the consistency model in the dichotomy of ACID versus BASE models. However, in this section, we will dive into the definition of ACID to understand more about the degree of compliance with such properties. We will see that borders are fuzzy and we'll show how Redis is a reliable database with some assumptions. While there are several interpretations, we will stick to the original definition of ACID databases from the famous paper *Principles of Transaction-Oriented Database Recovery*, released in 1983 by Andreas Reuter and Theo Härder. Far from educating you on the properties of ACID transactions, we will recap the original definitions at the beginning of the following sections to introduce Redis's features in the context of such properties.

Atomicity

All of the actions included in a transaction must be executed indivisibly: either all actions are properly reflected in the database or nothing has happened. No changes are reflected in the database, and the user must, whatever happens, know which state he or she is in.

Redis supports transactions, intended as atomic executions of a series of commands that are either executed by the database and reflected in changes to data or discarded. Transactions in Redis are executed with the `WATCH`, `MULTI`, `EXEC`, and `DISCARD` commands. However, the definition implicitly requires that the property is fulfilled in all possible circumstances, so different types of failures have to be considered and analyzed. It is indeed true that if there is no error or failure, Redis transactions are either entirely executed at `EXEC` time or they can be purposefully discarded with `DISCARD`:

```
127.0.0.1:6379> MULTI
OK
127.0.0.1:6379(TX)> SET greetings hello
QUEUED
127.0.0.1:6379(TX)> DISCARD
```

```
OK
127.0.0.1:6379> GET greetings
(nil)
```

But if things can go wrong, they will. So, let's see what happens if Redis encounters a syntax error. If an error is reported **before the EXEC** command, the transaction is automatically discarded when one of the commands presents a syntax error. Commands are getting queued before the execution of the transaction, and when queuing a command, the syntax is checked:

```
127.0.0.1:6379> MULTI
OK
127.0.0.1:6379(TX)> SSET greetings hello
(error) ERR unknown command 'SSET', with args beginning with:
'greetings' 'hello'
127.0.0.1:6379(TX)> SET greetings hello
QUEUED
127.0.0.1:6379(TX)> EXEC
(error) EXECABORT Transaction discarded because of previous errors.
```

Commands may also fail **after the EXEC** command is called. For example, if a command is invoked against a non-suitable type, such as a `SET` command against a List data type, the failure will be reported at `EXEC` time. Let's consider the following example:

```
127.0.0.1:6379> LPUSH greetings hello hola
(integer) 2
127.0.0.1:6379> MULTI
OK
127.0.0.1:6379(TX)> SET hola mundo
QUEUED
127.0.0.1:6379(TX)> SADD greetings ciao
QUEUED
127.0.0.1:6379(TX)> EXEC
1) OK
2) (error) WRONGTYPE Operation against a key holding the wrong kind of
value
```

In the previous excerpt, we are trying to add an element to the List using the `SADD` command, suitable for Sets. The transaction reports an error at execution time for the second command but the first is successful. Let's verify the outcome by having a quick look at the keyspace:

```
127.0.0.1:6379> GET hola
"mundo"
127.0.0.1:6379> LRANGE greetings 0 -1
1) "hola"
2) "hello
```

The transaction has been partially executed, as reported: Redis does not stop the execution of the transaction, by design. One may object that checking the semantics of the commands queued to a transaction would be straightforward. However, such errors must be isolated and fixed at software implementation and testing time, so that Redis transactions can be lightweight by omitting such checks that would slow down the execution.

While the errors exposed so far are introduced by developers or administrators, database failures (a bug in the Redis code base causing a crash of the process) or system failures (an outage or a hardware failure) are impossible to anticipate and may abruptly interrupt any possible state of the database. When a failure such as a crash happens in the middle of a transaction (before the execution of `EXEC`), the transaction will be fully discarded. However, if the failure happens while the transaction is being persisted on disk to the **append-only file** (**AOF**), partial writes are possible, causing an incomplete transaction to persist on disk.

If on one side Redis minimizes the chances of hitting such errors by writing the transaction on disk using a single `write(2)` syscall, and even in the case of configuring the strictest `fsync` policy (`appendfsync always`), such errors are possible. Redis does not implement a double-write mechanism for data persistence, so this error cannot be automatically recovered at database restart when crash recovery is performed (when the AOF file is reloaded in memory). When detecting a partially written transaction in the AOF, Redis will report an error that can be fixed with the `redis-check-aof` tool, which offers the capability to rectify the AOF by removing any partial transactions, thereby allowing the server to restart correctly and discarding the incomplete transaction.

Let's test it with an example. Start a Redis or Redis Stack server using the `redis.conf` configuration file provided as follows. Note that the default configuration in Redis 7 is to allow servers to restart even in case of corruption, hence we are setting the value of `aof-load-truncated` to `no`:

```
appendonly yes
appendfsync always
aof-load-truncated no
logfile "/tmp/redis.log"
```

Execute a transaction:

```
127.0.0.1:6379> MULTI
OK
127.0.0.1:6379(TX)> SET hello world
QUEUED
127.0.0.1:6379(TX)> SET hola mundo
QUEUED
127.0.0.1:6379(TX)> EXEC
1) OK
2) OK
```

Now, shut down the server using the `SHUTDOWN` command and go have a look at the AOF file (with Redis 7, you will find it in a file named something like `appendonlydir/appendonly.aof.1.incr.aof`). Scroll to the bottom of the file and verify that the transaction has been registered:

```
MULTI
*3
$3
SET
$5
hello
$5
world
*3
$3
SET
$4
hola
$5
mundo
*1
$4
EXEC
```

Now simulate a corruption by editing it so you can, for example, remove the last command and the `EXEC` command, leaving it as follows:

```
MULTI
*3
$3
SET
$5
hello
$5
world
*3
```

In another console, tail the log file with the following:

```
tail -f /tmp/redis.log
```

Then restart the server, as done earlier. The server will fail to start, and the report will be as follows:

```
82974:M 04 Jul 2023 11:58:15.338 # Revert incomplete MULTI/EXEC
transaction in AOF file appendonly.aof.1.incr.aof
82974:M 04 Jul 2023 11:58:15.338 # Unexpected end of file reading
```

```
the append only file appendonly.aof.1.incr.aof. You can: 1) Make a
backup of your AOF file, then use ./redis-check-aof --fix <filename.
manifest>. 2) Alternatively you can set the 'aof-load-truncated'
configuration option to yes and restart the server.
```

Following the recommendation of the log, let's proceed to fix the AOF file:

```
redis-check-aof --fix appendonlydir/appendonly.aof.manifest

Start checking Multi Part AOF
Start to check BASE AOF (RDB format).
[...]
RDB preamble is OK, proceeding with AOF tail...
AOF analyzed: filename=appendonly.aof.1.base.rdb, size=89, ok_up_
to=89, ok_up_to_line=1, diff=0
BASE AOF appendonly.aof.1.base.rdb is valid
Start to check INCR files.
0x              42: Reached EOF before reading EXEC for MULTI
AOF analyzed: filename=appendonly.aof.1.incr.aof, size=73, ok_up_
to=23, ok_up_to_line=16, diff=50
This will shrink the AOF appendonly.aof.1.incr.aof from 73 bytes, with
50 bytes, to 23 bytes
Continue? [y/N]: y
Successfully truncated AOF appendonly.aof.1.incr.aof
All AOF files and manifest are valid
```

Now you can open the AOF file, verify what has happened, and restart the server successfully.

As seen in this section, running transactions in Redis is possible. While Redis by design lacks a transaction manager with automatic rollback and isolation levels, transactional behavior can be implemented on a standalone Redis server, and also in a clustered Redis or Redis Enterprise, under the assumption that data changed by the transaction is located in the same data partition or shard. Redis Cluster and Redis Enterprise Cluster do not support distributed transactions across multiple shards by design and for the benefit of performance.

Considering transactions in Redis, it is worth pointing out that support for transactions is not the typical requirement for which one would choose a NoSQL database. It is then important to note that in Redis, it is possible to execute multiple changes against collections atomically. In the following example, adding multiple pairs to a Hash dictionary is an atomic operation, and persisted to disk with a single write system call:

```
127.0.0.1:6379> HSET document:123 title "Talking about ACIDity"
content "Variadic commands are atomic"
(integer) 2
```

An operation that changes multiple properties in a JSON document is atomic, too:

```
127.0.0.1:6379> JSON.SET document:123 $ '{"title":"Talking about
ACIDity", "content":"JSON operations are atomic"}'
OK
```

Finally, multi-key commands are atomic too. The following is from the documentation of the `MSET` (`https://redis.io/commands/mset/`) command:

MSET is atomic, so all given keys are set at once. It is not possible for clients to see that some of the keys were updated while others are unchanged.

`MSET`, as a multi-key command, sets multiple field-value pairs at once:

```
MSET {user:123} "John Smith" {user:123}:address "Yigal Alon St 94, Tel
Aviv-Yafo, Israele"
```

Examples of multi-key commands are `BITOP`, `BLPOP`, `BRPOP`, `BRPOPLPUSH`, `MSETNX`, `RPOPLPUSH`, `SDIFF`, `SDIFFSTORE`, `SINTER`, `SINTERSTORE`, `SMOVE`, `SORT`, `SUNION`, `ZINTER`, `ZINTERSTORE`, `ZUNION`, `ZUNIONSTORE`, `ZDIFF`, and `ZDIFFSTORE`.

To complete this overview of Redis transactions, it is worth highlighting that both Lua scripts and functions and JavaScript functions exhibit transactional behavior since they are executed atomically, and the observations made in this section apply to the execution of such functions. You can refer to *Chapter 9*, *The Programmability of Redis Stack*, to learn more about this topic.

Consistency

A transaction reaching its normal end (EOT, end of transaction), thereby committing its results, preserves the consistency of the database. In other words, each successful transaction by definition commits only legal results.

The C in ACID is probably the most ambiguous property, as it appears as a restatement of the rest of the properties. If a transaction is atomic, isolated, and persisted, the transaction is also legal and recoverable in case of abrupt database termination. However, there is something more to point out. Sticking to the definition given by Wikipedia:

Consistency ensures that a transaction can only bring the database from one consistent state to another, preserving database invariants: any data written to the database must be valid according to all defined rules, including constraints, cascades, triggers, and any combination thereof. This prevents database corruption by an illegal transaction. Referential integrity guarantees the primary key–foreign key relationship.

From this, we can better see that the original definition is split into two parts:

- A transaction will bring the database from one consistent state to another.
- Database invariants are preserved.

While the second statement is self-explanatory in terms of the constraints (referential integrity, not null, ...) available in ACID databases and used as consistency criteria, the first statement brings the client applications into the picture to understand what a consistent transaction is. Clients are responsible for initiating transactions, enforcing integrity constraints, and executing operations in a consistent manner. Translating this to the database means that the database must fulfill the commands executed by the client in a way that the rules of the application are consistent, and the changes are committed when the client application decides to complete the transaction. Hence, the definition of consistency embraces applications as well in the definition of what consistency should look like. The C in ACID refers to logical consistency and, in short, guarantees that the database can map application business logic to the database while preserving the database invariants.

Translating the definition to Redis is immediate. Redis doesn't have such constraints, so it is possible to interpret the property and state that a Redis database will not be logically corrupted after a transaction is executed.

Isolation

Events within a transaction must be hidden from other transactions running concurrently. If this were not the case, a transaction could not be reset to its beginning for the reasons sketched earlier.

By design, as a single-threaded architecture database, Redis guarantees that the clients have exclusive access to the keyspace, either performing a single command or executing a `MULTI/EXEC` transaction. As mentioned, Redis does not implement a transaction manager and does not offer full isolation, and in addition, Redis does not implement locks that guarantee exclusive access to data structures. This implies that a transaction may commit changes to data that has been modified by a concurrent transaction. To give an example, a session may execute the following transaction:

```
127.0.0.1:6379> SET greeting hello
OK
127.0.0.1:6379> MULTI
OK
127.0.0.1:6379(TX)> APPEND greeting " world"
QUEUED
127.0.0.1:6379(TX)> EXEC
1) (integer) 11
127.0.0.1:6379> GET greeting
"hello world"
```

But we can execute the following lines from a terminal session:

```
127.0.0.1:6379> SET greeting hello
OK
127.0.0.1:6379> MULTI
OK
127.0.0.1:6379(TX)> APPEND greeting " world"
QUEUED
```

Then, from another terminal session, we change the value of the key as follows:

```
127.0.0.1:6379> SET greeting ciao
OK
```

Completing the transaction, you can verify that the desired change *within* the transaction has been affected by another session:

```
127.0.0.1:4321(TX)> EXEC
1) (integer) 10
127.0.0.1:4321> GET greeting
"ciao world"
```

Redis did not lock the `greetings` key, and the concurrent session has changed the key at will. There is another way to manage such situations: Redis offers the `WATCH` command, which allows clients to monitor specific keys for modifications. `WATCH` can be used in conjunction with transactions to implement optimistic locking. Transactions are rejected if the watched keys have been modified by other sessions before executing a transaction, providing a form of isolation. The previous example would then be improved as follows:

```
127.0.0.1:6379> SET greeting hello
OK
127.0.0.1:6379> WATCH greeting
OK
127.0.0.1:6379> MULTI
OK
127.0.0.1:6379(TX)> APPEND greeting " world"
QUEUED
127.0.0.1:6379(TX)> EXEC
(nil)
```

The transaction has been aborted and no change was completed.

Let's now consider the durability property and see what options exist to configure Redis as a durable database.

Durability

Once a transaction has been completed and has committed its results to the database, the system must guarantee that these results survive any subsequent malfunctions. Since there is no sphere of control constituting a set of transactions, the database management system (DBMS) has no control beyond transaction boundaries. Therefore the user must have a guarantee that the things the system says have happened have actually happened.

When working with in-memory caches, durability may not be a strong requirement. If any malfunction causes a crash of the process or the entire system suffers an outage, the cache can always be restarted without data and provisioned when the client hits a cache miss (lazy loading). Alternatively, it is possible to perform a full synchronization from a primary data source. On the other hand, it can be desirable to minimize cache misses to avoid latency spikes. In this case, a hot cache is required as soon as it is restarted after a failure. Redis has reliable persistence mechanisms that guarantee durability: the data can be persisted to a storage device and reloaded in memory at restart.

Let's dig into the journey of a write operation after it leaves the client, is stored in the primary memory (the keyspace), and needs to be persisted to disk:

1. The database invokes the `write(2)` syscall. This command is used to write the data to disk, so the data is transferred to the *OS buffer cache* first.
2. The database invokes the `fsync` syscall. This command transfers what is in the OS buffer cache to the *cache of the storage device.*
3. The disk controller persists the data from the cache to the *physical device* (solid state or rotational hard disk).

The buffer cache mentioned in steps 1 and 2 can be audited with `free`, as an example:

```
free -m
          total  used  free  shared   buff/cache   available
Mem:       7959  1145   692     330         6121        6097
Swap:      2047    14  2033
```

In Linux, Unix-like systems, and other OSs, the buffer cache serves as a memory cache that is used to improve the efficiency and performance of disk I/O operations. It is an intermediate layer between the filesystem and the physical disk managed by the kernel that temporarily stores the data that is read from or written to the disk. The buffer cache is enabled by default on Linux systems but can be bypassed by the application using the `O_DIRECT` or `O_SYNC` mode. When this happens, every `write(2)` operation is performed synchronously, and it doesn't return until the data has been physically written to the underlying storage device. Bypassing the buffer cache does not offer any granularity on the desired durability: every write operation is simply written to disk, which may be simply too slow. In addition, systems using the buffer cache protect the data against database crashes.

When the data is in the buffer cache, the keyspace is not the only existing copy of the data, and a subsequent crash of the Redis process, or Redis being killed manually or by the OOM killer, will not affect the data in the buffer cache, which can be flushed to disk by the OS soon afterward. Linux usually synchronizes the data in the buffer cache to disk autonomously every 30 seconds. However, if, between the `write` and the `fsync` operations, a system crash (an outage, as an example) occurs, data will inevitably be lost.

AOF and RDB

Redis can be configured as a durable data store enabling the AOF persistence with the `appendonly` parameter set to `yes`. Every change occurring in the database is appended to a text file in the same readable format of the protocol used by Redis (the RESP protocol). While there are several parameters affecting the behavior of the AOF feature, let's focus on the desired persistence policy, which can be configured as follows:

- `appendfsync no`: With this setting, the moment when the changes in the OS buffer cache are flushed to disk is not decided by Redis, which does not call `fsync`. Clients get the acknowledgment that the write operation is successful when the data is transferred to the buffer cache with `write(2)`. The OS flushes the buffer cache at will, usually every 30 seconds. Changes that occurred up to 30 seconds before an incident may not have reached the AOF file on disk and be lost.
- `appendfsync everysec`: Changes in the OS buffer cache are flushed to disk every second (fast but less safe). Changes that occurred up to one second before an incident may not have reached the AOF file on disk and be lost.
- `appendfsync always`: Every time changes to data occur in memory, they are appended to the AOF file. Write commands proceeding from single commands or pipelines from one or multiple clients enter in the latest event loop iteration, and at the end of the iteration, the file is flushed to disk. This is the safest option but also the slowest. However, as noted, when there are multiple parallel writes in the same loop iteration, Redis will attempt to perform a single `fsync` operation at the end of the loop, as this policy supports **group commit**. This enhancement guarantees that even with this strict durability setting, Redis can sustain hundreds of concurrent transactions per second and in case of failure, Redis will lose at most the latest group of commits.

Durability can also be achieved by means of RDB data snapshots, which are point-in-time copies of the data in memory using the `SAVE` (synchronous) or `BGSAVE` (asynchronous) commands. However, snapshots don't provide the same level of durability as AOF. Such dumps are collected at regular intervals and may have non-negligible effects on the performance of the database, so their periodic collection should be planned to cause minimal impact. Usually, dumps are collected every few minutes or hours. In this section, we will consider AOF as the mechanism guaranteeing maximum durability to a Redis server.

As said, Redis databases are not fully ACID-compliant because the atomicity of transactions is not guaranteed in case of a crash (crashes may be caused by the OOM killer, a bug, or a system failure). It is possible to detect and fix issues deriving from crashes when they cause incomplete transactions to be persisted using the `redis-check-aof` tool. An additional safety measure would be using storage devices with battery-backed RAID caching controllers.

A battery-backed RAID write caching controller plays a crucial role in database durability. It helps ensure that data modifications made by database transactions are safely stored on disk, even in the event of unexpected power failures or system crashes. When a database transaction needs to be persisted on disk, the controller first stores the changes in its volatile memory cache instead of immediately writing them to the disk. This caching technique improves performance by reducing the number of disk write operations.

However, to maintain durability and prevent data loss, the controller must periodically flush the cached data from memory to the disk. This is where the `fsync` command comes into play. The `fsync` command is issued by the database server to the storage system, specifically targeting the files associated with the modified data.

When the `fsync` command is received, the battery-backed write caching controller ensures that all the cached data is durably written to the disk before acknowledging the completion of the command to the server, and finally, to the client. By relying on the battery backup, the controller can safely complete the flushing process even if there is a power outage or system crash. The backup power source ensures that the cached data is written to the disk and not lost due to the loss of volatile memory.

In summary, the battery-backed write caching controller, in conjunction with the `fsync` command, provides a reliable mechanism to achieve durability in databases. It allows data modifications to be temporarily cached in volatile memory for performance reasons while ensuring that the changes are ultimately written to disk in a durable manner.

Guarantees of pipelines

Clients using pipelining sacrifice the ability to receive immediate feedback on the outcome of each command in exchange for improved speed. This means that before executing the next command, clients do not wait for a response to the previous command; pipelines are batches of commands, and Redis will return a batch of results. For these clients, it is not necessary to commit the data and provide a reply immediately, as they prioritize speed over receiving immediate responses. Nonetheless, even when using pipelining, data writes and fsyncs (depending on the configuration) always occur when concluding an iteration of the event loop. Basically, durability guarantees are preserved even when pipelines are used, and clients trade knowing the immediate outcome of the single command for speed.

We have concluded the discussion on the BASE and ACID properties and discovered how Redis fulfills such properties. In the next section, we will consider what configuration guarantees the highest consistency and availability, and expose the trade-offs and compromises with different settings.

Configuring Redis for durability, consistency, and availability

For those scenarios where reliability matters besides availability, you can consider the following configurations.

Configuring snapshots

Snapshots (also called Redis database snapshots, or RDBs) provide a consistent binary dump of the data stored in the keyspace and are used to perform data recovery to a specific point in time. You should set the following in the configuration file:

```
save 900 1000
dbfilename "dump.rdb"
```

These settings enable snapshots every 900 seconds if at least 1,000 keys have changed. This kind of persistence is good for point-in-time restores and is also considered a backup. So, from time to time, you should copy the RDB snapshot file to an external storage device on a different, possibly remote host (invoking a script with `cron`, as an example) to discard major incidents affecting the local storage device. This method cannot be considered valid to achieve a good **recovery point objective** (**RPO**); snapshots are expensive operations and are usually collected every few hours. Configuring AOF persistence is the way to go.

Configuring AOF

As mentioned, the best RPO can be achieved when AOF is configured:

- `appendfsync everysec`: Changes in the OS buffer cache are flushed to disk every second (fast but less safe)
- `appendfsync always`: Every write is flushed to disk as it occurs (safer but slower)

However, it is a well-known fact that persisting every single write operation to disk is time- and resource-expensive. You can test yourself with a simple benchmark using the `redis-benchmark` tool. The following command executes 100,000 `SET` commands and uses a randomly generated key out of 10,000 possible keys. By default, the command simulates 50 clients and supports pipelining. Pipelining groups together multiple commands that are sent as a batch by the client and set to 16 commands:

```
redis-benchmark -t set -r 10000 -n 100000 -P 16
```

Running the benchmark with different persistence configurations leads to the following results, tested on commodity hardware such as a laptop. Note that a meaningful benchmark should be run from a separate host to understand the maximum throughput. However, in this case, we are interested in the relative numbers achieved with different configurations, so the benchmark can be executed locally to the database.

When `appendfsync` is configured to `everysec`, the benchmark will report the following summary:

```
Summary:
  throughput summary: 118483.41 requests per second
  latency summary (msec):
    avg       min       p50       p95       p99       max
  6.539     0.904     6.215     8.455    40.511    43.199
```

When `appendfsync` is configured to `always` instead, the benchmark will report the following:

```
Summary:
  throughput summary: 15339.78 requests per second
  latency summary (msec):
    avg       min       p50       p95       p99       max
  51.397    11.080    56.255    62.175    65.151    73.023
```

Flushing every change to disk causes *dramatically negative impacts* on the throughput, so it must be used wisely and benchmarked in advance.

Now run this simple benchmark with increasing iterations and note the pressure on the storage device in the case of setting AOF to `everysec`:

```
iostat -c 100 -w 1
              disk0           cpu      load average
    KB/t  tps  MB/s   us sy id    1m    5m   15m
   49.71  200  9.71   18  6 75  2.90 2.86 3.02
   90.35   51  4.50   19  6 75  2.90 2.86 3.02
   92.54   52  4.68   19  6 75  2.90 2.86 3.02
  134.70   40  5.24   20  6 74  2.90 2.86 3.02
   48.02  167  7.81   24 10 66  2.99 2.88 3.02
```

Then compare with the system metrics when setting AOF to `always` and note how the `tps` increases and how the rest of the metrics vary:

```
sh-3.2# iostat -c 100 -w 1
              disk0           cpu      load average
    KB/t  tps  MB/s   us sy id    1m    5m   15m
   75.33  155 11.40   17 14 69  2.58 2.46 2.95
    7.61  653  4.86   16  9 74  2.58 2.46 2.95
   13.54  775 10.25   19 11 70  2.58 2.46 2.95
    7.77  646  4.90   14 11 75  2.58 2.46 2.95
    6.91  632  4.27   14  8 77  2.58 2.46 2.95
```

The `appendfsync always` configuration, together with a battery-backed caching controller, is the safest from the perspective of RPO. When using such a configuration, it is mandatory to make additional considerations:

- What is the *relative read/write rate*? If using Redis mostly for read operations, a conservative AOF persistence setting may be acceptable.
- Is Redis deployed in a *clustered mode* (Redis OSS Cluster, or a clustered database in Redis Enterprise Cluster)? Deploying Redis shards on multiple hosts, hence writing shards' related AOF files in parallel to multiple storage devices, increases the I/O bandwidth available.

- Can I *tolerate losing some data* (write operations executed during, at most, a one-second-long lapse of time)? When Redis is used as a primary database to store sessions or authentication tokens, losing a limited number of data structures may be acceptable.

Choosing the desired durability is usually a function of other requirements and hardware capabilities. Redis, as a real-time and in-memory data store, can be configured to not lose any single key, but it must be kept in mind that trading performance for durability must be evaluated accurately.

Let's see now how service availability fits into the same picture.

Configuring high availability

We have gone through the principal consistency settings to ensure that data is preserved up to the latest change and discovered how to increase the throughput by allowing a relaxed persistence configuration. Consistency is not everything we need to take care of, though, because guaranteeing the availability of the database is crucial. Redis implements several mechanisms to perform failover to a replica:

- Manual failover
- Automated failover using Sentinel
- Automated failover in a Redis Cluster with replication enabled
- Built-in automated failover in Redis Enterprise and Redis Cloud

We will discuss the differences in the next chapter, but regardless of the chosen Redis deployment, what matters is the consistency of the replica with the master copy of the data, and this does not depend on the chosen flavor of Redis (OSS or Enterprise) or a specific configuration. Replication is performed using an asynchronous protocol to maximize the performance. This means the following:

1. The client application performs a write operation to the Redis database.
2. The master server (or shard, if the database is clustered) executes the commands and eventually persists it to disk according to the desired RDB or AOF persistence method.
3. The client application is acknowledged.
4. Only then, the operation enters a buffer of commands that are replicated.

This rough sketch of the replication sequence of events implies that the replica server will run behind the master, depending on the throughput on the master replica, the network bandwidth, and the host resources, among other reasons. It is evident that a replica server that is lagging behind the master, in case of a master crash, may not have the latest changes, and when promoted to be the new master, will not offer a fully consistent copy of the data that was stored by the master. As discussed, this may not be an issue in those use cases where data loss is tolerated (if a bunch of authentication tokens is lost, this will cause those users or APIs to have to authenticate again). Nonetheless, users may want to preserve consistency in the master as well as in the replica, so failovers are guaranteed to preserve all the data that was written by application clients.

Configuring consistency

Redis offers two settings to maximize the consistency of replicas: `WAIT` and `WAITAOF`. `WAIT` can be used when we want to make sure that everything written previously has been replicated to the desired number of replicas. The signature of the command is as follows:

```
WAIT numreplicas timeout
```

Consider what is indicated by the documentation:

Note that WAIT does not make Redis a strongly consistent store: while synchronous replication is part of a replicated state machine, it is not the only thing needed. However, in the context of Sentinel or Redis Cluster failover, WAIT improves real-world data safety.

`WAIT` does not guarantee that when it reports a failure, the previous data was not replicated. `WAIT` may report false negatives (data is replicated, but `WAIT` fails because of a connectivity issue between the master and the replica/s) and in such a case, when `WAIT` fails, it is up to the application client to verify what has happened and manage the failure accordingly (check the replica, or re-execute a command if idempotent, as an example, such as `SADD`, `ZADD`, or `HSET`).

`WAITAOF` is similar to `WAIT`, but in addition to the guarantee that data has been replicated, it also reports when the local copy and/or the replicas have fsynced the change to disk:

```
WAITAOF numlocal numreplicas timeout
```

Using the `WAITAOF` command together with the most conservative AOF policy on both the master and the replica/s (`appendfsync always`) is the safest combination of options that users can configure to achieve consistent replicas and guarantee no data loss, at the price of non-negligible performance impacts.

Summary

Redis not only can be adopted safely as a primary database in many use cases, but it is also the best option in many terms. Secondary indexing of Hash and JSON documents together with the ability to perform complex and hybrid multi-field queries and with basic analytical processing capabilities makes Redis, Redis Stack, and the commercial Enterprise and Cloud versions full-fledged data management systems with full support for scalability and availability. While NoSQL databases don't generally fulfill the ACID properties but privilege availability over consistency, we have gone through the assumptions that help maximize the consistency of Redis databases against crashes, either in the standalone or replicated deployments.

Compromising on data integrity, consistency, and durability may not be an option, and in this chapter, you have learned to achieve the most durable configuration in Redis with the safest (but much less performing) AOF persistence policy. You have also discovered that making multiple changes to single data structures rather than using `MULTI`/`EXEC` transactions reduces the risk of incomplete transactions logged in the AOF (but incomplete transactions can also be rolled back before restarting a crashed server). Adopting a battery-backed RAID cache controller can offer additional guarantees that data is persisted even in case of power loss. Finally, you have been introduced to the replication guarantees when `WAIT` or `WAITAOF` are used so that replicas are consistent with master servers.

Even with the most conservative setup, configuration, and usage, Redis does not strictly fulfill the ACID properties per the standard and official definition (there is no transaction manager with support for isolation levels and rollbacks, to give an example). Instead, with the right assumptions, it is possible to maximize consistency and availability while achieving the desired performance.

In summary, we have discovered how Redis can be used as a unique data store, thus removing the need for both having a primary database and configuring a real-time secondary store as a cache. Redis as a primary database is a database that doesn't need a cache.

In *Chapter 12, Managing Development and Production Environments*, you will see how Redis technology can be used along the entire software engineering life cycle when traditional requirements such as availability and scalability are demanded, in addition to learning how to manage development and production environments in an easy and integrated way. You will learn how to set up Redis Stack for high availability and scalability, and understand what the benefits are of using the Redis Enterprise data platform and the managed Redis Enterprise Cloud flavor to forget about managing your data layer so you can focus on what matters: being successful at implementing and deploying your application and resting assured that your database will adapt to changing workloads with the maximum degree of availability.

12

Managing Development and Production Environments

Until now, you've ventured on a comprehensive exploration of Redis Stack. You've explored its capabilities as a document store, understood its potential as a vector database, and delved into its prowess as a time-series database. You've stepped into the fascinating world of probabilistic data structures and uncovered the deep programmability features of Redis Stack. You've been introduced to RedisInsight, a powerful data management GUI, and weighed the advantages of using Redis Stack as a primary database.

As you transition to this final chapter, it's essential to build upon what you've learned and dive deeper into the architectural nuances of Redis Stack. When discussing architecture, you must consider the target environments, such as production, development, testing, and validation environments. Each of these has unique needs and characteristics.

The primary distinctions between these environments are the following:

- Total cost of ownership (TCO)
- High availability (HA)
- Scalability
- Security

To culminate this journey, a critical step awaits you: migrating from a development environment with Redis Stack to a more robust production setting. Here, you have choices. You can transition to either Redis Enterprise or Redis Cloud, to achieve better performance and resilience. Redis Cloud, in particular, is a fully managed **Database as a Service (DBaaS)** solution provided by Redis. It offers the same convenience and reliability as Redis Enterprise but without the need for operational management. Both paths provide opportunities to elevate your Redis solutions, ensuring they meet the demands of real-world production scenarios. Let's dive into how to make the best choice for your needs and execute a seamless migration.

In this section of the final chapter, you will zero in on these pivotal aspects:

- Redis Stack as a development environment
- Preparing for production with Redis Enterprise
- Redis Cloud – an enterprise-ready Redis DBaaS

To begin, let's discuss the prerequisites for following this chapter.

Technical requirements

For the practical demonstrations outlined in this chapter, it is best to have Redis Stack Server 7.2 or a later version installed on your local development environment. Utilizing Redis Cloud might not be appropriate for these exercises, the reason being that Redis Cloud, as a fully managed service, abstracts away many architectural complexities that one would encounter with a local setup. This chapter specifically addresses the manual configuration of Redis Stack to achieve HA and scalability—features that are inherently and seamlessly managed in Redis Cloud. Thus, a local installation of Redis Stack is essential in your local development environment for the purposes of this guide.

Redis Stack as a development environment

When working with Redis Stack, achieving HA, scalability, and security might seem like a steep hill to climb. There's a lot to set up and monitor; however, don't be daunted! Even if you're just getting your feet wet, having a roadmap can be invaluable. That's why I've compiled a mini-guide for you. While it won't magically turn Redis Stack into an enterprise-grade solution, it will give you a solid foundation of general guidelines and recommendations to move in the right direction. Consider it your compass in the sometimes complex world of Redis Stack optimization.

HA

Let's start with HA. In Redis Stack, HA is achieved by increasing the number of Redis Stack instances configured as replicas. These replicas listen to and follow a primary instance. To set this up, specify the IP address and port of the primary instance, and all replicas will receive updates.

Typical configuration parameters within the Redis Stack configuration file include the following:

```
replicaof <masterip> <masterport>
masterauth <master-password>
masteruser <username>
replica-serve-stale-data yes
replica-read-only yes
```

It's crucial to note that replicas receive updates asynchronously, which means that the replica instance can be slightly lagging behind the master instance, depending on the throughput and the network bandwidth. In addition, in case of issues such as a crash on the master instance, there's a possibility of data loss.

However, certain measures can be implemented to mitigate this. For example, you can configure the master to only return a write acknowledgment to the application after the data has been replicated on at least *n* replicas. Moreover, it's possible to set a timeout, after which the primary instance will return an error acknowledgment to the application. The configuration parameters to achieve this behavior are shown here:

```
min-replicas-to-write 1
min-replicas-max-lag 10
```

If these two conditions are not met, the application receives an error, and the write is aborted. You will find more insights in this area in *Chapter 11, Using Redis Stack as a Primary Database*.

However, this alone doesn't ensure HA. If the primary shard fails, the replica shards will also find themselves in an inconsistent state due to the absence of the primary instance. HA mechanisms account for this by promoting one of the *n* replicas to become the primary in the event of a primary shard malfunction. This is precisely the role of **Redis Sentinel**, which is already integrated into Redis Stack.

So, what does it involve? Essentially, you initiate another Redis Stack process specifying the dedicated Sentinel configuration file, which includes references to the primary and replica shards.

To start a Redis Stack process as Redis Sentinel, do as follows:

```
redis-stack-server /path/to/sentinel.conf -sentinel
```

Alternatively, a specific Redis Sentinel command can be used, as follows:

```
redis-sentinel /path/to/sentinel.conf
```

Typical configuration parameters within the Sentinel configuration file include the following:

```
sentinel monitor mymaster 127.0.0.1 6379 2
sentinel down-after-milliseconds mymaster 60000
sentinel failover-timeout mymaster 180000
sentinel parallel-syncs mymaster 1
sentinel monitor resque 192.168.1.3 6380 4
sentinel down-after-milliseconds resque 10000
sentinel failover-timeout resque 180000
sentinel parallel-syncs resque 5
```

Redis Sentinel incorporates a mechanism to elect a replica shard as the primary, often referred to as the master. To ensure this election can take place, the number of Sentinel instances should be odd, starting from three. However, this doesn't mean you need precisely three Redis Stack shards to manage your data. It's entirely feasible to have a primary shard and a secondary shard, with HA managed by Redis Sentinel spread across at least three distinct nodes/processes.

This setup implies that you would be managing at least five Redis Stack processes in total: the primary shard (data), its replica (synchronized by the primary—data), and the three Sentinel processes overseeing HA. In this way, if the primary shard malfunctions, Sentinel detects the issue and elects a new primary shard.

The next diagram provides a representation of an architecture based on Redis Stack with Redis Sentinel:

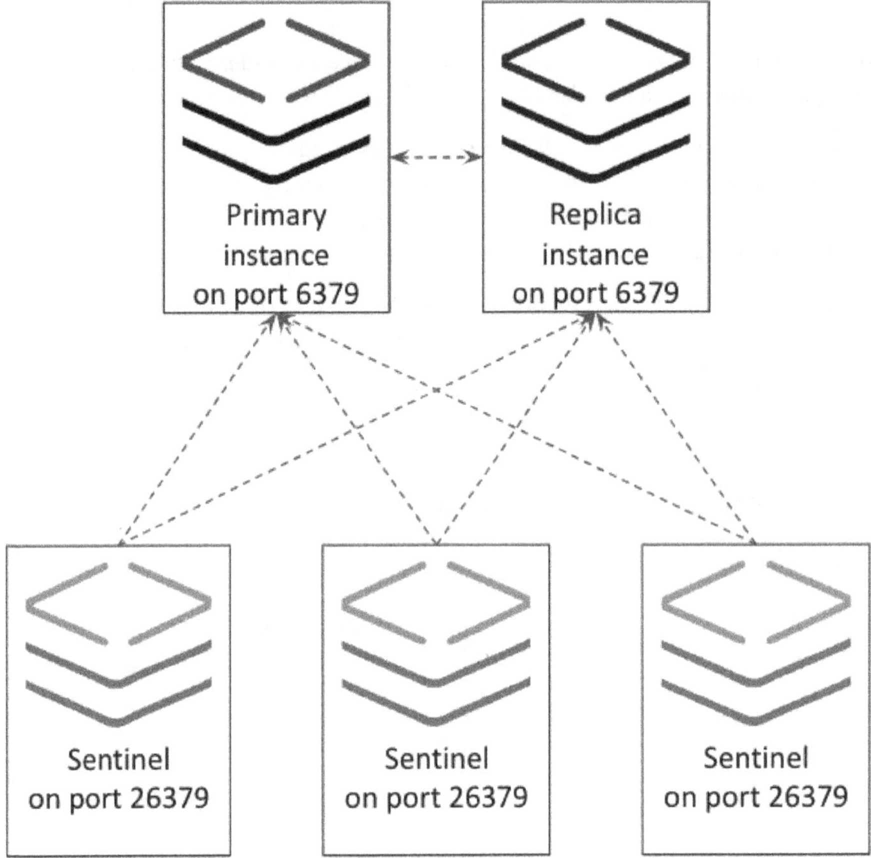

Figure 12.1 – Redis Stack architecture in HA with Redis Sentinel

In this configuration, each Redis Stack process resides on its own server, just as the Redis Sentinel processes do. This ensures a clear separation between the data and the HA functionality offered by Sentinel.

Now that we've delved into the intricacies of HA with Redis Stack, it's time to shift our focus to another critical aspect: scalability. As your system grows, so do its demands, and understanding how to scale effectively is key.

Scalability

When we talk about scalability in Redis Stack, we're diving into the concept of clustering, also known as sharding, a method to distribute a dataset across multiple Redis Stack shards. Imagine having a dataset: instead of having it on one instance, you can split it, say, between three shards, each managing roughly 33% of the data.

Inside Redis Stack, data is organized within a grid of 16,384 slots, known as hash slots. If you're running a single Redis Stack instance, all of these slots reside within that sole shard. But with three shards? The first shard takes care of slots ranging from 0 to 5460, the second manages slots from 5461 to 10921, and the third shard manages slots from 10922 to 16383.

So, how does Redis Stack decide where to place data? Remember—Redis Stack is a key-value store; the key, used to identify the data, is also fed into a hashing function, CRC16. The result of this function, when applied to the modulo operation with the total number of slots (16,384), gives a number between 0 and 16,383. Based on this number, Redis Stack determines which shard the data will reside in. It's this mechanism that enables scaling Redis architecture across dozens or even hundreds of nodes.

The clustering mechanism is intrinsic to Redis Stack. However, to harness it, you'll need to enable specific configuration parameters, as listed next:

- `cluster-enabled: <yes/no>`
- `cluster-config-file: <filename>`
- `cluster-node-timeout: <milliseconds>`

The concept of a node is introduced, mainly because scalability often requires additional resources. This is achieved by dynamically adding nodes to the cluster. While Redis Stack auto-manages cluster configurations on default ports and saves them to the file specified by `cluster-config-file`, setting up a cluster is a hands-on task. You'll have to provide a list of IP and port pairs, using the following command:

```
redis-cli --cluster create 127.0.0.1:7001 127.0.0.1:7002
127.0.0.1:7003
```

From here, a diagram of Redis Stack's clustered architecture will be showcased:

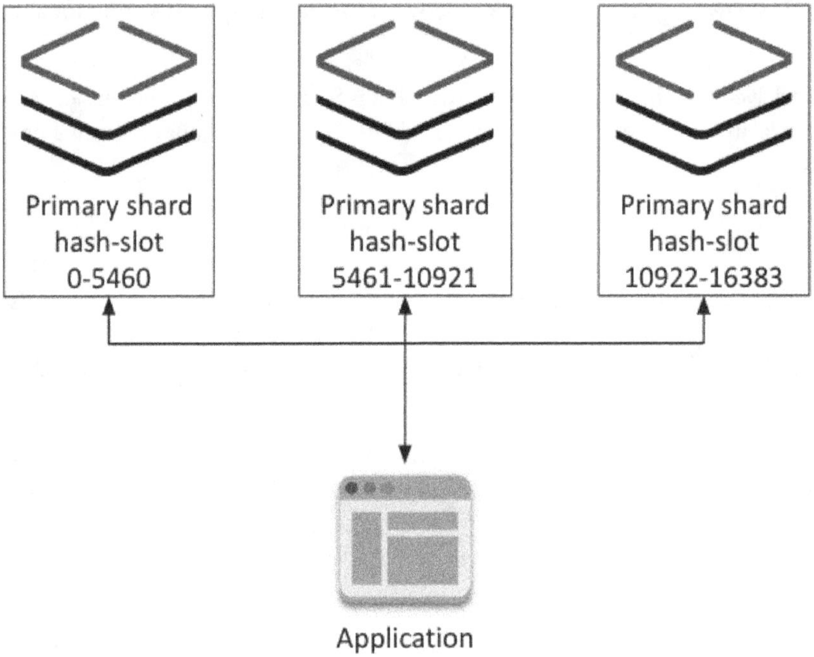

Figure 12.2 – Redis Stack with cluster enabled

Noticeably, if a node fails, it inevitably results in the loss of the respective range of hash slots and the associated data.

Nonetheless, just as with Sentinel, Redis Cluster allows for replication, enhancing the cluster's HA. To achieve this, you'll have to double the nodes, maintain identical configurations, and specify the number of replicas during cluster creation. The command is an extension of the previous one:

```
redis-cli --cluster create 127.0.0.1:7001 127.0.0.1:7002
127.0.0.1:7003 127.0.0.1:7004 127.0.0.1:7005 127.0.0.1:7006 --cluster-
replicas 1
```

Redis Stack then decides which nodes will have the primary shards and which ones will host the replica shards. Using the preceding command, you end up with a cluster comprising three primary instances and three replicas. An illustrative architecture of a replicated Redis Stack cluster is depicted next:

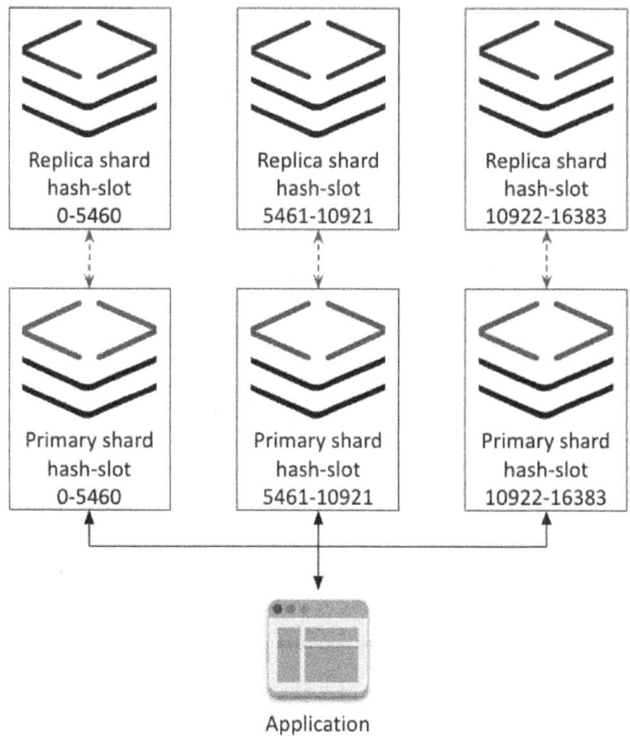

Figure 12.3 – Redis Stack with cluster replication enabled

Lastly, with the `redis-cli` tool, you can inspect cluster nodes, shards, and the distribution of hash slots.

Here, we're inspecting the nodes:

```
redis-cli -p 7001 CLUSTER NODES
617fa344e767a4da7fad53e4dd2bc9918e54116e 127.0.0.1:7002@17002 master -
0 1692355469644 2 connected 5461-10922
06993fd4dcdba94b58d540fcc227fc10928b4026 127.0.0.1:7003@17003 master -
0 1692355468640 3 connected 10923-16383
9809cc52a20317a39cceae6da394c6fd42d112f8 127.0.0.1:7001@17001
myself,master - 0 1692355467000 1 connected 0-5460
```

And here, we're inspecting the shards:

```
redis-cli -p 7001 CLUSTER SHARDS
1) 1) "slots"
   2) 1) "5461"
      2) "10922"
   3) "nodes"
   4) 1)  1) "id"
```

```
            2) "617fa344e767a4da7fad53e4dd2bc9918e54116e"
            ...
2) 1) "slots"
   2) 1) "0"
      2) "5460"
   3) "nodes"
   4) 1)  1) "id"
            2) "9809cc52a20317a39cceae6da394c6fd42d112f8"
            ...
3) 1) "slots"
   2) 1) "10923"
      2) "16383"
   3) "nodes"
   4) 1)  1) "id"
            2) "06993fd4dcdba94b58d540fcc227fc10928b4026"
            ...
```

Here, we're inspecting the distribution of the hash slots:

```
redis-cli -p 7001 CLUSTER SLOTS
1) 1) (integer) 0
   2) (integer) 5460
   3) 1) "127.0.0.1"
      2) (integer) 7001
      3) "9809cc52a20317a39cceae6da394c6fd42d112f8"
      4) (empty array)
2) 1) (integer) 5461
   2) (integer) 10922
   3) 1) "127.0.0.1"
      2) (integer) 7002
      3) "617fa344e767a4da7fad53e4dd2bc9918e54116e"
      4) (empty array)
3) 1) (integer) 10923
   2) (integer) 16383
   3) 1) "127.0.0.1"
      2) (integer) 7003
      3) "06993fd4dcdba94b58d540fcc227fc10928b4026"
      4) (empty array)
```

It might also be helpful to determine in advance which hash slot a key will belong to. Run the following command to ascertain this:

```
redis-cli -p 7001 CLUSTER KEYSLOT myname
(integer) 12807
```

What we've explored so far should give you a clear sense of what's required to achieve a foundational level of scalability with a Redis Stack architecture. And now that we've delved into the intricacies of scalability, it's crucial to shift our focus to another paramount aspect: security.

Security

Another significant topic in Redis Stack is security. For Redis Stack, the concept of security must be addressed from two fundamental perspectives: architectural and data-centric. These two aspects can be summarized with two acronyms: *TLS* and *ACL*.

In this section of the chapter, we will delve into both themes, starting with architectural security and then moving on to safeguarding our data.

Transport Layer Security

Transport Layer Security, commonly known as **TLS**, is a mechanism designed to ensure secure communications by encrypting information exchanged between two entities. The **Internet Engineering Task Force** (**IETF**) developed TLS as a means to unify internet security protocols.

Beyond its definition, the crucial takeaway is that the TLS protocol facilitates secure, encrypted transmission. Only the sender and receiver can decipher the message.

Within Redis Stack, there are two types of communication. The first, often termed "external," is between the application and Redis Stack. The second, "internal," takes place among Redis Stack processes, be they local or remote; for instance, between the primary shard and its replica. It's paramount to note that Redis Stack should never be exposed directly. Instead, requests should be mediated through designated backend services using client libraries supported by Redis Stack. So, when we mention "application," we're referencing the backend application, never the frontend. There's a configuration parameter for this in the `redis.conf` file, appropriately named `bind`. This should always point to an internal network interface, avoiding public IPs. The default, as expected, is the loopback interface:

```
bind 127.0.0.1
```

Returning to TLS, its mechanism relies on certificates. On one end, these encrypt data, and on the other, they decrypt it, all the while confirming the data's integrity—ensuring it hasn't been altered during transmission. To enable TLS communication in Redis Stack, the following certificates are essential:

- CA certificate
- Server certificate and private key
- Diffie-Hellman parameters file

These files should be specified in the `redis.conf` configuration, like so:

```
tls-cert-file /path/to/redis.crt
tls-key-file /path/to/redis.key
```

```
tls-ca-cert-file /path/to/ca.crt
tls-dh-params-file /path/to/redis.dh
```

Beyond these, the `tls-port` parameter defines which port Redis Stack will listen to for TLS connections. Notably, setting the TLS port doesn't automatically disable the non-TLS one. To do so, you need to set it to `0`:

```
port 0
tls-port 6379
```

The configurations previously described secure Redis Stack concerning external communication. When it comes to internal communication, things are more straightforward. For both replication (from primary shard to replica) and HA, as well as scalability, the basic configurations remain consistent and are therefore inherited.

For replication, in addition, you'll need the following:

```
tls-replication yes
```

For HA, Sentinel will employ the same replication parameter, `tls-replication`. For scalability, which implies clustering, the additional necessary parameter is this:

```
tls-cluster yes
```

These settings ensure messages are encrypted and decrypted and that their integrity is validated. While these steps bolster security, be advised that they might slightly affect performance.

Redis Stack also supports so-called mutual certificate authentication (mTLS), which allows an application to authenticate without using credentials (username and password) but through a certificate. This mode is automatically activated when TLS directives are enabled and can also be specifically turned off using the following parameter in the `redis.conf` configuration file:

```
tls-auth-clients no
```

While certificate-based authentication provides a robust and seamless way of ensuring security in Redis Stack, there are scenarios where you might lean toward more traditional authentication methods. This brings us to the realm of the **access control list** (**ACL**).

ACL

Redis employs an ACL to manage and restrict commands and key access for certain connections. Clients are required to authenticate by submitting a username and password when connecting. Once authenticated, the connection is bound to the user's predefined restrictions. Additionally, Redis can automatically authenticate new connections using a pre-set "default" user, typically the default setting. This approach also means that connections not explicitly authenticated are limited to a certain range of functionalities, as determined by the configuration of the default user.

The first step in data protection is to require access credentials. This can be set directly within Redis Stack's configuration file, `redis.conf`, using the following parameter:

```
requirepass <yourSecretPassword>
```

After setting the password, Redis Stack can be accessed using this command:

```
AUTH <yourSecretPassword>
```

Here, no username is specified, because, for backward-compatibility reasons, the default is `default`. However, ACL rules allow you to define users and assign them rules. Let's start by creating a new user and assigning them a password:

```
ACL SETUSER mirko >ortensi on
```

With this command, we've created a user, `mirko`, with a password, `ortensi`, and activated it with the on directive. If you don't specify the on directive, the user is created but not enabled. To activate the user, use the following:

```
ACL SETUSER mirko on
```

Then, the user can authenticate as previously described using the `AUTH` command, specifying both the username and password.

Now, once users are defined, you can dictate how they interact with the data, either broadly or with finer granularity by allowing or restricting certain commands. We'll start broadly using command categories:

```
ACL CAT
```

The expected output would be this:

```
 1) "keyspace"
 2) "read"
 3) "write"
 4) "set"
 5) "sortedset"
 6) "list"
 7) "hash"
 8) "string"
 9) "bitmap"
10) "hyperloglog"
11) "geo"
12) "stream"
13) "pubsub"
14) "admin"
15) "fast"
```

```
16) "slow"
17) "blocking"
18) "dangerous"
19) "connection"
20) "transaction"
21) "scripting"
```

The preceding list categorizes the command groups. For instance, the `"stream"` category pertains to all commands accessing data for streams. The `"read"` category covers all read-only commands, regardless of the data structure targeted, while `"write"` covers all write commands.

These categories simplify basic rule-setting. For example, let's create a second user, `luigi`, granting them read-only privileges for all keys, while `mirko` will get write privileges for all keys:

```
ACL SETUSER luigi >fugaro on +@read ~*
ACL SETUSER mirko +@write ~*
```

Now, before testing our ACLs with the respective user credentials, let's view the ACL rules set so far:

```
127.0.0.1:6379> ACL LIST
```

This is the expected output:

```
1) "user default on nopass sanitize-payload ~* &* +@all"
2) "user luigi on sanitize-payload #hashed_password ~* +@read"
3) "user mirko on sanitize-payload #hashed_password ~* +@write"
```

As can be observed, there are three rules defined. The first pertains to the `default` user, who does not have a password and possesses full access permissions (`~* &* +@all`, a detailed explanation of which will follow shortly). The second rule is for the user `luigi`, who is restricted to read-only commands, while the third is designated for the user `mirko`, granting them write-only permissions. To illustrate, let's proceed by accessing the system as `mirko` and entering some sample data, as demonstrated next:

```
127.0.0.1:6379> AUTH mirko ortensi
OK
127.0.0.1:6379> keys *
(error) NOPERM User mirko has no permissions to run the 'keys' command
127.0.0.1:6379> set name mirko
OK
127.0.0.1:6379> keys *
(error) NOPERM User mirko has no permissions to run the 'keys' command
127.0.0.1:6379> get name
(error) NOPERM User mirko has no permissions to run the 'get' command
```

As we can observe, the user `mirko` is only permitted to write and execute write commands. The `keys *` command is strictly a read-only command; thus, the user cannot view the keys stored in Redis Stack, let alone those they have written themself.

Now, let's try authenticating with the user `luigi`, as follows:

```
127.0.0.1:6379> AUTH luigi fugaro
OK
127.0.0.1:6379> keys *
1) "name"
127.0.0.1:6379> get name
"mirko"
127.0.0.1:6379> set name luigi
(error) NOPERM User luigi has no permissions to run the 'set' command
```

Another clearer and more straightforward method to determine what a specific user is allowed to do involves executing the `ACL GETUSER` command, as illustrated next:

```
127.0.0.1:6379> ACL GETUSER mirko
```

This is the expected output:

```
 1) "flags"
 2) 1) "on"
    2) "sanitize-payload"
 3) "passwords"
 4) 1)
"96f06e7ea22b73fa289b759b6a8c43f130aade97fa23e388d1a4288afe8607d2"
 5) "commands"
 6) "-@all +@write"
 7) "keys"
 8) "~*"
 9) "channels"
10) ""
11) "selectors"
12) (empty array)
```

As we have observed, the process of writing rules is indeed straightforward, yet it adheres to a specific syntax. ACL rules can be applied to commands, categories, keys, and data types. What follows is a comprehensive list of directives to tailor ACL rules according to specific requirements:

- `+command`: Enables a specific command
- `-command`: Disables a specific command
- `+@category`: Allows all commands under that category

- `-@category`: Disallows all commands under that category
- `allcommands`: An alias for `+@all`
- `nocommands`: An alias for `-@all`
- `~keyPrefix`: Allows access to keys with a certain prefix
- `%R~keyPrefix`: Read-only access for keys with a prefix
- `%W~keyPrefix`: Write-only access for keys with a prefix
- `%RW~keyPrefix`: Read-write access for keys with a prefix
- `allkeys`: An alias for `~*`

From the provided list, certain rules have been excluded, such as the `"on"` and `"off"` directives for enabling and disabling a user account. Additionally, the `">"` rule for password creation and the `"<"` rule for password removal are not present. For a more comprehensive understanding of ACL rules and in-depth insights, you can refer to the online documentation on the Redis Stack website at the following link: `https://redis.io/docs/management/security/acl/`.

While we've touched on the HA, scalability, and security of Redis Stack, it's worth noting that there are certain limitations when it comes to automation and additional configurations. These tweaks could potentially enhance the management experience of a Redis Stack-based solution.

Limitations

As we have observed, achieving HA requires manually configuring additional Redis Stack processes in Sentinel mode. To ensure these processes function effectively and consistently, it's crucial to isolate them on separate servers. This isolation ensures they don't interfere with the standard operation of Redis Stack and the provision of data access services. From an infrastructural perspective, this can lead to increased costs.

Continuing on the subject of HA, there is a distinct absence of support for geographically distributed deployment. This lack of support hinders the implementation of critical scenarios such as **disaster recovery** (**DR**) and **business continuity** (**BC**). Such scenarios typically employ well-recognized patterns, including the Active-Passive and Active-Active models. The ability to deploy across various geographical locations is essential for ensuring data availability and resilience in the face of potential regional outages or disasters. Implementing these recognized patterns not only aids in the efficient recovery of data post-disruption but also guarantees uninterrupted service delivery to the end users. It's a fundamental feature expected in modern-day data management and service deployment architectures.

When it comes to scalability, although it is simpler than the Sentinel mode in terms of configuration, Redis Cluster presents its own challenges. For instance, when adding more nodes, the cluster does not automatically handle key re-balancing and re-sharding. Manual intervention is necessary. Moreover, the topology of nodes that make up the cluster must be predefined during the configuration phase.

Given these nuances, organizations face a critical decision. If the priority is HA only, then Sentinel mode could be the preferred choice. On the other hand, if scalability and increased throughput are paramount, then the Cluster mode (with managed HA behind the scenes) becomes the more appropriate selection. Note that the Sentinel configuration is not compatible with the Cluster setup.

From a security standpoint, there is a noticeable absence of support for two prominent user management protocols: **Lightweight Directory Access Protocol** (**LDAP**) and **Security Assertion Markup Language 2** (**SAML2**). Additionally, there lacks a comprehensive solution for user profile management outside the confines of ACL rules, even though they undoubtedly offer value.

As initially indicated, Redis Stack may be well suited for a development environment. For production settings, where greater integrations and heightened focus on automation, reliability, and security are demanded, seeking alternative solutions would be advisable.

The capabilities and features of Redis Stack, together with the well-known ease of use and real-time performance of Redis, are available in two commercial versions: **Redis Enterprise** and **Redis Cloud**. The former caters to so-called on-premises production environments, while the latter is essentially Redis Enterprise, but it's offered as a service through major cloud providers such as **Google Cloud Platform** (**GCP**) and **Amazon Web Services** (**AWS**). This offering allows users to leverage the robust features of Redis Enterprise on these popular cloud platforms. The Redis Cloud alternative is fully managed by Redis (the company) and is positioned as a DBaaS solution. In contrast, Microsoft Azure integrates Redis Enterprise directly into its solution catalog, naming it Azure Cache for Redis. Azure further distinguishes its offering by providing specialized tiers, including Enterprise and Enterprise Flash, tailored to different usage needs and performance requirements.

Preparing for production with Redis Enterprise

As we've observed, Redis Stack is ideal for local development environments. However, when the application needs to intersect with architectural and infrastructural requirements, it's prudent to adopt an enterprise-grade Redis solution—specifically, Redis Enterprise. From an application perspective, the libraries and frameworks supported by Redis remain consistent. But what are the distinctions between Redis Stack and Redis Enterprise?

The differences are manifold, some being quite apparent, while others are subtler. They range from TCO, multitenancy support, HA, scalability, security, and performance to monitoring.

In the following sections, we will delve into these aspects to comprehend the added value that Redis Enterprise brings to such contexts. Before doing so, let us first explore Redis Enterprise from an architectural standpoint.

Redis Enterprise architecture

Redis Enterprise is built on a shared-nothing architecture, a type of distributed computing structure where each node in a computer cluster—comprising a processor, memory, and storage unit—handles update requests independently. This design aims to prevent conflicts and contention for resources among nodes.

A Redis Enterprise cluster consists of an odd number of nodes, starting with a minimum of three. The requirement to have an odd number of nodes is due to the necessity for a quorum, as a master node is elected for the cluster's management. This sophisticated management is facilitated by a set of additional components that are not present in Redis Stack, allowing for a more streamlined and precise governance of the architecture. These components include the proxy, the cluster manager, the REST API, the admin console, and the `redis-cli` tool, collectively referred to as the control plane. The proxy is also part of the data plane, along with the shards. The proxy is a component responsible for handling (persistent) connections to the actual Redis shards. It efficiently distributes data requests to the relevant shards, ensuring data is fetched or stored where it is meant to be.

On the other hand, the cluster manager is a set of components that oversees and maintains the topology of the cluster nodes and the shards within them. Any change in topology, be it the addition or removal of a node or shard, is automatically handled by the cluster manager. This means that potential failures of an entire node, proxy, or even a single shard are automatically addressed and rectified by the cluster manager. It ensures automatic rebalancing and resharding of the dataset, making sure data remains available and consistent.

Lastly, the REST API serves as an interface to interact with the cluster manager via the HTTP/S protocol. This facilitates configuration management, especially when looking to automate certain processes or procedures.

Next, we will provide a graphical representation of a Redis Enterprise cluster:

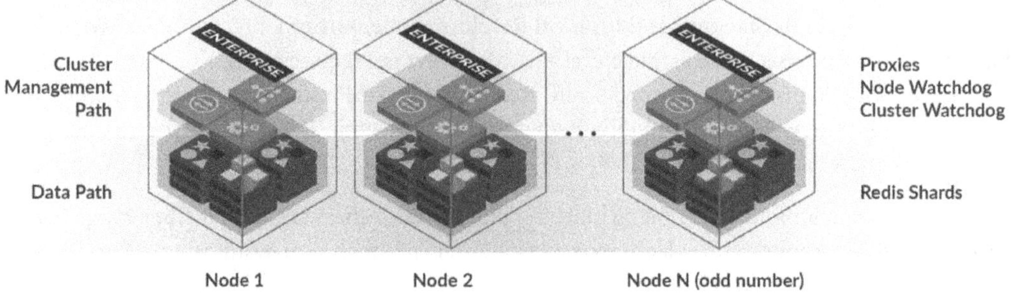

Figure 12.4 – Redis Enterprise cluster

Another significant distinction when compared to Redis Stack is the support for multi-tenancy.

A multi-tenancy architecture

When initiating a Redis Stack process, what one effectively obtains is a shard, essentially a database to store data. From the application perspective, meaning from the client's side, the Redis Stack database is accessible through an IP address and a port. Upon establishing the connection, data reading and writing can commence. This implies that multiple applications connected to the same Redis Stack instance can read from and write to the same dataset, posing the risk of data overwriting or accessing data that it might not be intended for. This risk arises from the absence of a context or, more accurately, the lack of a tenant concept.

However, with Redis Enterprise, the concept of a tenant is introduced. In this framework, every Redis database has its distinct shards. It's crucial to highlight that a shard equates to an operating system-level process; hence, having separate processes ensures both data and resource isolation, safeguarding CPU, memory, and the data itself against potential conflicts.

Multi-tenancy allows a single Redis Enterprise cluster to serve multiple customers, organizations, and applications by provisioning multiple databases, referred to as tenants. This means that each tenant's data and configurations remain isolated and invisible to other tenants, ensuring both data security and functional independence. For each tenant, a unique network endpoint (**fully qualified domain name**, or **FQDN**) is assigned. In this manner, the application will use this endpoint as the sole connection address to the Redis database, eliminating the need to connect to a specific node or shard. This streamlined approach not only enhances the ease of integration but also ensures consistent connection practices across multiple application instances, ensuring optimal performance and reducing potential points of failure. The endpoint is delivered through the Proxy component, which, by default, is situated on a singular node under the `single` policy. Nonetheless, to enhance performance further and mitigate the risk of a **single point of failure** (**SPOF**), the Proxy component can also be scaled utilizing various policies, including the following:

- `single`: Only one proxy service will be up and only in one node
- `all-master-shards`: A proxy service will be up in all nodes where there is at least one primary shard
- `all-nodes`: A proxy service will be up in all nodes

This multi-tenancy capability enhances both operational efficiency and scalability by enabling diverse applications or user groups to share a common infrastructure without compromising on data segregation or performance. This not only optimizes resource usage but also simplifies management and scaling procedures.

Each tenant uniquely identifies a Redis database, which might be represented by a single shard or multiple shards. This configuration is contingent on whether HA mechanisms have been enabled and whether data distribution across multiple shards (sharding) is in effect.

Next is a diagram representing the structure of a Redis Enterprise database:

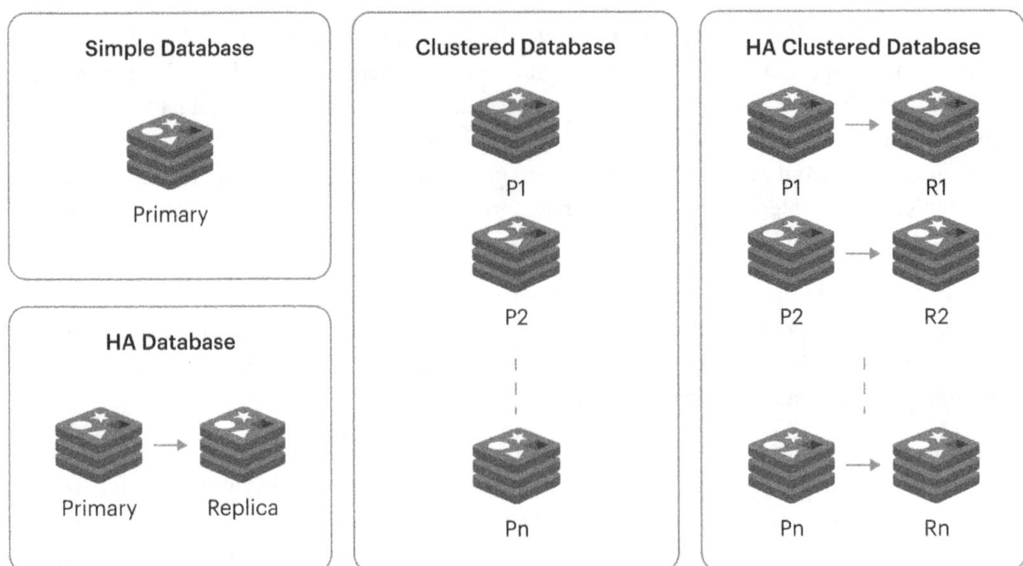

Figure 12.5 – Redis Enterprise database in its all topologies

Before delving into the detailed scenarios depicted in the diagram, let's take a systematic approach and first examine how HA is managed and implemented.

HA

In technical terms, a database, or, more specifically, a "tenant," can be represented by a single shard, often referred to as the primary shard.

In Redis Enterprise, HA is activated by setting the `replication` property to `true`. When this is initiated, the cluster manager establishes a replica shard (continually fed by the primary shard). The main goal of this replica shard is to seamlessly take over operations if, for any reason, the primary shard becomes unavailable. Strategically, in Redis Enterprise, the replica shard is always located on a different node from the primary shard, adhering to an anti-affinity placement policy.

This policy can be fine-tuned, allowing for the replica shard node not only to be different but also to belong to a separate rack or even a distinct physical server (especially relevant if nodes are managed as virtual machines). While the replica shard placement mechanism can account for individual data center infrastructures, when extended across multiple data centers or regions, especially in cloud infrastructure, it can lead to networking challenges. As a result, such a layout can become complex and is typically not advised.

Does this mean that DR and BC scenarios can't be implemented? Quite the contrary, but the approach requires a paradigm shift.

As mentioned in a previous section, it is viable to implement Redis Enterprise deployments by leveraging two prominent patterns: Active-Passive and Active-Active.

This implementation strategy involves deploying two or more distinct and independent Redis Enterprise clusters that are federated with each other, facilitating either unidirectional (Active-Passive) or bidirectional (Active-Active) communication to ensure seamless data synchronization.

The Active-Active pattern allows for data to be read from and written to all databases participating in this topology. However, it's crucial that applications always interface with the geographically closer cluster to minimize latency, ensuring optimal performance.

Conversely, the Active-Passive pattern ensures that all data reads and writes are confined exclusively to the database designated as Active. The Active counterpart then shoulders the responsibility of synchronizing data to the database replica labeled as Passive.

Furthermore, there exists an alternative pattern named Active-Read-Replica. This configuration permits data to be read from both clusters but restricts write operations exclusively to the Active cluster.

For organizations concerned with DR, the Active-Passive and Active-Read-Replica patterns are the preferred choice. On the other hand, when focusing on BC strategies or geographically distributed services (retail, real-time inventory, mobile banking, and more), the Active-Active pattern emerges as the preferred choice.

Moreover, these patterns can be adeptly deployed within cloud infrastructures. This includes utilizing multi-regional environments within a single cloud provider or even spanning multiple cloud providers. Notably, with the Redis Cloud service, Redis commits to an impressive **service-level agreement** (**SLA**) of 99.999% uptime and HA.

Let us now delve into how scalability is adeptly managed within the framework of Redis Enterprise.

Horizontal and vertical scalability and dynamic auto-tiering

As observed in *Figure 12.5*, a Redis database can be configured for HA by activating the replica shard. Regarding scalability, as previously described in the Cluster mode of Redis Stack, it is achieved by distributing the dataset across multiple shards. This distribution can be approached in two distinct manners:

- **Vertical scaling**: This involves distributing data across multiple shards within the same original node or server. This approach clearly necessitates proper sizing of nodes that constitute the cluster to accommodate multiple shards. The sizing is dictated by the desired throughput, which impacts the CPU and the volume of data that needs to be managed. A shard within Redis Enterprise is optimized to such an extent that it requires only a single CPU to guarantee outstanding performance. From a RAM perspective, the requirements vary based on specific application storage needs. Next is a representation of how data can be distributed across multiple shards utilizing vertical scalability:

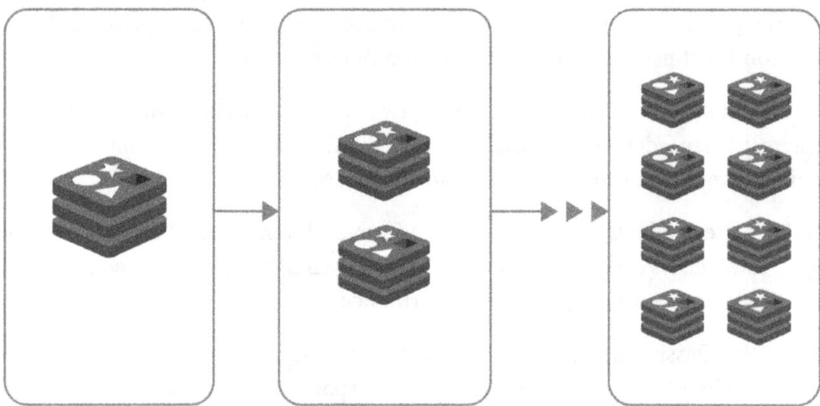

Figure 12.6 – Vertical scaling in Redis Enterprise

- **Horizontal scaling**: This involves distributing data across multiple shards located on different nodes, thereby preventing the exhaustion of resources on any individual node or server. Moreover, the operational flexibility of the Cluster Manager component of Redis Enterprise allows for the addition of more nodes if the overall available resources are deemed insufficient. It might not be obvious, but you can further optimize workload distribution by leveraging both vertical and horizontal scalability methods, as depicted in the subsequent diagram:

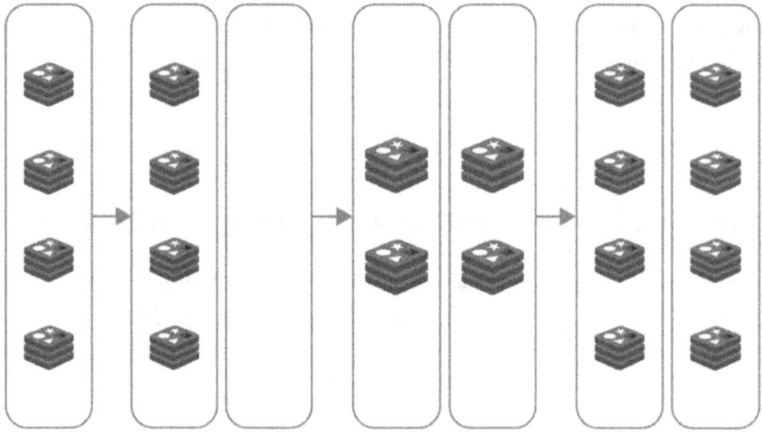

Figure 12.7 – Horizontal and vertical scaling in Redis Enterprise[3]

Regardless of the scalability type selected, Redis Enterprise takes on the responsibility of automatically managing not only the placement of shards according to anti-affinity mechanisms (often referred to as **resharding**) but also the positioning of keys within the calculated hash slots (known as **rebalancing**).

Beyond their automatic nature, these mechanisms are entirely transparent to applications, ensuring that they don't experience any disconnection errors or service interruptions. In essence, this sophisticated architecture provides both robustness and seamless scalability, allowing technical teams to focus on their application logic rather than infrastructure intricacies.

Discussing infrastructure, especially when addressing RAM, costs can become a significant and sometimes prohibitive factor. As long as the volume of data remains within the magnitude of gigabytes, the associated infrastructure expenses are manageable. However, when scaling to the realm of tens or even hundreds of terabytes, these costs can skyrocket. In the interest of cost reduction TCO, Redis Enterprise offers a solution to extend RAM capacity by leveraging **solid-state drives** (**SSDs**) rooted in flash memory, such as NVMe, through a mechanism called Auto Tiering. With this, data storage is seamlessly managed by Redis Enterprise, ensuring that some portions of the data reside in RAM while others are allocated to the flash memory. It's essential to understand that this flash memory functions similarly to RAM—it's volatile and ephemeral. From an administrative perspective, one merely needs to specify the percentage of data to be managed in RAM versus that on the flash memory. Subsequently, the Auto Tiering mechanism autonomously handles the allocation process.

Security hardening

Another fundamental distinction between Redis Stack and Redis Enterprise pertains to security. The concepts elaborated upon in the preceding sections regarding architectural security remain applicable to the Enterprise version. However, what distinguishes the two is the approach to security management. Primarily, there's a web-based console that administrators can access to manage both the cluster and the databases. More importantly, this console allows for the administration and configuration of user accounts and user profiles through ACL mechanisms, and integration with Active Directory via the LDAP protocol. To facilitate user management, Redis Enterprise offers a range of predefined roles tailored for standard operations, as depicted in the subsequent screenshot:

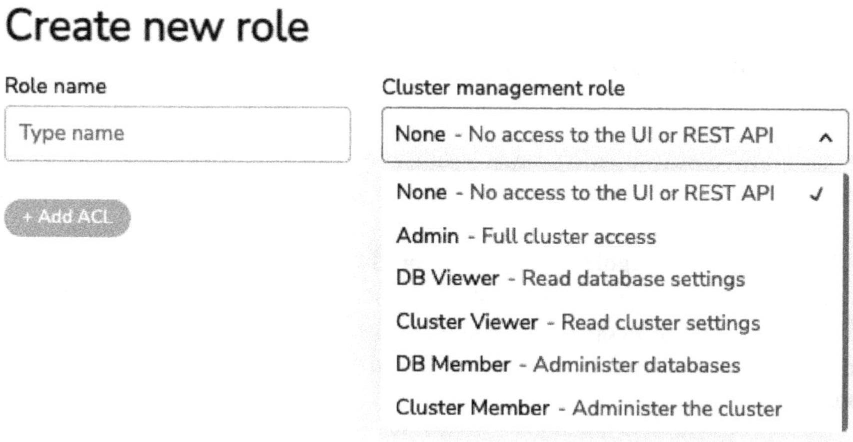

Create new role
Role name
Type name
+ Add ACL
Cluster management role
None - No access to the UI or REST API
None - No access to the UI or REST API ✓
Admin - Full cluster access
DB Viewer - Read database settings
Cluster Viewer - Read cluster settings
DB Member - Administer databases
Cluster Member - Administer the cluster

Figure 12.8 – Redis Enterprise standard roles

As can be discerned from the preceding screenshot, there are read-only roles intended to inspect the settings of both the cluster and the databases, as well as write roles that grant permissions to modify the configurations of these entities.

The web console also facilitates the guided creation of custom ACLs, achieved through an ACL-builder tool. These ACLs can be designated during the establishment of new roles, enabling user profiling to be tailored according to specific requirements. Additionally, these very roles and ACLs can be mapped to users set up via LDAP. This effectively bridges the gap between profiles and roles available in Active Directory and those defined within Redis Enterprise.

The LDAP configuration is a setting that must be implemented at the cluster level, as with certificates. The management of certificates has been further enhanced with the introduction of a revocation mechanism in accordance with the **Online Certificate Status Protocol** (**OCSP**). Additionally, recent versions of Redis Enterprise have introduced the capability to encrypt so-called "internode" traffic; that is, communication between the various nodes that constitute the cluster. This security precaution also extends to Active-Active and Active-Passive configurations, ensuring safe synchronization across multiple regions. This complements the comprehensive TLS support at the control plane and data plane and for the Redis Enterprise discovery service.

Beyond the web console as an administration tool, Redis Enterprise also provides a command-line utility named `rladmin`. This tool allows for the management of the cluster, databases, and their configurations, as well as fine-tuning settings that further optimize the performance of Redis.

Given the extensive range of commands and configurations that can be set, you can refer to the official Redis documentation website for in-depth information:

`https://docs.redis.com/latest/rs/references/cli-utilities/rladmin/`

Another paramount aspect following security is the capability to monitor the performance and health of the Redis Enterprise architecture, and this is exactly what you will learn in the next section.

Observability and monitoring

In the evolving landscape of modern distributed systems, observability and monitoring are indispensable components to ensure consistent performance, health, and reliability. Observability encompasses the capacity to inspect the internal states of a system from its external outputs, serving as a compass for administrators to navigate through the complex interdependencies of services. Monitoring, a subset of observability, involves the regular tracking and notification of key metrics and system health indicators. These components work symbiotically, wherein monitoring provides the ongoing stream of data, and observability aids in deriving insights from it. The comprehensive integration of both allows administrators to not only detect anomalies but also diagnose root causes, facilitating proactive interventions and continuous system optimization.

With Redis Enterprise, monitoring and observability are elevated to a more sophisticated level, tailored for its high-performance architecture. Redis Enterprise exposes an endpoint that offers metrics in the **OpenMetrics** format, which is widely adopted by tools such as Prometheus. This structured format ensures that metrics are presented in a standardized manner, enabling easy integration with a plethora of observability platforms. As a result, administrators can seamlessly integrate Redis Enterprise's metrics into any monitoring system that supports the OpenMetrics format, allowing for a comprehensive view of its performance and health. Additionally, the robustness of Redis Enterprise's built-in features, coupled with third-party monitoring tools, ensures that administrators can efficiently track **key performance indicators** (**KPIs**), resource utilization, and any potential anomalies, guaranteeing optimal system health and performance.

In the realm of monitoring solutions, **Grafana Cloud** stands out due to its direct integration capabilities with Redis Enterprise. This integration is not just superficial but offers a comprehensive suite of dashboards tailored to serve specific monitoring needs, be it a general overview, individual node status, or granular database performance. To harness the power of this integration, one must deploy the Grafana agent on every node within the Redis Enterprise cluster. Once installed, the agent is responsible for transmitting metrics specific to each Redis database. The transmission pathway is established by configuring the Prometheus endpoint, unique to each database. Next is a representative YAML configuration that illustrates the setup process:

```
integrations:
 ...
logs:
 ...
metrics:
 configs:
 - name: integrations
  remote_write:
  - basic_auth:
    password: <YOUR_TOKEN>
    username: <YOUR_UID>
   url: https://<GRAFANA_ZONE>.grafana.net/api/prom/push
  scrape_configs:
   - job_name: integrations/redis-enterprise
    metrics_path: /metrics
    scheme: https
    tls_config:
      insecure_skip_verify: true
    static_configs:
     - targets: ['<YOUR_REDIS_DB_ENDPOINT>:8070']
    relabel_configs:
     - source_labels: []
      regex: .*
      target_label: redis_cluster
      replacement: 'redis.foogaro.cloud'
 ...
```

Upon successful configuration and data collection, the metrics can be visualized within a Grafana dashboard. The presentation of these metrics is not just numerical but is depicted in a comprehensive and intuitive layout, as illustrated in the subsequent dashboard screenshot:

Figure 12.9 – Redis Enterprise monitoring using Grafana integration and dashboards

This dashboard goes beyond merely presenting raw data. Instead, it organizes and visualizes the information in a structured and intuitive layout. Such an arrangement is particularly conducive to efficient monitoring, allowing for swift identification of trends, anomalies, or potential areas of concern.

Redis Enterprise emerges as the ideal solution for transitioning from a local development environment to a production setting. This platform not only provides a robust framework for ensuring seamless migration but also emphasizes the stability and performance necessary for high-demand production scenarios. It is noteworthy to mention that Redis Enterprise serves as the foundational technology behind Redis Cloud, a fully managed Redis service. We will delve deeper into the features and capabilities of Redis Cloud in the subsequent section.

Redis Cloud – an enterprise-ready Redis DBaaS

Redis Cloud serves as a fully managed cloud service designed to optimize the performance, scalability, and reliability of Redis deployments, abstracting the complexities of infrastructure management and ensuring seamless scalability without compromising on speed or integrity.

With built-in HA, data persistence options, and robust security features, Redis Cloud is architected to meet the demands of mission-critical applications. Its automatic failover guarantees that your applications remain operational and responsive, even during unforeseen system disruptions.

Furthermore, for those prioritizing infrastructure flexibility, Redis Cloud provides cross-platform support, allowing enterprises to integrate it within multi-cloud strategies or on-premises environments with ease. This agility ensures that businesses remain resilient and adaptive in an ever-evolving technological landscape.

Often, before adopting a new technology, organizations prioritize obtaining a cost estimate, commonly referred to as the TCO.

TCO is a crucial factor for organizations when evaluating technological solutions. Redis Cloud, as a fully managed cloud service, presents several distinct advantages that contribute to an optimized TCO:

- **Infrastructure management and maintenance**: Redis Cloud assumes the responsibilities of infrastructure provisioning, maintenance, and updates. This removes the need for internal teams to handle these tasks, leading to savings in labor costs, infrastructure investments, and operational overhead.
- **Scalability and performance**: Redis Cloud is designed for seamless scaling, ensuring that your application can handle growth without needing constant reconfigurations or upgrades. This scalability reduces future costs associated with system expansions or performance tuning.
- **HA**: The built-in automatic failover and data persistence features minimize the risks and potential costs of downtime. Whether it's a minor disruption or a major outage, Redis Cloud's resilience ensures that your business processes aren't adversely impacted.
- **Security**: Robust security features, including end-to-end encryption, advanced access controls, and compliance certifications, reduce the risk (and thus potential costs) of data breaches or leaks. Investing in a secure platform such as Redis Cloud can save considerable sums that might otherwise be spent addressing security incidents.
- **Cross-platform support**: Flexibility in deployment across various cloud providers means that businesses can select the most cost-effective infrastructure solutions for their specific needs, rather than being locked into a particular platform or provider.
- **Dedicated support**: The support provided by the Redis team means that issues can be addressed promptly, reducing the time and resources your enterprise might otherwise spend troubleshooting.
- **Predictable pricing**: With clear and transparent pricing models, budgeting for Redis Cloud becomes more straightforward, eliminating unexpected costs or overages.
- **Optimized resource utilization**: Redis Cloud ensures that resources are utilized optimally, ensuring you get the most out of what you pay for. This efficiency means fewer wasted resources and more value for money.

In sum, the long-term savings in labor, operations, security, and infrastructure lead to a lower TCO for a managed solution such as Redis Cloud. It's an investment that pays dividends in terms of performance, security, and operational simplicity.

As previously highlighted in earlier sections, Redis Cloud is accessible on GCP and AWS. The Azure cloud provides Redis Enterprise directly integrated into its product catalog solutions.

On each of these platforms, Redis Enterprise is available as a fully managed service. Additionally, Redis Cloud is seamlessly integrated into the marketplaces of these cloud providers. Organizations can leverage the native billing systems of the respective cloud platforms or burn down their existing cloud commitments, streamlining procurement while optimizing spend.

Having observed the advantages of Redis Cloud's offerings, let's delve into the specifics of accessing the service itself. The initial step involves visiting the `https://app.redislabs.com/` website and proceeding with registration. One can either utilize the authentication systems provided by Google and GitHub or opt for **single sign-on** (**SSO**). Notably, Redis Cloud offers a free 30 MB plan, ideal for initial exploration without any expense. When you're ready, you can easily scale up your plan for any use case and any size, even up to practically unlimited capacity.

Upon successful login, the next imperative action is to establish a subscription. This subscription serves as your designated environment, which the Redis DevOps team will set up, paving the way for subsequent database creations. Let's now explore, step by step, the process of establishing our environment and availing the benefits of the free tier:

1. Navigate to the official *Redis Labs* website at `https://app.redislabs.com/` and initiate the login process.
2. Once on the home page, click on the **Create Subscription** button to begin your subscription setup.
3. To benefit from the complimentary offering, choose the **Essentials** plan.
4. Identify and select your preferred cloud provider, such as Google Cloud, from the available list.
5. Opt for the closest geographical region for optimal performance; in my case, I chose **Europe Belgium**.
6. Proceed by choosing the free tier, which provides a capacity of 30 MB. This option is typically set as the default.
7. If you possess a promotional coupon code, this would be the stage to input it.
8. Assign a meaningful name to your subscription. Remember—your subscription acts as your working environment in Redis, so choose a name that reflects its purpose.
9. Finalize by clicking on **Create Subscription**.

With the subscription in place, you're now set to establish your inaugural database on Redis Cloud at no cost:

1. To commence, click the **New Database** button.
2. Designate an appropriate name for your database.
3. Decide upon and select the type of solution that aligns with your requirements.
4. Note that persistence is not available within the free tier.
5. Opt for a data eviction policy. If uncertain, you can retain the default setting, which is `volatile-lru`.

6. Either designate a secure password for database connectivity or make sure to document the one automatically generated by the system.
7. To activate, simply click on the **Activate Database** button.

Within a matter of seconds, your database will be operational, and the access endpoint will be readily accessible, as depicted in the subsequent screenshot:

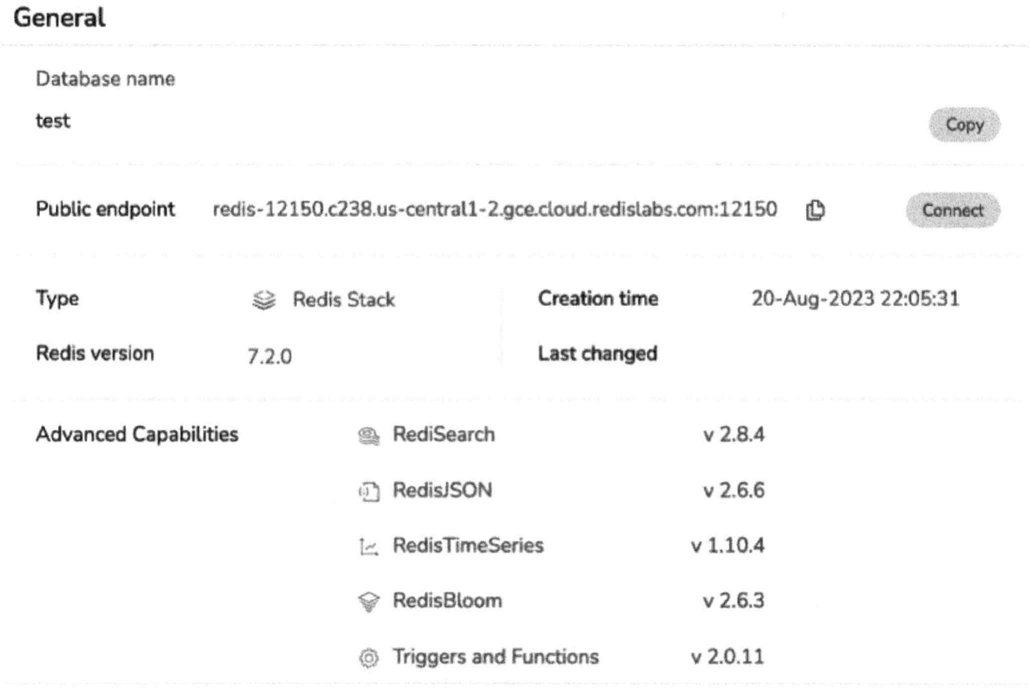

General

Database name
test
Copy

Public endpoint redis-12150.c238.us-central1-2.gce.cloud.redislabs.com:12150 Connect

Type Redis Stack
Creation time 20-Aug-2023 22:05:31
Redis version 7.2.0
Last changed

Advanced Capabilities
RediSearch v 2.8.4
RedisJSON v 2.6.6
RedisTimeSeries v 1.10.4
RedisBloom v 2.6.3
Triggers and Functions v 2.0.11

Figure 12.10 – Redis Cloud database

Redis Cloud presents two distinct plans for users. The **Essentials** plan encompasses all the necessary features for building and scaling fast applications, offering these services at a fixed monthly rate. On the other hand, the **Pro** plan is designed for more demanding applications, offering flexible pricing with scaling options to accommodate varying needs and usage intensities.

> **Note**
>
> Exciting news awaits you! We are thrilled to present a special $100 promo coupon code for Redis Cloud. To claim this awesome offer, simply navigate to the **Credits** section located in the **Billing & Payments** panel on the left side of your screen and enter the code `STACKBOOK`. Don't miss out on this fantastic opportunity to enhance your Redis Cloud experience!

However, it's essential to note that the Redis Cloud portal isn't the sole avenue for managing subscriptions and databases. For those looking for more automated or programmatically driven approaches, Redis Cloud provides a cloud API. Additionally, integration with **Infrastructure as Code** (**IaC**) systems, such as **Terraform** and **Pulumi**, is available, ensuring seamless deployment and management for developers and system administrators alike.

In essence, Redis Cloud stands as a testament to the commitment of Redis to offer enterprise-level solutions that empower organizations to harness the full potential of their data, while simplifying operations and ensuring optimal performance.

Summary

In this last chapter, we delved into Redis Stack, emphasizing its role as a robust development environment. We explored the pivotal aspects of scalability and HA, which ensure the seamless operation and adaptability of Redis systems. The topic of security hardening emerged as a cornerstone, introducing tools such as ACL and TLS to protect data.

Transitioning to Redis Enterprise, we highlighted its proficiency in supporting production environments with features such as multi-tenancy architecture and dynamic auto-tiering. This section also emphasized advanced HA mechanisms and further security refinements.

Last, but not least, this chapter introduced Redis Cloud, a fully managed DBaaS solution, touching upon the crucial concept of TCO. We outlined the numerous benefits of Redis Cloud and its flexible IaC offerings and concluded with an overview of its three distinct plans. In essence, this chapter provided you with a holistic understanding of the Redis ecosystem, from development tools to enterprise-ready solutions.

Index

A

B

C

G

H

I

M

N

O

P

S

T

U

V

W

Packtpub.com

Subscribe to our online digital library for full access to over 7,000 books and videos, as well as industry leading tools to help you plan your personal development and advance your career. For more information, please visit our website.

Why subscribe?

- Spend less time learning and more time coding with practical eBooks and Videos from over 4,000 industry professionals
- Improve your learning with Skill Plans built especially for you
- Get a free eBook or video every month
- Fully searchable for easy access to vital information
- Copy and paste, print, and bookmark content

Did you know that Packt offers eBook versions of every book published, with PDF and ePub files available? You can upgrade to the eBook version at packtpub.com and as a print book customer, you are entitled to a discount on the eBook copy. Get in touch with us at customercare@packtpub.com for more details.

At www.packtpub.com, you can also read a collection of free technical articles, sign up for a range of free newsletters, and receive exclusive discounts and offers on Packt books and eBooks.

Other Books You May Enjoy

If you enjoyed this book, you may be interested in these other books by Packt:

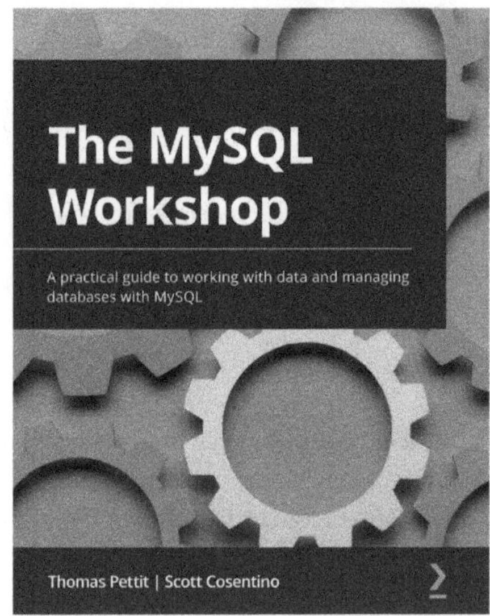

The MySQL Workshop

Thomas Pettit, Scott Cosentino

ISBN: 9781839214905

- Understand the concepts of relational databases and document stores
- Use SQL queries, stored procedures, views, functions, and transactions
- Connect to and manipulate data using MS Access, MS Excel, and Visual Basic for Applications (VBA)
- Read and write data in the CSV or JSON format using MySQL
- Manage data while running MySQL Shell in JavaScript mode
- Use X DevAPI to access a NoSQL interface for MySQL
- Manage user roles, credentials, and privileges to keep data secure
- Perform a logical database backup with mysqldump and mysqlpump

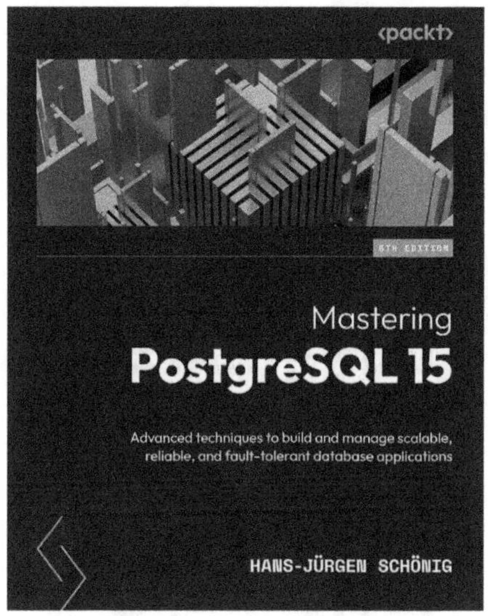

Mastering PostgreSQL 15 - Fifth Edition

Hans-Jürgen Schönig

ISBN: 9781803248349

- Make use of the indexing features in PostgreSQL and fine-tune the performance of your queries
- Work with stored procedures and manage backup and recovery
- Get the hang of replication and failover techniques
- Improve the security of your database server and handle encryption effectively
- Troubleshoot your PostgreSQL instance for solutions to common and not-so-common problems
- Perform database migration from Oracle to PostgreSQL with ease

Packt is searching for authors like you

If you're interested in becoming an author for Packt, please visit `authors.packtpub.com` and apply today. We have worked with thousands of developers and tech professionals, just like you, to help them share their insight with the global tech community. You can make a general application, apply for a specific hot topic that we are recruiting an author for, or submit your own idea.

Share Your Thoughts

Now you've finished *Redis Stack for Application Modernization*, we'd love to hear your thoughts! Scan the QR code below to go straight to the Amazon review page for this book and share your feedback or leave a review on the site that you purchased it from.

`https://packt.link/r/1-837-63818-7`

Your review is important to us and the tech community and will help us make sure we're delivering excellent quality content.

Download a free PDF copy of this book

Thanks for purchasing this book!

Do you like to read on the go but are unable to carry your print books everywhere?

Is your eBook purchase not compatible with the device of your choice?

Don't worry, now with every Packt book you get a DRM-free PDF version of that book at no cost.

Read anywhere, any place, on any device. Search, copy, and paste code from your favorite technical books directly into your application.

The perks don't stop there, you can get exclusive access to discounts, newsletters, and great free content in your inbox daily

Follow these simple steps to get the benefits:

1. Scan the QR code or visit the link below

`https://packt.link/free-ebook/9781837638185`

2. Submit your proof of purchase
3. That's it! We'll send your free PDF and other benefits to your email directly

Printed in the USA
CPSIA information can be obtained
at www.ICGtesting.com
CBHW082014240424
7491CB00008B/49